T0008971

THE CODE BREAKER

YOUNG READERS EDITION

THE CODE BREAKER

YOUNG READERS EDITION

JENNIFER DOUDNA AND THE RACE TO UNDERSTAND OUR GENETIC CODE

WALTER ISAACSON

with Sarah Durand

Simon & Schuster Books for Young Readers

NEW YORK LONDON TORONTO SYDNEY NEW DELHI

SIMON & SCHUSTER BOOKS FOR YOUNG READERS
An imprint of Simon & Schuster Children's Publishing Division
1230 Avenue of the Americas, New York, New York 10020

This book is a work of fiction. Any references to historical events, real people, or real places are used fictitiously. Other names, characters, places, and events are products of the author's imagination, and any resemblance to actual events or places or persons, living or dead, is entirely coincidental.

Text © 2021 by Walter Isaacson
This young readers edition is adapted from *The Code Breaker* by Walter Isaacson, published by Simon & Schuster in 2021
Adaptation by Sarah Durand
Diagram on p. 19 from iStock/Getty Images
Cover illustration © 2022 by Lucia Picerno
Cover design by Laura Eckes © 2022 by Simon & Schuster, Inc.
All rights reserved, including the right of reproduction in whole or in part in any form.
SIMON & SCHUSTER BOOKS FOR YOUNG READERS
and related marks are trademarks of Simon & Schuster, Inc.
For information about special discounts for bulk purchases, please contact
Simon & Schuster Special Sales at 1-866-506-1949 or business@simonandschuster.com.
The Simon & Schuster Speakers Bureau can bring authors to your live event. For more information or to book an event, contact the Simon & Schuster Speakers Bureau at 1-866-248-3049 or visit our website at www.simonspeakers.com.
Also available in a Simon & Schuster Books for Young Readers hardcover edition
Interior design by Hilary Zarycky
The text for this book was set in Jensen.
Manufactured in the United States of America
0223 OFF
First Simon & Schuster Books for Young Readers paperback edition March 2023
2 4 6 8 10 9 7 5 3 1
Library of Congress Cataloging-in-Publication Data
Names: Isaacson, Walter, author. | Durand, Sarah, author.
Title: The code breaker young reader's edition / Walter Isaacson, Sarah Durand.
Description: First edition. | New York : Simon & Schuster Books for Young Readers, 2022. | Includes bibliographical references. | Audience: Ages 8-12 | Audience: Grades 4-6 | Summary: "Walter Isaacson's #1 *New York Times* bestselling history of our third scientific revolution: CRISPR, gene editing, and the quest to understand the code of life itself, is now adapted for young readers" — Provided by publisher.
Identifiers: LCCN 2021042297 (print) | LCCN 2021042298 (ebook) | ISBN 9781665910668 (hardcover) | ISBN 9781665910675 (paperback) | ISBN 9781665910682 (ebook)
Subjects: LCSH: Doudna, Jennifer A. | CRISPR (Genetics)—Juvenile literature. | Gene editing—Juvenile literature. | Genetics—Research—Juvenile literature.
Classification: LCC QH437.5 .I83 2022 (print) | LCC QH437.5 (ebook) | DDC 576.5—dc23
LC record available at https://lccn.loc.gov/2021042297
LC ebook record available at https://lccn.loc.gov/2021042298

To the memory of Alice Mayhew and Carolyn Reidy.
What a joy it was to see them smile.

CONTENTS

Introduction

⸻❊❊❊⸻

In July 2019, a doctor at a hospital in Nashville, Tennessee, inserted a large needle into the arm of a thirty-four-year-old Black woman from a small town in central Mississippi. Victoria Gray, a mother of four children, wasn't getting her yearly vaccination against the flu or donating blood to someone in need. She was becoming the first person in the United States to receive an infusion of cells that had been taken from her blood and altered using a revolutionary gene-editing technology called CRISPR-Cas9. These transformed cells were now being reinserted into her body in an attempt to cure her of the sickle cell disease that had given her debilitating pain since she was a baby.

Sickle cell anemia is a genetic condition caused when a single piece of a person's **DNA** (out of more than three billion pairs!) mutates. "DNA" is short for "deoxyribonucleic acid," and it's the molecule inside every organism that carries the genetic instructions for growth and development. When DNA mutates in a sickle-cell patient, it leads to a defect in the hemoglobin protein, the part of the blood that carries oxygen from our lungs to the rest of our bodies. A normal version of hemoglobin protein forms round and smooth blood cells that move easily through our arteries and veins. But the problematic hemoglobin protein caused by sickle cell anemia forms long fibers that cause the red blood cells to clump together and fold into the shape of a sickle, or a kind of hook. When this happens, oxygen does not get to a person's tissues and organs, and they experience severe pain.

About one hundred thousand sickle-cell patients live in the US, and they are mainly African Americans. Today, most of these people live past age fifty, but in the 1970s, life expectancy was less than twenty years old. The fact that Victoria Gray might live a long life was a relief to her family, but it didn't change the fact that suffering from a chronic illness could be agonizing.

Before her infusion, doctors had taken stem cells—which are special cells your body makes before you are born—from Victoria Gray's blood. Then they edited them using CRISPR technology to activate the production of a certain gene that would allow Victoria Gray's blood cells to produce healthy hemoglobin that would heal the defective sickle cells. Hopefully, her body would soon contain enough working hemoglobin to make round, smooth cells outnumber the sickle cells.

When Victoria Gray was injected, her heart rate shot up, and for a while she had trouble breathing.

"There was a little scary, tough moment for me," she said. "After that, I cried. But it was happy tears."[1]

Victoria Gray was optimistic, and so was her family. Maybe, just maybe, for the first time in her whole life, she wouldn't be in pain.

A few months after she was injected with her edited cells, Gray drove up to the Nashville hospital to see if the therapy was working. She was hopeful. Ever since she'd gotten the edited cells, she hadn't needed any blood transfusions or experienced any sudden pain. Inside the hospital, a nurse drew multiple tubes of Victoria's blood. Gray waited nervously, but then her doctor came in to give her the news.

"I am super-excited about your results today," he said, adding that there were signs that she was starting to make healthy hemoglobin.

In fact, about *half* her blood contained hemoglobin that could heal her defective sickle cells!

In June 2020, Gray got some even more exciting news: the treatment seemed to be lasting. After nine months, she still had not suffered any sickle-cell pain attacks, nor did she need any further blood transfusions. Tests showed that 81 percent of her bone marrow cells were producing the good hemoglobin, meaning the gene edits were still working.[2]

"High school graduations, college graduations, weddings, grandkids—I thought I wouldn't see none of that," she said after getting the news. "Now I'll be there to help my daughters pick out their wedding dresses."[3]

Could this be an amazing milestone in human history? Could a special type of treatment, cooked up in a lab, help cure genetic diseases in humans? Is it possible that conditions such as blindness and sickle cell anemia that were once believed to be incurable—even fatal—can now be reversed? Maybe CRISPR will be able to cure certain types of cancer caused by rogue cells that reproduce and attack tissues, or maybe it will even stop a mysterious, deadly virus like the coronavirus. Is it possible that CRISPR will even help *prevent* illnesses by eliminating them from the genetic code? If we can change genes in a lab with CRISPR, can we use those improved genes to make humans smarter, stronger, faster, and more resistant to disease?

One of the greatest pioneers in modern science knows the answer to all those questions. The scientist at the forefront of this exciting new technology is Jennifer Doudna (pronounced "DOWD-nuh"), a woman whose groundbreaking discoveries in chemistry allowed her to win the Nobel Prize in Chemistry—one of the most important awards in the world—in 2020. Her work illustrates that the key to innovation is connecting a curiosity about basic science to the practical work of creating tools that can be applied to our lives. As this book will show, scientists like Jennifer Doudna move discoveries from the inside of a lab to the inside of your home.

Doudna's life offers an up-close look at how science works. Her story helps answer: What actually happens in a lab? To what extent do discoveries depend on individual genius, and how has teamwork become more critical? And has the competition for individual prizes, money, and fame stopped people from working together for the common good?

Most of all, Doudna's story conveys the importance of *basic* science, meaning quests that are curiosity-driven rather than geared toward immediate, practical results. Curiosity-driven research plants the seeds—sometimes in unpredictable ways—for later discoveries.[4] For example, a few scientists decided to research basic physics simply because it excited them, and their discoveries eventually led to the invention of the microchip. Similarly, the findings of a handful of researchers who took an interest in an astonishing method that bacteria use to fight off viruses helped generate a revolutionary gene-editing tool that humans now use in their own struggle against viruses.

Jennifer Doudna is the perfect example of that brand of curiosity. Hers is a tale filled with the biggest of questions, from the origins of the universe to the future of the human race. Yet it begins with a sixth-grade girl who loved searching for "sleeping grass" and other fascinating phenomena amid the lava rocks of Hawaii, and who came home from school one day to find on her bed a detective tale about the people who discovered what they believed to be "the secret of life."

PART ONE
The Origins of Life

CHAPTER ONE

Hilo

⸺⸺⸺✠⸺⸺⸺

I f she had grown up in any other part of America, Jennifer Doudna might have felt like a regular kid. But in Hilo, an old town in a volcano-filled region on Hawaii's "Big Island," the fact that she was blond, blue-eyed, and lanky made her feel like a complete freak. Her classmates called her a haole, a negative term for people who weren't Native Hawaiians. Feeling so different made her become skeptical of others and careful about the situations she chose to get herself into, even though later in life she became very friendly and open to new experiences.[1]

Her family often told Doudna and her sisters stories about their ancestors. One of the more popular tales involved one of Doudna's great-grandmothers, who was part of a family of three brothers and three sisters. The parents could not afford for all six children to go to school, so they decided to send the three girls. One daughter became a teacher in Montana and kept a diary that has been handed down over the generations. Its pages were filled with tales of determination, hard work, and long hours in the family store, and other frontier pursuits.

"She was crusty and stubborn and had a pioneering spirit," said Doudna's sister Sarah, who now has the diary.

In fact, she was a little like her great-granddaughter Jennifer Doudna.

Doudna was also one of three sisters, although there were no brothers. As the oldest, she was spoiled by her father, Martin Doudna, who sometimes referred to his children as "Jennifer and the girls." She was born February 19, 1964, in Washington, DC, where her father worked as a speechwriter for the Department of Defense. More than anything else, he wanted to be a professor of American literature, so he moved to Ann Arbor, Michigan, with his wife, a community college teacher named Dorothy, and enrolled at the University of Michigan.

When he earned his PhD, Martin applied for fifty jobs and got only one offer, from the University of Hawaii at Hilo. He borrowed $900 from his wife and moved his family there in August 1971, when Doudna was seven.

That's when Doudna began to feel alone and isolated, especially at school.

In the third grade, she was so unloved by her classmates that she had trouble eating, and she developed all sorts of digestive problems that she later realized were stress related. Kids teased her every day—especially the boys, because unlike them she had hair on her arms. To protect herself, she escaped into books and developed a defensive layer.

There's an internal part of me they'll never touch, she told herself.

Many creative people—including Leonardo da Vinci, Albert Einstein, Oprah Winfrey, and Malala Yousafzai—grew up feeling slightly alienated from their surroundings. Like them, Doudna started to become curious about where humans belong in the universe. Digging deep and reading everything she could get her hands on, Doudna tried to figure out who she was in the world and how we all got here.

Fortunately, this loneliness did not last forever. Life began to get better halfway through third grade, when her family moved from the heart of Hilo to a new development of houses that had been carved into a forested slope on the edge of the Mauna Loa volcano. She switched from a large school, with sixty kids per grade, to a smaller one with only twenty. There they studied US history, a subject that made her feel more connected to her roots and less like an outsider.

"It was a turning point," she recalled.

Doudna thrived so much that by the time she was in fifth grade, her math and science teacher urged her to skip a grade. Her parents agreed and moved her into sixth grade, and that year she finally made a close friend, a girl with whom she has kept in close contact her whole life. Lisa Hinkley (now Lisa Twigg-Smith) was from a classic mixed-race Hawaiian family: part Scottish, Danish, Chinese, and Polynesian. She knew how to handle the bullies.

"When someone would call me a . . . haole, I would cringe," Doudna recalled. "But when a bully called Lisa names, she would turn and look right at him and give it right back to him. I decided I wanted to be that way."

One day in class the students were asked what they wanted to be when they grew up. Lisa proclaimed that she wanted to be a skydiver. Doudna thought that was so cool. Lisa was bold in a way Doudna had never been. So Doudna told herself she needed to learn to be brave, and soon she started to be. Doudna and Lisa spent their afternoons riding bikes and hiking through sugarcane fields, where the biology was lush and diverse, with moss and mushrooms, peach and arenga palms. They found meadows filled with lava rocks covered in ferns, and in the lava-flow caves there lived a species of spider with no eyes. Doudna wondered, *How did this spider come to be?* She was also intrigued by a thorny vine called *hilahila* or "sleeping grass," because its fernlike leaves curl up when touched.[2]

We all see the wonders of nature every day, whether it be a plant that moves or a sunset that reaches its pink finger rays into a sky of deep blue. The key to true curiosity is pausing to think about the causes. What makes a sky blue or a sunset pink or a leaf of sleeping grass curl?

Doudna was curious about all those things and more, and she soon found someone who could help answer such questions. Her parents were friends with a biology professor named Don Hemmes, and he and Doudna's family loved to go on nature walks together. They especially liked hunting for mushrooms, which was Hemmes's scientific interest. After photographing the fungi, he would pull out his reference books and show Doudna how to identify them. He also collected microscopic shells from the beach, and he would work with her to categorize them so that they could try to figure out how they evolved.

Doudna's exploration also continued at home. Her father bought her a horse, a chestnut male named Mokihana after a Hawaiian tree with a fragrant fruit. She joined the soccer team, playing halfback, a position that had been hard to fill because it required a runner with long legs and lots of stamina. At school, math was her favorite class because it felt like detective work.

Although she began doing well academically, she did not feel that teachers at her small school on the outskirts of Hilo expected much of her. She had an interesting response to that, though—the lack of challenges made her feel free to take more chances.

"I decided you just have to go for it," she recalled. "It made me more willing to take on risks, which is something I later did in science when I chose projects to pursue."

Her father was the one person who *really* pushed her. He saw his oldest daughter as his soul mate in the family, the intellectual who was bound for college and an academic career like him. Doudna felt like she was the son he'd always wanted to have, and that was why he treated her a bit differently than he treated her sisters.

Doudna's father was a huge reader who would check out a stack of books from the local library each Saturday and finish them by the following weekend. Often he would bring home a book for Doudna to read. And that is how a paperback copy of James D. Watson's *The Double Helix* ended up on her bed one day when she was in sixth grade, and was waiting for her when she got home from school.

Doudna picked up the book, looked at it, and put it aside, thinking it was just some silly story she'd breeze through and soon forget. When she finally got around to it on a rainy Saturday afternoon, though, she was hooked. In *The Double Helix*, Watson writes how as a twenty-three-year-old biology student from the American Midwest he ended up at Cambridge University in England and bonded with the biochemist Francis Crick. In 1953, he and Crick won the race to discover the double helix, the two strands that wind around each other and make up the structure of DNA. Doudna loved how the book reveals fascinating, groundbreaking science at the same time it tells a gossipy account of the adventures of famous professors doing lab experiments, then playing tennis and drinking afternoon tea.

In addition to his own personal story, Watson related the fascinating tale of Rosalind Franklin, a structural biologist and **crystallographer**, which is a scientist who studies the arrangement of atoms in solids. Watson sometimes wasn't very kind to Franklin in the book, referring to her as "Rosy," a name she never used, and poking fun at her serious appearance and chilly personality. Yet he was respectful of her mastery of the complex science and beautiful art of using X-rays to discover the structure of molecules.

Doudna sped through the pages, enthralled with what was an intensely personal detective drama, filled with vividly portrayed characters. *The Double Helix* taught her about ambition, competition in the pursuit of nature's inner truths, and the importance of solid research. She also noticed how badly Rosalind Franklin was treated, in a condescending way that a lot of women endured during the 1950s. But what struck her more was that a woman could be a great scientist.

"It may sound a bit crazy," Doudna said later, "but reading the book was the first time I really thought about it, and it was an eye-opener. Women could be scientists."[3]

The book also led Doudna to realize something awe-inspiring about nature. There were biological mechanisms that governed living things, including the wondrous phenomena that caught her eye when she hiked through the Hawaiian rain forest. As she hunted for mushrooms and palms and spiders with no eyes, the ideas from the book made her grasp the fact that you could also discover the reasons behind why nature works the way it does.

Doudna's career would be shaped by the insight that is at the core of *The Double Helix*: the shape and structure of a chemical molecule determine what biological role it can play in the world. This is an amazing discovery for those who are interested in uncovering the fundamental secrets of life. In a larger sense, her career would also be molded by the realization that she was right when she first saw *The Double Helix* on her bed and thought that it was a detective mystery.

"I have always loved mystery stories," she noted years later. "Maybe that explains my fascination with science, which is humanity's attempt to understand the longest-running mystery we know: the origin and function of the natural world and our place in it."[4]

Even though Doudna's school didn't encourage girls to become scientists, she decided that was what she wanted to do. Driven by curiosity, a passion to understand how nature works, and a competitive desire to turn discoveries into inventions, Doudna would help make what James Watson would call the most important biological advance since the discovery of the double helix.

CHAPTER TWO

Genes and DNA

------- ⟨⟨⟨⟩⟩⟩ -------

The paths that led Watson and Crick to the discovery of DNA's double helix structure were pioneered a century earlier, in the 1850s, when the English naturalist Charles Darwin published his book *On the Origin of Species* and Gregor Mendel, a priest in Brno (now part of the Czech Republic), began breeding peas in the garden of his abbey. Together their discoveries gave birth to the idea of the **gene**, an entity that makes up part of a strand of an organism's DNA and that carries the traits the organism passes on to future generations.[1]

Charles Darwin had originally planned to follow the career path of his father and grandfather, who were well-respected doctors. But he found himself horrified by the sight of blood, and he quit medical school. Ever since he was eight years old, when he began collecting specimens of living things from the countryside near his home, his true passion had been to be a **naturalist**. He got his opportunity in 1831 when, at age twenty-two, he was offered the chance to take a round-the-world voyage on a ship called the HMS *Beagle*.[2]

In 1835, four years into the ship's five-year journey, the *Beagle* explored the Galápagos Islands, off the Pacific coast of South

America. There Darwin collected the skeletons of birds including finches, blackbirds, grosbeaks, mockingbirds, and wrens. Two years later, after he'd returned to England, he was informed by an ornithologist (a biologist who studies birds) that the birds were, in fact, different species of finches. Darwin began to formulate the theory that these very different birds had all evolved from a common ancestor.

He knew that horses and cows near his childhood home in rural England were occasionally born with slight variations, and over the years breeders would carefully select cows that could produce calves with the most desirable traits. Perhaps, he thought, other creatures in nature evolved in the same way. He decided to call this process "natural selection."

In certain isolated places, such as the islands of the Galápagos, he wondered if a few mutations (changes in the species' biology) would occur in each generation that would strengthen that species as a whole. For example, suppose a species of finch had a beak suited for eating fruit, but then a drought destroyed the fruit trees. Birds with beaks better suited for cracking nuts would live and pass on their traits, while the fruit-eating birds would die out. The mechanism of natural selection would lead to bird species well adapted to their environments. If a species could eat, it could survive and reproduce. Darwin wrote, "The results of this would be the formation of a new species."

The realization that species evolve through mutations and natural selection left a big question to be answered: On a microscopic level, how did this happen? How could a beneficial variation in the beak of a finch or the neck of a giraffe occur, and *then* how could it get passed along to future generations? Darwin thought that organisms might hold tiny particles that contained hereditary information, and he speculated that the information from a male and female blended when they bred.

Unfortunately, his logic ran into a problem. If these tiny bits of hereditary information combined, wouldn't new, beneficial qualities be blended with less-beneficial qualities, which would ultimately dilute all the positive traits? If good traits were constantly compromised over time because they mixed with bad ones, how did strong traits pass on? How did species survive and thrive?

Darwin had in his personal library a copy of a little-known scientific journal that contained an article, written in 1866, with the answer. But he never got around to reading it, nor did almost any other scientist at the time.

The author was Gregor Mendel, a monk born in 1822 to farmers in Moravia, in what is now the eastern part of the Czech Republic. Mendel had a garden and had developed an obsessive interest in breeding peas. His plants had seven traits that came in two variations: yellow or green seeds, white or violet flowers, smooth or wrinkled seeds, and so on. By careful selection, he produced purebred vines that had, for example, only violet flowers or only wrinkled seeds.

The following year he experimented with something new: breeding plants with differing traits, such as those that had white flowers with those that had violet ones. It was a difficult task that involved cutting each plant with small tools and using a tiny brush to transfer pollen. The work paid off, though, and what his experiments showed was momentous. There was no blending of traits. Tall plants crossbred with short ones did not result in medium-sized offspring, nor did purple-flowered plants crossbred with white-flowered ones produce pale lavender plants. Instead, all the offspring of a cross between a tall plant and a short plant were tall. The offspring from plants with purple flowers that had been crossbred with white-flowered plants grew only purple flowers. Mendel called these surviving aspects the **dominant traits**; the ones that did not prevail he called **recessive**.

An even bigger discovery came the following summer when he produced offspring from his hybrids. Although the first generation of plants had displayed only the dominant traits (such as all purple flowers or tall stems), the recessive trait reappeared in the next generation. And his records revealed a pattern: in this second generation, the dominant trait was exhibited in three out of four cases, with the recessive trait appearing once. When a plant inherited two dominant versions of the gene or a dominant and a recessive version, it would show the dominant trait. But if it happened to get two recessive versions of the gene, it would display that less common trait.

Mendel wrote up his findings and presented his paper in 1865 to forty farmers and plant-breeders in a science society, and they published it in the society's annual journal. The article was hardly noticed until 1900, at which point it was rediscovered by scientists performing similar experiments.[3] The findings of Mendel and these later scientists led to the concept of a unit of heredity, which a Danish botanist in 1909 called a "gene."

Over many decades, scientists studied living cells to try to determine where genes were located. Scientists initially assumed that genes were carried by proteins. After all, proteins do most of the important tasks in organisms, including making up an organism's structure, regulating its functions, and facilitating its growth. Researchers eventually figured out, however, that it is another common substance in living cells—**nucleic acids**—that are the workhorses of heredity. These molecules are composed of building blocks called **nucleotides**, and nucleotides are made up of a sugar group, a phosphate (a basic elemental substance) group, and one of four substances called **bases**. When the nucleotides are strung together in chains, they form a strand of nucleic acid. These nucleic acid molecules come in two varieties: ribonucleic acid (RNA) and a similar molecule whose sugar lacks one oxygen atom. Thus that molecule is called deoxyribonucleic acid, which is our old friend DNA.

The primary discovery that DNA housed all genes was made in 1944 by the bacteriologist Oswald Avery and his colleagues at the Rockefeller Institute Hospital, in New York City, which is now known as the Rockefeller University. They took DNA from a strain of bacteria, mixed it with another strain, and showed that the DNA passed down certain traits to the next generation. The next step in solving the mystery of life was figuring out how DNA did this. That required determining the exact structure of DNA, including how all its atoms fit together and what shape resulted.

This discovery was made in 1953 by two Cambridge University scientists named James D. Watson and Francis H. C. Crick.[4]

Or was it?

Watson and Crick met in the fall of 1951 in Cambridge University's Cavendish Lab. Despite a twelve-year age difference and the fact that Watson was American and Crick was British, they immediately clicked. Both shared the belief that discovering the structure of DNA would provide the key to the mysteries of heredity. Almost immediately they were lunching together at a pub near the lab called the Eagle, where they talked to each other so loudly that they were given their own room so that they wouldn't bother the other customers.

Around the same time Watson and Crick were experimenting and lunching, a brilliant thirty-one-year-old English biochemist named Rosalind Franklin came to work at King's College London. Born to a wealthy, educated family in London, she became a chemist and crystallographer. Her clothes weren't fancy or fashionable, which caused men to comment negatively on her appearance. But she was also a focused scientist who had an important skill: she had learned how to use X-rays to study chemical structures.

Franklin claimed she had taken pictures of DNA, but she refused to share them with anyone. In November 1951, though, she scheduled a lecture to summarize her latest findings. James Watson took the train down to London from Cambridge to watch.

"She spoke to an audience of about fifteen in a quick, nervous style," he recalled. "There was not a trace of warmth or frivolity in her words. And yet I could not regard her as totally uninteresting. Momentarily I wondered how she would look if she took off her glasses and did something novel with her hair."

It was the 1950s, after all, and women were valued for their looks, not their scientific genius.

Watson told Crick about the presentation the next morning. As he listened, Crick started scribbling diagrams, declaring that Franklin's data indicated a structure of two, three, or four strands twisted in a helix, a shape that looks like a spiral staircase. He thought that, by playing with different models based on what he'd sketched, they might soon discover the configuration of DNA. Within a week they had built a model that they thought provided a solution: three strands swirled in the middle, with their four bases jutting outward from the center.

Unfortunately, the model seemed to have some flaws, namely that some of the atoms they'd laid out were crushed together a little too closely.

Watson and Crick invited Maurice Wilkins to come up to Cambridge and take a look at their models and drawings, and Rosalind Franklin decided to come along as well. They arrived the next morning and, without saying much in the way of hellos, Crick began to display the triple-helix structure. Franklin immediately saw that it had errors. She told Crick his team was wrong and insisted that her pictures of DNA did not show that the molecule was the shape of a helix. Though her photos of DNA may not have shown this, on that point she would turn out to be incorrect. DNA is helical. But her other two objections were correct: the twisting strands that Watson and Crick had placed in the center had to be on the outside, not the inside, and their model did not contain enough water.

Watson and Crick realized they were in error, and they were embarrassed. Then the director of the Cavendish Lab found out about their mistake, and they were ordered to stop working on DNA. Their model-building components were packed up and sent to Rosalind Franklin and another scientist in London.

Watson and Crick turned to other projects, but they couldn't stop thinking about the fact that other people were hard at work searching for the structure of DNA while they weren't. They decided to monitor the work of other scientists, particularly one named Linus Pauling whose son Peter was a young student in their Cambridge lab.

One day in December 1952, Peter Pauling wandered into the lab, put his feet up on a desk, and dropped the news that Watson had been dreading. In his hand was a letter from his father in which Linus Pauling mentioned that he had come up with a structure for DNA and was about to publish it.

Pauling's paper arrived in Cambridge in early February. Peter got a copy first and walked into the lab to tell Watson and Crick that his father's solution was similar to the one they had tried: a three-chain helix with a backbone in the center. Watson grabbed the paper from Peter's coat pocket and began to read.

"At once I felt something was not right," Watson recalled. "I could not pinpoint the mistake, however, until I looked at the illustrations for several minutes."

Watson realized that some of the atomic connections in Pauling's proposed model would not be stable. As he discussed it with Crick and others in the lab, they became convinced that Pauling had made a big mistake—the same mistake Rosalind Franklin had pointed out to them. They got so excited that they quit work early that afternoon to dash off to the Eagle to celebrate.

After that, Watson and Crick decided they had no time to waste. Nor could they continue to let Franklin and other scientists do all the work. So Watson took the train down to London one afternoon, carrying his early copy of Pauling's paper. He walked into Rosalind Franklin's lab as she was bending over a light box measuring a crystal-clear X-ray image of DNA. She gave him an angry look, but he launched into a summary of Pauling's paper.

For a few moments they argued about whether DNA was likely to be a helix, with Franklin still doubtful. Watson interrupted her, and Franklin got even angrier. Just then another scientist named Maurice Wilkins walked by the lab, sensed a fight about to start, and pulled James Watson aside to have some tea and calm down. While they were speaking, he confided that Franklin had taken some pictures of a wet form of DNA that provided new evidence of its structure. He then went into another room and retrieved a print of what became known as "Photo 51."

Wilkins had gotten hold of the picture in a valid way: he was the PhD advisor of the student who had worked with Franklin to take it. What was less appropriate was showing it to Watson without Franklin's permission. Watson recorded some of the key data from the photograph and took those notes back to Cambridge to share with Crick. The photograph indicated that Franklin had been correct in arguing that the backbone strands of the structure were on the outside rather than on the inside of the molecule. But she was still wrong in resisting the possibility that DNA formed a helix.[5]

Watson and Crick soon received more of Franklin's data. She had submitted a report on her work to Britain's Medical Research Council, and a member of the council shared it with them. Although Watson and Crick had not exactly stolen Franklin's findings, they had once again used her work without her permission.

By then Watson and Crick had a pretty good idea of DNA's structure. It had two sugar-phosphate strands that twisted and spiraled to form a double-stranded helix. Extending in from these strands were the four bases in DNA: **adenine, thymine, guanine,** and **cytosine**, now commonly known by the letters A, T, G, and C. A sugar-phosphate strand with its base of A, T, G, or C is called a nucleotide, and the order of these nucleotides is called a DNA sequence.

DNA

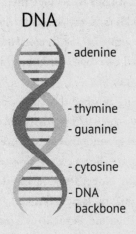

- adenine

- thymine
- guanine

- cytosine

- DNA backbone

Watson and Crick were also lucky to work in a lab of scientists with different specialties; one of them, a quantum chemist, confirmed that adenine (A) would pair with thymine (T), and guanine (G) would pair with cytosine (C). The exciting result of this structure was that when the two strands split apart, they could perfectly duplicate themselves. In other words, the structure Watson and Crick were proposing would permit the molecule to pass along the information encoded in itself.

Just like that, they knew how heredity worked. The structure of DNA allowed it to carry a genetic code that it could pass on when it split.

Watson encouraged the technicians in the machine shop at the Cavendish Lab to work faster on the DNA model. By this point everyone was on top of the world, and in a couple of hours the workers had finished making the shiny metal plates that were part of the model. With all the parts now on hand, it took Watson only an hour to arrange them so that the atoms matched with Franklin's X-ray data and the laws of chemical bonds. As Watson wrote in *The Double Helix*, "Francis winged into the Eagle to tell everyone within hearing distance that we had found the secret of life."

Watson and Crick finished their paper on the last weekend of March 1953. It was only 975 words, typed by Watson's sister.

Because of their groundbreaking discovery of the structure of DNA—and because they were the first scientists to publish correct findings—the Nobel Prize in Physiology or Medicine was awarded in 1962 to James Watson, Francis Crick, and Maurice Wilkins. Rosalind Franklin was not eligible because she had died in 1958, at age thirty-seven, of ovarian cancer. She may have developed cancer because of her repeated exposure to the radiation produced by all the X-rays she'd used in her research. If she had survived, the Nobel committee would have faced an awkward situation because each prize can be awarded to only three winners.

Even though Franklin had died in 1958, after Jennifer Doudna read *The Double Helix*, the scientist never left Doudna's mind. Here was a female scientist whose contributions to one of the greatest discoveries in scientific history had been used without her permission. She had been made fun of for her looks and dismissed for her passion, and then she had died before she could win the recognition she deserved. Rosalind Franklin had been an outsider just like Jennifer Doudna was. Franklin had been a part of the race to discover the truths of life, fighting against others who'd wanted to push her aside and win acclaim by announcing their findings first. As Doudna headed into high school, she wondered if she would fade into the background like Rosalind Franklin had—or if the time had come for a female scientist to shine.

CHAPTER THREE

The Education of a Biochemist

J ennifer Doudna would later meet James Watson, work with him on occasion, and be exposed to how difficult and complicated he could be. But her reactions when she first read his book as a sixth grader were simple. His work made her realize that it was possible to peel back the layers of nature's beauty and discover, as she says, "how and why things worked at the most fundamental and inner level." Everything in life was made up of molecules. The chemical components and structure of these molecules governed what they did.

The book also confirmed her hunch that science could be fun. All the previous science books she'd read had "pictures of emotionless men wearing lab coats and glasses." The tale of Watson and Crick and Franklin was one of competition and collaboration, of letting data dance with big ideas, and of being in a race with rival labs. All of that made sense to her, and it would continue to do so throughout her career.[1]

In high school Doudna got a chance to do a few biology experiments about DNA, including one that involved breaking apart salmon sperm cells and stirring their gooey contents with a glass rod. In tenth grade she was inspired by an energetic chemistry teacher who made the experiments seem like great adventures, and later she was inspired by a woman she heard lecture on the biochemical reasons why cells become cancerous.

But most of all, Doudna never forgot the long hikes in the rain forest—the environment that wove together her childhood curiosity about the eyeless spiders in the lava tubes, the sleeping grass that curled when you touched it, and the human cells that became cancerous. These things were all connected to the detective story of the double helix.

She decided that she wanted to study chemistry at college. Like many female scientists of the time, though, she met resistance. When she explained her college goals to her school's guidance counselor, he shook his head.

She paused and stared at him.

"Girls don't do science," he asserted. He then discouraged her from even taking the College Board chemistry test. "Do you really know what that is, what that test is for?" he asked.

"It hurt me," Doudna recalled, but it also made her determined. *Yes, I will do it,* she told herself. *I will show you. If I want to do science, I am going to do it.*

She applied to Pomona College in Claremont, California, just east of Los Angeles. Pomona had a good program in chemistry and biochemistry. She was admitted and enrolled in the fall of 1981. At first, she was unhappy there. Having skipped a grade in school, she was now only seventeen.

"I was suddenly a small fish in a very big pond," she recalled, "and I doubted I had what it took."

She was also homesick for Hawaii and, once again, felt out of place. Many of her classmates came from wealthy Southern

California families and had their own cars, while she was on a scholarship and worked part-time to pay her living expenses. In those days, it was expensive to call home long distance. Her parents didn't have a lot of money, so they told her to call collect (meaning they'd pay for it) but only once a month.

Doudna had been eager to major in chemistry, but soon began to doubt she could handle it. Perhaps her high school counselor had been right. Her general chemistry class had two hundred students, most of whom had gotten a five on the Advanced Placement chemistry test. It made her question whether she'd set her sights on something that was just not achievable. And because she was so competitive, college chemistry didn't appeal to her if she was just going to be a so-so student. She didn't want to become a chemist if she couldn't reach the top.

Doudna thought about changing her major to French, but when she went to talk to her French teacher about it, the teacher asked her what her current major was. When Doudna replied that it was chemistry, the teacher told her to stick with it.

"She was really insistent," Doudna said. "She said 'If you major in chemistry, you'll be able to do all sorts of things. If you major in French, you will be able to be a French teacher.'"[2]

Doudna's attitude improved the summer after her freshman year when she got a job working in the lab of her family friend Don Hemmes, the University of Hawaii biology professor who had taken her on nature walks when she was a child. He was using high-powered microscopes to investigate the movement of chemicals inside cells. Hemmes was also studying the evolution of tiny shells. An active scuba diver, he would scoop up samples of the smallest shells, almost microscopic in size, and his students would help him put them in sticky resin and slice thin sections to analyze them under a microscope. Doudna was so fascinated during her time with Hemmes that she started keeping a lab notebook for the first time.[3]

In Pomona College's chemistry classes, most of the experiments were conducted by following what was basically a recipe. There was a procedure you had to stick to, and there was only one right answer or result. The work in Don's lab wasn't like that. In fact, it was like an amazing adventure where you didn't know the answer you were meant to get. It gave Doudna a taste of the thrill of curiosity and discovery. It also helped her see what it would be like to be part of a community of scientists, making advances and piecing them together to decipher the ways that nature worked.

When Doudna returned to Pomona in the fall for her sophomore year, she was more mature and confident, and she made friends, fit in better, and became more assured of her ability to do chemistry. As part of her work-study program, Doudna had a series of jobs in the college chemistry labs. Most did not interest her because they did not explore how chemistry intersected with biology. But that changed after her junior year, when she got a summer position in the lab of her advisor, Sharon Panasenko, a biochemistry professor.

Panasenko was studying a topic that matched Doudna's interest in the mechanisms of living cells: how some bacteria found in soil can send out chemical signals that allow them to communicate with each other and join forces when they are starved for nutrients. Panasenko asked Doudna to help figure out how those chemical signals worked.

"I have to warn you," Panasenko told her, "that a technician in my lab has been working on growing these bacteria for six months, and he hasn't been able to make it work."

Doudna was not intimidated, and she began trying to grow the bacteria in large baking pans rather than the usual petri dishes. One night she put her preparations into the incubator. She came in the next day, and when she peeled back the foil on the particular baking dish that lacked nutrients, she was stunned to see these beautiful structures that looked like little footballs. She had succeeded where the other technician had failed.

"It was an incredible moment," she said, "and it made me think I could do science."

When it came time to apply to graduate school, Doudna did not initially think about Harvard, despite being the top student in her physical chemistry class. She didn't believe she could get in. But her father pushed her to apply.

"You certainly won't get in if you don't try," he said.

She *did* get in, and Harvard even offered her a lot of money to help with her living expenses.

Before she moved across the country to Cambridge, Massachusetts, she spent part of the summer traveling in Europe using the money she had saved from her work-study program at Pomona College. When Doudna got back in July 1985, she went right to Harvard so that she could begin working before classes started. Like other universities, Harvard required graduate chemistry students to work each semester in the lab of a different professor. The goal of these rotations was to allow students to learn different techniques and then select a lab for their dissertation research, which is the final, lengthy project required for someone to earn a PhD.

Doudna called Roberto Kolter, who was head of the graduate studies program, to ask if she could begin her rotations in his lab. A young Spanish specialist in bacteria, he had a big smile, wireless glasses, and a joyful way of speaking to people. His lab was international, with many of the researchers from Spain or Latin America, and Doudna was struck by how young and politically active they were. Maybe she was inspired because of her recent trip abroad, but she thought the diversity reflected the global nature of modern science. It became the way her labs would look for the rest of her career.

Kolter assigned Doudna to study how bacteria make molecules that are toxic to other bacteria. She was responsible for **cloning** (making an exact DNA copy of) genes from the bacteria and testing their functions. She thought of a new way to set up the process, but Kolter told her it wouldn't work. Doudna was stubborn, though, and she went ahead with her idea. It worked, and she got the clone. Kolter was surprised but supportive, and Doudna was delighted. This bold move was a step in overcoming the insecurity that she still had inside her.

Doudna began to work in the lab of Jack Szostak, a young Harvard molecular biologist who was studying DNA in yeast. Doudna got to watch him perform experiments, hear his thought process, and admire the way he took risks. The key aspect of his intellect, she realized, was his ability to make unexpected connections between different fields. Most of all, her experiments with him gave her a glimpse of how the science that happens in a lab can be used in the outside world.

Doudna's first experiment plunged her into the growing field of genetic engineering. Yeast cells can easily take up pieces of

DNA and incorporate them into their genetic makeup. Knowing this, Doudna engineered strands of DNA that contained a **sequence** (the chain-like order of the nucleotides in DNA) that matched a sequence in the yeast. With a little electric shock, she opened up tiny passageways in the cell wall of the yeast, allowing the DNA that she'd made to wriggle inside. It then combined with the yeast's DNA.

She had created a tool that could edit the genes of yeast!

CHAPTER FOUR

RNA

━━━━━━━━━━━━━⦸⦸⦸━━━━━━━━━━━━━

When Jennifer Doudna's lab rotation ended in the spring of 1986, she asked Jack Szostak if she could stay on and do her PhD research under him. Szostak agreed—but he made one thing clear. He was about to undertake a big move and was no longer going to focus on DNA in yeast. While other biochemists were getting excited about sequencing DNA for the Human Genome Project—an international, publicly funded effort to map all the genes in human DNA—he had decided to shift his lab's attention to ribonucleic acid, also known as "**RNA**." He suspected that RNA might reveal secrets about the biggest of all biological mysteries—the origins of life.

RNA is a molecule in living cells that is similar to DNA, but each nucleotide has one more oxygen atom in the sugar-phosphate backbone, and one of RNA's four bases is different. RNA might be less famous than DNA, but it does an essential job for DNA, carrying out its coded instructions. In fact, DNA doesn't do much work. It mainly stays at home in the nucleus of our cells, protecting the information it encodes and occasionally reproducing itself. RNA, on the other hand, takes DNA's coded information and goes out and makes real products, such as proteins.

These proteins come in many types. **Fibrous proteins**, for example, help form structures such as bones, muscles, hair, fingernails, tendons, and skin. **Membrane proteins** relay signals within cells and between adjacent cells. But the most fascinating type of proteins are **enzymes**. They serve as catalysts, which means they regulate the chemical reactions in all living things.

In the late 1980s, two scientists named Thomas Cech and Sidney Altman independently discovered that proteins were not the only molecules that could be enzymes. In fact, some forms of RNA acted as enzymes because they could split themselves after accelerating a chemical reaction. Cech and Altman called these catalytic RNAs "**ribozymes**,"[1] and their discovery was such huge and exciting news that it won them the Nobel Prize.

This finding had pretty cool implications. If some RNA molecules could store genetic information and speed up chemical reactions, they might be more fundamental to the origins of life than DNA, which cannot naturally replicate itself without the presence of proteins.[2] After all, an essential quality of living things is that they have a method to reproduce. If they can't do that, they cease to exist. Therefore, if you want to make the argument that RNA might be the foundational molecule for every living thing in the world, it helps to show *how* it can replicate itself. This was the project that Szostak and Doudna embarked upon.[3]

Both Doudna and Szostak knew that switching their focus to RNA was risky, but they didn't want to follow the herd researching DNA. Like Jennifer Doudna's great-grandmother in Montana, they yearned to pioneer something new, to explore a frontier that was a bit neglected but that they thought was exciting. Szostak had a guiding principle: *Never do something that a thousand other people are doing.* That appealed to Doudna.

"It was like when I was on the soccer field and wanted to play a position that the other kids didn't," she says. "I learned from Jack that there was more of a risk but also more of a reward if you ventured into a new area."

By this point Doudna knew that the most important clue for understanding a natural phenomenon was to figure out the structure of the molecules involved. That would require her to employ some of the principles that Watson and Crick and Franklin had used to unravel the structure of DNA. First, she asked questions. Next, she built models. Through the whole process, she enlisted the help of colleagues. Though, unlike Watson and Crick, she asked permission to use their work! She made many, many mistakes along the way, but ultimately, Doudna was able to create an RNA enzyme, or ribozyme, that could stitch together little RNA pieces. Then she and Szostak were able to engineer a ribozyme that could splice together a copy of itself.

"This reaction demonstrates the feasibility of RNA-catalyzed RNA replications," she and Szostak wrote in a 1998 paper for *Nature.*

The biochemist Richard Lifton later called this paper a "technical tour de force,"[4] and it sealed Doudna's place as a rising star in the complex world of RNA research. This scientific area was still very mysterious, but over the next two decades, the understanding of how little strands of RNA behaved would become increasingly important.

As a young PhD student, Doudna mastered the special combination of skills that distinguished Szostak and other great scientists: she was good at doing hands-on experiments and at asking the big questions. She knew that God was in the details but also in the big picture. What also stood out for Szostak was Doudna's willingness, even eagerness, to tackle challenges. That became evident near the end of her tenure in Szostak's lab in 1989, when Doudna realized that in order to understand the workings of a piece of RNA, she would have to fully uncover its structure, atom by atom.

"At that time, RNA structure was viewed as so difficult that it was maybe impossible to figure out," Szostak recalled. "Hardly anyone was trying anymore."[5]

Doudna wanted to.

Interestingly, James Watson—whose work had so fascinated Doudna as a child—was also hot on the trail to uncover the structure of RNA. In the summer of 1987, he'd organized a seminar at his laboratory in Cold Spring Harbor on Long Island, New York, to discuss "the evolutionary events that may have given rise to the living organisms that now exist on earth."[6] In other words, how did life begin?

This is a big question, so Watson narrowed his focus. At the conference, he wanted to explore the recent discoveries showing that certain RNA molecules could replicate themselves. Szostak was invited, but he was unavailable, so an invitation went out to Doudna to present the work that they were doing on engineering a self-replicating RNA molecule. When she got the letter addressed to "Dear Ms. Doudna" (she was not yet Dr. Doudna) and signed by Watson, she not only immediately accepted; she also had it framed.

Jennifer Doudna was only twenty-three, and she was about

to make a presentation at a scientific conference for the first time. Not only that, but one of her heroes, James Watson, would be sitting in the front row.

The talk she gave was based on the paper she had written with Szostak. It was highly technical but very exciting, and, as she spoke, Watson eagerly listened and took notes.

"I was so incredibly nervous that my palms were sweating," she recalls.

At the end of her speech, Watson stood up, walked toward her, and offered his congratulations. Another scientist whose work had paved the way for Doudna and Szostak's paper also leaned over and whispered, "Good job."[7]

Doudna was floored by their praise. Clearly, her work with Szostak was moving the scientific community's understanding of RNA in a hugely positive direction.

At some point during the conference, Doudna took a walk down Bungtown Road, which wanders through the laboratory's campus. Along the way, she saw a slightly stooped woman walking toward her. The woman was the biologist Barbara McClintock, who had been a researcher at Cold Spring Harbor for more than forty years and had recently been awarded the Nobel Prize for her discovery of **transposons**, known as "jumping genes," which can change their position within the DNA strand. Doudna paused when she saw McClintock, but she was too shy to introduce herself.

"I felt like I was in the presence of a goddess," she said years later, still in awe. "Here's this woman who's so famous and so incredibly influential in science acting so unassuming and walking toward her lab thinking about her next experiment. She was what I wanted to be."

CHAPTER FIVE

The Twists and Folds of Structural Biology

⎯⎯⎯⎯ ⌇⌇⌇ ⎯⎯⎯⎯

Ever since she had puzzled over the touch-sensitive leaves of the sleeping grass on her walks as a child in Hawaii, Doudna had been passionately curious about the underlying mechanisms of nature. How did chemical reactions cause biological activity?

The field of biochemistry—which is the study of the chemical processes that direct the activity of all organisms—provided many answers by showing Doudna how the molecules in living cells behave. But there is a specialty that looks even deeper into nature: **structural biology**. Using imaging techniques such as X-ray crystallography—which is what Rosalind Franklin had used to find evidence of the structure of DNA—structural biologists try to discover the three-dimensional shapes of molecules and how they function.

Doudna realized that she would need to learn more about structural biology if she truly wanted to understand how some RNA molecules could reproduce themselves.

"To figure out how these RNA do chemistry," she says, "I needed to know what they looked like."

She was aware that such work would be an echo to what

Franklin had done with DNA, and the parallel pleased her. But Doudna's interest went beyond a thirst for scientific knowledge. She also sensed that once you figured out the structure of certain molecules, that discovery might lead to groundbreaking genetic technologies that could help prevent and cure diseases—or more.

Doudna's new pursuit meant that it was time to move on from the lab of Jack Szostak, who admitted that he was not a visual thinker or an expert in structural biology. In 1991, Doudna considered where and with whom she could do her postdoctoral work. There was one obvious choice—the structural biologist who had just shared the Nobel Prize for discovering ribozymes, the kind of RNA that she and Szostak had been studying— Thomas Cech (pronounced "check") of the University of Colorado in Boulder. Like Rosalind Franklin, he was using X-ray crystallography to explore each nook and cranny of the structure of RNA. Plus, Doudna had already met Cech. He was the man who'd whispered "Good job" after her sweaty-palmed lecture at Cold Spring Harbor in the summer of 1987.

There was one other reason why Doudna decided to go to Boulder for her postdoctoral work. In January 1988 she had married a Harvard Medical School student named Tom Griffin, who'd been working in a lab next to hers. Griffin loved Colorado, and they decided to move there in the summer of 1991.

At first the marriage worked well enough. Doudna bought a mountain bike, and she and Tom enjoyed riding together along Boulder Creek. She also took up Rollerblading and cross-country skiing. But her true passion was science, and her husband didn't share her single-minded focus. Science for him was a day job, and he didn't want to spend his spare time in a lab. He was interested in music and books, and while Doudna respected his hobbies, she didn't share them.

"I'm someone who's thinking about science all the time," she says. "I'm always focused on what's cooking in the lab, the next experiment, or the bigger question to pursue."

After a few years, they decided to divorce. Doudna was obsessed with what her next experiment was going to be, and Tom didn't have that same intensity.

Luckily, Doudna knew that keeping busy would allow her to adjust to her new life change. She was on a scientific mission to determine the three-dimensional structure of RNA, and if she could do that, she'd show how its twists and folds bring atoms together and cause chemical reactions that allow the RNA to replicate.

She wasn't starting from scratch. During the 1970s, biologists had figured out the structure of a smaller and simpler RNA molecule. But little progress had been made in the twenty years since then because scientists found it difficult to isolate and get images of bigger RNAs. Colleagues told Doudna that getting a good image of a large RNA molecule would be too difficult and she was crazy to even try. What she planned to do was a high-risk venture that involved going to a region of the playing field where few others wanted to run. But if she succeeded, there would be a huge payoff for science.

Doudna was determined. She knew that the first step was to crystallize the RNA, which meant converting a liquid RNA molecule into a well-organized solid structure. Then she could use X-ray crystallography and other imaging techniques to figure out its components and shapes.

Helping her was a quiet but cheery graduate student named Jamie Cate. He had been using X-ray crystallography to study the structure of proteins, but when he met Doudna, he joined her quest to focus on RNA.

"I told him about the project I was working on, and he got very interested," she says. "It was really out there. We had no idea what we were going to find."

Unlike Tom Griffin, Cate loved to focus on lab work. He and Doudna talked every day about how to crystallize the RNA, and soon they were continuing their discussions over coffee and sometimes dinner.

While they were getting to know each other, they made a breakthrough that resulted from one of those small mistakes that often happen in science. One day a technician was working with Doudna to try to make crystals, and she put the experiment into an incubator that was not working properly. When the technician and Doudna realized what had happened, they assumed the experiment was spoiled. Then they looked at the samples through a microscope; there were crystals growing.

"That was the first breakthrough showing us that to get these crystals we had to elevate the temperature," Doudna says.

Shortly after the faulty incubator incident, another advance showed the enduring power of being in the same location as other smart people. Tom and Joan Steitz, a husband-and-wife team of Yale biochemists who were studying RNA, were in Boulder for a year. Tom liked hanging around the lunchroom of the Cech lab holding a mug of coffee. One morning, Doudna mentioned to him that she had been able to obtain crystals of the RNA molecule she was researching but that they tended to break down too quickly when they were exposed to X-rays. Steitz replied that in his Yale lab he had been testing a new technique for cooling crystals. He arranged for Doudna to fly to Yale and spend time with the researchers in his lab there who were pioneering the technique.

When she got to Yale, she discovered that the process worked beautifully. Doudna immediately knew she had the answer for how to solve the structure of RNA.

Her visit to Tom Steitz's lab at Yale helped convince Doudna to accept a job there in the fall of 1993 as a professor. Not surprisingly, Jamie Cate wanted to accompany her, so she contacted the Yale administration and helped arrange for him to transfer there as a graduate student in her lab. By using the supercooling techniques, Doudna and Cate were able to create crystals that could work well with X-rays. They ran into a few problems along the way, but together they solved them. Soon they began the process of creating maps of RNA and then building models of potential structures, just as Watson and Crick had done for DNA in the early 1950s.

Unfortunately, when their work was reaching its climax in the fall of 1995, Doudna got a call from her father. He had been diagnosed with melanoma, an aggressive form of skin cancer, and it had traveled to his brain. He told her that he had only three months to live. Doudna spent the rest of that fall flying back and forth from Yale to Hilo, a journey of more than twelve hours. Chunks of time at her father's bedside were interspersed with hours on the phone with Cate. Each day, Cate would send her new images, and they would talk about ways to interpret it.

"It was an incredible time of highs and lows and intense emotional swings," she recalls.

Fortunately, her father was genuinely curious about her work, and that made the ordeal less difficult. In between periods of crippling pain, he would ask her to give him the latest images she had received. She would walk into his bedroom, and he would be lying there looking at the latest data. Before they could discuss his health, he would ask her questions.

During a visit that November, which lasted through Thanksgiving, an RNA map arrived from Yale that she realized was good enough to nail down the structure of the RNA molecule. She could actually see how the RNA was folded up into an amazing three-dimensional shape. She and Cate had been working on it for more than two years—while countless colleagues had declared that what they were doing was impossible—and now the latest data showed that they had triumphed.

Her father was completely bedridden by then and could barely move. But she walked into his bedroom and showed him a color printout she had made from a data file of the latest map.

It looked like a green ribbon that was twisted into a really cool shape.

"It looks like green fettuccini," he joked.

The visit clarified how time had strengthened her relationship with her father. She knew how deeply she was going to miss sharing her discoveries with him when he was gone. He took science seriously, and he took her seriously. Like her, he was attracted to all the details, but he also sought the bigger picture.

When Martin Doudna died a few months later, Doudna and her mother and sisters went with friends on a hike to scatter his ashes high up in the Waipio Valley near Hilo. The name means "curving water," and the river that winds through the lush wilderness has many gorgeous waterfalls. Among those friends joining them were Don Hemmes, the biology professor who'd mentored Doudna, and her closest childhood friend, Lisa Hinkley Twigg-Smith.

"As we released his ashes into the wind," Twigg-Smith recalled, "[a] hawk . . . soared overhead."[1]

Doudna's father's death coincided with her first major scientific success. She and Cate, along with their lab colleagues, were able to determine the location of every atom in a certain RNA molecule. Just as the double-helix structure of DNA had revealed how it could store and transmit genetic information, the structure Doudna and her team had discovered explained how RNA could be an enzyme and be able to slice, connect, and copy itself.[2]

When their paper was published, Yale sent out a press release that attracted the notice of a local New Haven, Connecticut, television station. After trying to explain what a ribozyme is, the news anchor reported that it had baffled scientists because they had never been able to see its shape.

"But now a team led by Yale scientist Jennifer Doudna finally was able to capture a snapshot of the molecule," the anchor proclaimed.

The story featured a young, dark-haired Doudna in her lab, showing off a blurry image on her computer screen.

"We hope our discovery will provide clues as to how we might be able to modify the ribozyme so that it can repair defective genes," she said.

Though she didn't think about it much at the time, it was a momentous statement and marked the beginning of her quest to translate basic science about RNA into a tool that could edit genes.

Over the next two decades, many people would contribute to the development of gene-editing technologies. What distinguishes Doudna's tale is that, by the time she entered the field of gene editing, she had already established her reputation and earned distinction in the most basic underlying science: the structure of RNA.

CHAPTER SIX

Going West

In September 1996, *Science* published the article that Doudna and her colleagues had written about their discovery of RNA's structure.[1] By that time, Doudna and Jamie Cate were more than scientific partners and coauthors; they had also started dating. They got married in the summer of 2000 at the Melaka Beach Hotel on the Big Island of Hawaii. Two years later, they had their only child, Andrew.

By then, Cate had become an assistant professor at MIT, so he and Doudna were commuting between New Haven and Cambridge, Massachusetts. By train the trip is less than three hours, but for a new couple who worked long hours, it was exhausting. They decided to see if they could get appointments in the same town.[2] Harvard offered Doudna a position in the Department of Chemistry and Chemical Biology, which had just been renamed and was growing. She went there as a visiting professor, and on the first day the dean handed her an offer letter for a permanent position. With Cate at nearby MIT, it seemed to be an ideal arrangement.

Then she got a call from the University of California at Berkeley—all the way across the country. Her first reaction was to turn down any offer that took her so far away again, but when she told Cate, he was pleasantly surprised.

"You should call them back," he said. "Berkeley is nice."

She did, and soon she and Cate arranged a trip there. When they visited Berkeley's campus, Doudna didn't want to move there. But Cate became more enthusiastic. He enjoyed the West Coast and thought Cambridge was not laid-back enough for his tastes. He didn't like that the director of his lab wore a bow tie every day, and he was happier at the thought of being at Berkeley, where the energy level was mellow. Doudna quickly warmed up to the idea, and by the summer of 2002, they had moved.

During Doudna's first semester at Berkeley, in the fall of 2002, there was an outbreak in China of a virus that causes fever, muscle aches, difficulty breathing, and coughing. Called severe acute respiratory syndrome (SARS), the disease stopped being an imminent threat after eighteen months, but during that time it killed close to eight hundred people around the world. Many viruses are composed of DNA, but SARS contained RNA. This newly discovered virus intrigued Doudna, and she became interested in how the RNA in some viruses—such as circular, studded **coronaviruses**—allows them to take over the protein-making machinery of cells.

Doudna also became interested in a phenomenon known as **RNA interference**, or RNAi. Normally, the genes encoded by the DNA in cells send messenger RNAs (RNA molecules that carry genetic information copied from the DNA, also called mRNA) to direct the building of a protein. RNA interference does just what the name implies: small molecules find a way to mess with these mRNAs, and so the proteins don't get built.

RNA interference happens with the help of an enzyme known as "Dicer." Dicer snips a long piece of interfering RNA into short fragments. Then, after joining up with some other structures in the cell, these little interfering RNA fragments head out on a search-and-destroy mission, seeking out a mRNA molecule that has matching letters (bases). The mRNA is chopped up in a scissors-like fashion. This silences the genetic information carried by the messenger RNA.

Researchers did not understand how Dicer was able to cut RNA into precisely the right letter sequences to disrupt a specific gene, so Doudna set out to discover its molecular structure. As she had done at Yale, she turned to X-ray crystallography to map out Dicer's composition. She ultimately determined that Dicer acted like a measuring ruler, with a clamp at one end that it used to grab on to a long RNA strand, and an axe at the other end, which it used to chop the segment at just the correct length.

Doudna and her team published a paper in 2006 showing how part of the Dicer enzyme could be replaced to create tools that would shut off many different genes.[3] The fact that Dicer could be altered was a very useful discovery that permitted researchers to use RNAi to determine the function of certain genes and to regulate their activities for medical purposes.

In the age of coronaviruses, there is another role that RNA interference may play. Throughout the history of life on our planet, some organisms (though not humans) have evolved to use RNAi to fight off viruses.[4] Doudna wondered: Perhaps there could be a way to use RNAi to protect humans from infections? There was evidence that there might be a way, and researchers hoped that drugs based on RNA interference might someday be a good option for treating severe viral infections, including those caused by new coronaviruses.[5]

A few months after Doudna's article, a paper published in a little-known journal described a different virus-fighting mechanism that exists in nature. It was written by a Spanish scientist who had discovered the mechanism in microorganisms like bacteria, which have a far longer and even more brutal history of fighting viruses than we humans do. At first, the handful of scientists studying this bacterial virus-fighting system assumed that it worked through RNA interference. They would soon discover that the microorganism phenomenon was even more interesting.

PART TWO
CRISPR

CHAPTER SEVEN

In the Lab with CRISPR

I n 1990, Francisco Mojica, a graduate student at the University of Alicante on the Mediterranean coast of Spain, began studying single-celled organisms called archaea that are similar to bacteria. The particular archaea he worked with thrive in ponds that are ten times saltier than the ocean. Mojica was looking at the genes that he thought might explain the organism's love of salt.

As discussed earlier, strands of DNA are made up of sequences of nucleotides, and each nucleotide has a base of A, T, C, or G. One day in his lab, Mojica spotted fourteen identical DNA sequences that were repeated at regular intervals. They seemed to be palindromes, meaning they read the same backward and forward.[1]

At first he assumed that he had made a mistake. But by 1992, his data was still showing these regularly spaced repeats, and Mojica began to wonder if anyone else had found something similar. Google did not yet exist, so he went to the library and searched through scientific journals. Eventually he stumbled upon a paper by a Japanese scientist who had observed the same phenomenon in *E. coli* bacteria.

Although it is also a single-celled organism, *E. coli* is very different from archaea, so it was surprising that both had these repeated sequences. Mojica figured the phenomenon couldn't be random; it had to serve some biological purpose. Bacteria and archaea don't contain much genetic material, and they cannot afford to waste a lot of it on sequences that have no important function. He launched a research group to study these mysterious repeated sequences, but it was difficult to get funding.

"I was told to stop obsessing about repeats, because there were a lot of those type of phenomena in organisms, and mine were probably nothing special," he says.

He kept studying them, though, and by 1997, he and other researchers had found these repeated sequences in twenty different species of bacteria and archaea. Many different names for the repeated sequences had sprouted, but the one that stuck was something Mojica came up with when he was driving home from his lab one evening. It was CRISPR, for "clustered regularly interspaced short palindromic repeats." Although the clunky phrase was almost impossible to remember, the acronym CRISPR was, indeed, crisp and crispy. It sounded friendly rather than too scientific or odd.

When he got home, he asked his wife what she thought of the name.

"It sounds like a great name for a dog," she said. "Crispr, Crispr, come here, pup!" He laughed and decided it would work.

In August 2003, Mojica was still hard at work figuring out the role CRISPRs played, but this time he was studying bacteria rather than archaea. He was on vacation in the beach town of Santa Pola, about twelve miles south of Alicante, staying at the house of his wife's parents. The holiday was not his idea of a good time. He loved his family, but he hated crowds and the heat. While his wife lay on the beach working on her tan, he would drive up to his lab in Alicante for the day, where he would analyze sequences from *E. coli* bacteria.[2]

What fascinated him were the "spacers," which were regions of normal-looking DNA segments that were nestled in between the repeated CRISPR segments. He took the spacer sequences of *E. coli* and ran them through databases. What he found was intriguing: the spacer segments matched sequences that were in the genetic material of viruses that attacked *E. coli*. He found the same thing when he looked at other bacteria with CRISPR sequences; the spacer segments in the bacteria matched the genetic material in viruses that attacked those bacteria.

One evening, when he was sure about his discovery, he explained it to his wife.

"I just discovered something really amazing," he said, after he got back to the beach house. "Bacteria have an immune system. They're able to remember what viruses have attacked them in the past."

She laughed, admitted she didn't quite understand, but said she believed it must be important because he was so excited.

He replied, "In a few years, you'll see this thing that I've just discovered will be written about in newspapers and in history books."

That part she did not believe.

The truth is that what Mojica had stumbled upon was a battlefront in the longest-running, most intense war on this planet, the fight between bacteria and the viruses—known as "**bacteriophages**" or "phages"—that attack them. Phages are the largest category of viruses in nature and are by far the most plentiful biological entity on earth. In fact, there exist a trillion phages for every single grain of sand.[3] Almost from the beginning of life on this planet, bacteria have developed elaborate methods for defending against viruses, and the viruses have sought ways to fight back.

Viruses work by invading an organism's cells and taking over the cell's machinery, so the virus can reproduce. Mojica found that bacteria with CRISPR spacer sequences seemed to be immune to the virus that had the same sequence. Bacteria without the spacers *did* get infected, though. It was clear that CRISPR was an amazing defense system, but there was something even cooler: the bacteria with CRISPR appeared to adapt to new threats. When new viruses came along, the bacteria that survived the attacks from those viruses were able to incorporate some of the virus's genetic material. Not only did this allow the bacteria to resist future attacks from the same kind of virus, but it also meant that the bacteria's *offspring* would be immune to that virus. Mojica recalls being so overcome by emotion at this realization that he got tears in his eyes.[4] The beauty of nature can sometimes do that to you.

The fact that bacteria could pass immunity to their offspring was an astonishing discovery, but unfortunately no one seemed to care at first. Three scientific publications rejected the papers he wrote about his realization, saying his research wasn't valid or his findings not important. Two years after Mojica had first identified that CRISPR was a type of immune system, he was finally published.

As is often the case in the history of science, discoveries can have unexpected applications. A scientist like Mojica may dive into research because they are curious about something, and be amazed later when it leads to a major finding. His prediction to his wife that his discovery would someday be in history books proved to be correct. Mojica's paper was the beginning of a wave of articles providing evidence that CRISPR was, indeed, an immune system that some bacteria adapted whenever they got attacked by a new type of virus.

Within a year, researchers at the US National Center for Biotechnology Information extended Mojica's theory by showing that some enzymes called "Cas" (short for "CRISPR-associated") enzymes could grab bits of DNA out of the attacking viruses and insert them into the bacteria's own DNA. This is sort of like cutting and pasting a mug shot of dangerous viruses.[5] But the researchers got one thing wrong. They speculated that the CRISPR defense system worked through RNA interference. In other words, they thought that bacteria used the mug shots to find a way to interfere with the virus's mRNAs (which carry out the instructions encoded by the virus's DNA).

Others thought so, too. And that's why Jennifer Doudna— one of the world's leading experts on RNA interference—got a call in early 2006 from another Berkeley professor she had heard of but didn't know.

That scientist was Jillian Banfield, a microbiologist who— like Francisco Mojica—was interested in tiny organisms found in extreme environments. Microbiologists are scientists who study microscopic living things. A friendly Australian who loved to collaborate with other scientists, Banfield was studying bacteria that her team had found in a very salty lake in Australia, in a hot geyser in Utah, and in the extremely acidic waste draining from a California copper mine into a salt marsh.[6]

When Banfield sequenced the DNA of her bacteria, she kept finding examples of the clustered repeated sequences known as CRISPRs. She was among those who assumed that the CRISPR system worked by using RNA interference. When she typed "RNAi and UC Berkeley" into Google, Doudna's name was the top result, so Banfield gave her a call. They agreed to meet for tea.

Doudna had never heard of CRISPR. In fact, she thought that Banfield was saying "crisper." After hanging up, she did a quick online search and found just a few articles about it. When she got to the point in an article where it said CRISPR stood for "clustered regularly interspaced short palindromic repeats," she decided to wait for Banfield to explain it to her.

The two scientists met on a windy spring day at a stone table in the courtyard of the Free Speech Movement Café, a soup-and-salad hangout at the entrance to Berkeley's undergraduate library. Banfield had printed out papers about CRISPR. She realized that, in order to figure out the function of these CRISPR sequences, it made sense to collaborate with a biochemist such as Doudna, who could analyze them in a laboratory.

Once the two women started talking, they became increasingly excited and began to talk faster. At the café table, Banfield drew a string of diamonds and squares that represented segments of the DNA she had found in her bacteria. The diamonds, she said, all had identical sequences, but the interspersed squares each had unique sequences.

"It's like they are diversifying so fast in response to *something*," she told Doudna. "I mean, what was causing these strange clusters of DNA sequences? How did they actually work?"

Until then, CRISPRs had largely been the focus of microbiologists such as Mojica and Banfield, who study living organisms. These scientists had come up with elegant theories about CRISPR—some of them correct—but they had not done controlled experiments in test tubes to figure out the structures of the molecules. If you could find out what CRISPR was made of, you might be able to uncover exactly how it worked. The time was right for a biochemist and structural biologist like Jennifer Doudna to jump in.

And jump in she did.

At first Doudna didn't have anyone in her lab to work with her. So she looked around and hired Blake Wiedenheft, a charming student from Montana who loved the outdoors. He had also worked with microorganisms from extreme environments, and he had collected samples from places as varied as the rugged, volcanic Kamchatka Peninsula in Russia and the boiling acid springs in Yellowstone National Park. Soon he was joined by Martin Jinek (pronounced "YEE-nik"), an expert in crystallography who had a singular focus and a fierce independence. Originally from the Czech Republic, he wanted nothing more than to figure out the structure of complexes that combined RNA and enzymes, and he thrived when he worked without much hands-on direction.[7]

Wiedenheft threw himself into his work in Doudna's lab with the joyful passion he displayed as an outdoorsman. At lunchtime he would go on a hard-core bike ride, then work through the afternoon and evening still wearing his cycling gear, wandering around the lab in his helmet. He once spent forty-eight hours straight on an experiment, sleeping next to it. He was willing to charge headlong into techniques he had never used before, and he leaned on Jinek to show him how. Wiedenheft was a microbiologist who wanted to learn crystallography, and Jinek was a crystallographer who wanted more experience working with living cells. They took an instant liking to each other.

Doudna decided that her lab's goal would be to dissect the CRISPR system into its chemical components and study how each worked. She and Wiedenheft chose to focus first on the CRISPR-associated enzymes.

Let's pause for a quick refresher course.

Enzymes are a type of protein. Their main function is to act as catalysts that regulate chemical reactions in the cells of living organisms, from bacteria to humans. There are more than five thousand biochemical reactions that are handled by enzymes, including breaking down starches and proteins in the digestive system, causing muscles to contract, sending signals between cells, regulating metabolism, and—most important for this discussion—cutting or splicing DNA and RNA.

By 2008, scientists had discovered a handful of enzymes produced by genes that are adjacent to the CRISPR sequences in a bacteria's DNA. These CRISPR-associated (Cas) enzymes enable the system to cut and paste new memories of viruses that attack bacteria. These enzymes also create short segments of RNA, known as **CRISPR RNA** (crRNA), that can guide a scissors-like enzyme to a dangerous virus and cut up its genetic material. Presto! That's how the clever bacteria create an immune system that can adapt to new threats!

The notation system for these Cas enzymes was still in development in 2009, largely because they were being discovered in different labs. Eventually they were standardized into names such as Cas1, Cas9, Cas12, and Cas13.

Doudna and Wiedenheft decided to focus on what became known as Cas1. It's the only Cas enzyme that appears in all bacteria that have CRISPR systems, which indicates that it performs a fundamental function. Cas1 had another advantage for a lab that was using X-ray crystallography to try to discover how the structure of a molecule determines its functions: it was easy to get Cas1 to crystallize.

Wiedenheft was able to isolate the Cas1 gene from bacteria and then clone it and crystallize it. But he was stuck when he tried to figure out the exact crystal structure, because he did not have enough experience using X-ray crystallography. That's where Jinek came in. Together they visited the nearby Lawrence Berkeley National Laboratory, where Jinek helped analyze the data so they could build an atomic model of the Cas1 protein.

They discovered that Cas1 has a distinct fold, indicating that it is the mechanism that bacteria use to cut off a snippet of DNA from invading viruses and incorporate it into their CRISPR arrangement. This new sequence then acts as the key to the memory-forming stage of the immune system. In June 2009, the team published their discovery in a paper that was the Doudna Lab's initial contribution to the CRISPR field. It was the first explanation of a CRISPR mechanism based on a structural analysis of one of its components.[8]

CHAPTER EIGHT

The Yogurt Makers

Some people say that science is the parent of invention, meaning that scientific principles and discoveries lead to new products and technologies. But often it's the opposite. Invention can act as the parent of science when new techniques or developments lead to a greater understanding of the principles behind those discoveries. For example, the creation of the steam engine allowed scientists to understand **thermodynamics** (the science that deals with the relations between heat and other forms of energy)—not the other way round. Orville and Wilbur Wright developed the first successful plane, and their invention helped advance the field of **aerodynamics** (the science of how objects move through air).

The colorful history of CRISPR provides another great tale about how, at times, inventions and technology lead to a greater understanding of the science that helped make them. In this case, it involves yogurt.

As Doudna and her team began working on CRISPR in the early 2000s, two young food scientists on different continents were studying CRISPR with the goal of improving ways to make yogurt and cheese. Rodolphe Barrangou in North Carolina and Philippe

Horvath in France worked for Danisco, a Danish food ingredient company that makes starter cultures, the collection of microorganisms that help ferment milk in order to make other dairy products. Starter cultures for yogurt and cheese are made from bacteria, and the greatest threats to the $40 billion global yogurt market are viruses that can destroy bacteria. So Danisco was willing to spend a lot of money for research into how bacteria defend themselves against these viruses. The company has a rich historical record of the DNA sequences of bacteria it has used over the years, and that is how Barrangou and Horvath—who first heard of Mojica's research into CRISPR at a conference—became part of the relationship between basic science and business.

Barrangou was born in Paris, and the country's rich culinary tradition gave him an enthusiasm for food. He also loved science, and in college he decided to combine his passions. He enrolled at North Carolina State University in Raleigh and got his master's degree in the science of pickle and sauerkraut fermentation. He went on to get his doctorate there, married a food scientist he met in class, and followed her to Madison, Wisconsin, when she went to work at the Oscar Mayer meat company. Madison is also home to a Danisco unit that produces hundreds of megatons of bacteria cultures for fermented dairy products per year, including yogurt. In 2005, Barrangou took a job there as a research director.[1]

Years before, he had become friends with another French food scientist, Philippe Horvath, who was a researcher at a Danisco laboratory in central France. Horvath was developing tools to identify the viruses that attack different strains of bacteria, and the two men began a long-distance collaboration to study CRISPR.

They would talk by phone two or three times a day as they plotted their plans. Their method was to study the CRISPR sequences of bacteria in Danisco's vast database, starting with *Streptococcus thermophilus*, the bacteria that is the great workhorse of the dairy culture industry. Barrangou and Horvath compared the bacteria's CRISPR sequences with the DNA of the viruses that attacked them. The beauty of Danisco's historic collection of bacteria data was that there were bacteria strains from every year since the early 1980s, so the researchers could observe the changes that occurred to the bacteria over time.

Horvath and Barrangou noticed that in the bacteria that had been collected soon after a big virus attack, there were new spacers with sequences from those viruses, indicating that the bacteria had acquired these sequences to prevent future attacks. Because the immunity was now part of the bacteria's DNA, it was passed down to all future generations.

After one specific comparison done in May 2005, they realized they had nailed the relationship between the bacteria's CRISPR sequences and the virus's DNA.

"We saw there was a hundred-percent match between the CRISPR of the bacterial strain and the sequence of the virus that we knew had attacked it," Barrangou recalls.[2]

They then accomplished something very useful: they showed that they could engineer the bacteria's immunity by creating and adding their own spacers. In addition, they proved that CRISPR-associated (Cas) enzymes were critical for acquiring new spacers and fighting off attacking viruses.

In 2005, the two French food scientists used these discoveries to apply for and get one of the first patents granted for

CRISPR-Cas systems. A patent is a document that gives a person the right to prevent other people from making, using, or selling an invention for a certain number of years. In this case, Danisco used that patent to create an exclusive way for CRISPR to vaccinate its bacterial strains. Almost two years later, Barrangou and Horvath produced a paper about CRISPR for the journal *Science*.

"That was a great moment in time," Barrangou says. "Here we were, workers at an unknown Danish company, sending a manuscript on a little-known system in an organism that no scientist cares about. Even to get reviewed was amazing. And we got accepted!"[3]

The article helped kick interest in CRISPR into a higher orbit. Jillian Banfield, the Berkeley biologist who had enlisted Doudna at the Free Speech Movement Café, immediately called Barrangou. They decided to do what pioneers in emerging fields often do: start an annual conference. The first conference— organized by Banfield and Blake Wiedenheft—met in late July 2008 in Berkeley's Stanley Hall, where Doudna's lab was. Only thirty-five people attended, including Francisco Mojica, who came from Spain to be a featured speaker.

Long-distance collaborations work well in science— especially in the CRISPR field, as Barrangou and Horvath showed. But being close physically can spark more powerful reactions; ideas come together when people have tea at places like the Free Speech Movement Café.

The conference rules were loose and trusting. People could talk informally about data they had not yet published, and the other participants would not take advantage of that. Each scientist helped the others, shared new insights, and never tried to step on the other researchers' toes. One conference attendee called the July meeting "our scientific Christmas party."[4]

The year of the inaugural conference produced a major advance. Two scientists from Chicago showed that the target of the CRISPR system was the virus's **genome** (an organism's full set of genetic information). In other words, CRISPR did not work through RNA interference by attacking the virus's messenger RNA, which had been the consensus when Banfield had first approached Doudna. Instead the CRISPR system targeted the *genome* of the invading virus.[5]

That had a holy-cow implication: if the CRISPR system was aimed at the DNA of viruses, then it could possibly be turned into a tool to edit genes. That discovery sparked a new level of interest in CRISPR around the world. If CRISPR could target and cut DNA, would it allow you to fix the cause of a genetic problem?

There was still a lot to figure out before that could happen. For example, scientists didn't know exactly how the CRISPR enzyme cut the DNA. And even though scientists had studied CRISPR in living cells, such as those of bacteria, a different approach was required to determine the essential components of the system. Biochemists needed to work with the molecules in a test tube, something that had not yet been done.

"When you do experiments in vivo [inside an organism], you're never completely sure what's causing things," one of the Chicago scientists said. "We cannot look inside a cell and see how things are working."

Basically, to understand each component fully, you need to take them out of cells and put them into a test tube, where you can control precisely what's there.

Who could do this? Jennifer Doudna. It was her specialty, and it was what Blake Wiedenheft and Martin Jinek were pursuing in her lab.

Unfortunately, the future of her lab was uncertain when she stepped away from it and made an unexpected career move.

CHAPTER NINE

Restless

⎯⎯⎯⎯⎯⎯ ⚬⚬⚬ ⎯⎯⎯⎯⎯⎯

In the fall of 2008, just after the first CRISPR conference, Jennifer Doudna was feeling restless with her contributions to science. She was forty-four, happily married, with a smart and polite seven-year-old son. Yet despite all her success—or maybe partly because of it—she was having a mild midlife crisis.

"I'd been running an academic research lab for fifteen years, and I started to wonder, 'Is there more?'" she recalls. "I wondered if my work was having an impact in the broader sense."

Despite the excitement of being at the front of the emerging field of CRISPR, she was eager to turn her scientific knowledge into therapies that could enhance human health. There were hints that CRISPR could someday allow humans to edit genes, which would have great practical value, but Doudna was feeling the tug to pursue projects that would have a more immediate impact. In short, she wanted the science she understood to allow her to become the parent of invention.

At first Doudna considered going to medical school so that she could work with patients and be involved in clinical trials. She also considered going to business school. Then she ran into a former academic colleague who had joined a San

Francisco biotech company called Genentech the year before.

The seed for Genentech was planted in 1972, when Stanford medical professor Stanley Cohen and biochemist Herbert Boyer of the University of California at San Francisco attended a conference in Honolulu. The conference was focused on a type of DNA in bacteria, and the results of the meeting would lead to the creation of **recombinant DNA technology**, which involves cutting pieces of DNA from different organisms and joining them together to create new genetic combinations. At the conference, Boyer gave a talk about his own discovery of an enzyme that could cut DNA strands very efficiently. Cohen then spoke about how to clone thousands of identical copies of a piece of DNA by introducing it into E. coli bacteria.

Bored and still a bit hungry after their conference dinner one night, Boyer and Cohen walked to a deli near Waikiki Beach. Over pastrami sandwiches, they brainstormed how to combine their discoveries to create a method for engineering and manufacturing new genes. They agreed to work together on the idea, and within four months they had spliced together DNA fragments from different organisms and cloned millions of them. This collaboration gave birth to the field of biotechnology and launched the genetic engineering revolution.[1]

A lawyer later approached them and, to their surprise, offered to help them file a patent application, which would give them the sole right to develop and sell their new technology. In 1974 they put their application through, and it was eventually approved.

In late 1975, a young businessman named Robert Swanson started making phone calls to scientists who might have been interested in starting a genetic engineering company. Swanson had so far been a complete failure at trying to start new companies. He was living in a shared apartment, driving a beat-up car, and surviving on cold-cut sandwiches. But he had read up on recombinant DNA and convinced himself that he had finally found a winning idea for a new business. As he went down his list of scientists alphabetically, the first one who agreed to meet him was Boyer. Swanson went to his office for what was supposed to be a ten-minute meeting, but he and Boyer ended up spending three hours together. They planned a new type of company that would make medicines out of engineered genes. Each agreed to put in $500 to cover the initial legal fees.[2]

They decided to call their new company Genentech, a mash-up of "genetic engineering technology." Genentech began making genetically engineered drugs and, in August 1978, exploded when it became the first company to make a synthetic version of insulin—a hormone that helps regulate blood sugar—to treat diabetes. Until then, producing one pound of insulin for diabetes treatment had required eight thousand pounds of pancreas glands taken from more than twenty-three thousand pigs or cows.

Genentech's success with insulin not only changed the lives of diabetics (and saved the lives of a lot of pigs and cows); it gave the entire biotechnology industry celebrity status. A portrait painting of a smiling Boyer appeared on the cover of *Time* with the headline THE BOOM IN GENETIC ENGINEERING, and by the time Genentech began recruiting Doudna in late 2008, the company was worth close to $100 billion. Her former colleague, who was now working on genetically engineering cancer drugs at Genentech, told her that he was loving his new role. His research was much more focused than when he'd been an academic, and he was working directly on problems that were going to lead to new treatments for diseases.

"So that got me thinking," Doudna says. "Rather than go back to school, maybe I should just go to a place where I could apply my knowledge."

Her first step toward becoming friendly with the Genentech team was to present a couple of seminars at the company to describe her work. Among those she met at one of the presentations was Sue Desmond-Hellmann, chief of product development. They had similar personalities, and both were eager listeners with quick minds and big smiles.

"When I was being recruited there, she and I sat down in her office and [she] told me she would be my mentor if I came to Genentech," Doudna says.

Doudna weighed her options and decided to accept the position at Genentech. When she did, she was told she could bring some members of her Berkeley team with her. Most of her lab partners decided to follow her, and they soon began to figure out what equipment to bring with them. They even started to pack it all up.

Unfortunately, as soon as Doudna began working at Genentech, in January 2009, she realized that she had made a mistake.

"I felt very quickly in my gut that I was in the wrong place," she says. "Every day and night, I felt I had made the wrong decision."

That January, she didn't sleep much. She kept a brave face at the office but was upset at home. She had trouble carrying out the most basic functions in her personal life. Her midlife identity crisis was quickly turning into a mild mental breakdown. She had always been a very measured person who kept her insecurities and occasional anxieties secret and under control. Until now.[3]

Her turmoil hit its peak after only a few weeks. On a rainy night in late January, she found herself lying awake in bed, so she got up and went outside in her pajamas. Then she sat in the rain in her backyard, getting soaked. Her husband found her wet and motionless and brought her back inside. Both wondered if she was clinically depressed. Doudna knew she wanted to go back to her research lab at Berkeley, but she feared that door had closed.

Her neighbor Michael Marletta, who was chair of the Chemistry Department at Berkeley, came to her rescue. Doudna called him the next morning and asked if he'd be able to come over. She sent her husband, Jamie, and their son, Andrew, away so she could have an emotional conversation privately. Marletta was immediately struck by how deeply unhappy Doudna looked, and he told her so.

"I bet you want to come back to Berkeley," he said.

"I think I may have slammed that door," she replied.

"No, you haven't," he reassured her. "I can help you come back."

Instantly her mood lifted. That night she could sleep again, knowing she was going back to where she was meant to be. She returned to her Berkeley lab at the beginning of March, after only two months away.

From this career mistake, Doudna became more aware of her passions and skills—and also her weaknesses. She liked being a research scientist in a lab. She was good at brainstorming with people she trusted. She was not good at navigating a corporate environment where the competition was for power and promotions rather than discoveries. But even though her brief stint at Genentech didn't work out, her desire to tie her research to the creation of practical new tools, and companies that could bring these tools to the world, would drive the next chapter of her life.

CHAPTER TEN

Building a Lab of People

There are two important parts involved in any scientific discovery: doing great research and building a lab that does great research.

Jennifer Doudna deeply enjoyed being a hands-on scientist who got to the lab early, put on latex gloves and a white coat, and performed experiments with pipettes and petri dishes. For the first few years after setting up her lab at Berkeley, she was able to do that most hours of the day. But by 2009, after her return from Genentech, Doudna realized that she had to spend more time cultivating the people in her lab rather than her bacterial cultures.

This transition from player to coach happens in many fields. Teachers become principals and baseball catchers get promoted to be general managers of major-league teams. When scientists become lab heads, their new managerial duties include hiring the right young researchers, mentoring them, going over their results, suggesting new experiments, and offering up the insights that come from experience.

Doudna was wonderful at these tasks. When considering candidates who might work in her lab, she made sure that her other team members believed they would fit in. The goal was to find people who were self-directed yet worked well with others. As her work on CRISPR grew, she found two PhD students with the right mix of eagerness and smarts to become core members of her team alongside Blake Wiedenheft and Martin Jinek.

The first was Rachel Haurwitz, who had grown up in Austin, Texas. When she'd come to Berkeley in 2008 after graduating from Harvard, she'd been eager to work in Doudna's lab because of her love for RNA. Almost immediately she was swept into the CRISPR orbit of Blake Wiedenheft, attracted by his magnetic personality, his love of the outdoors, and his joyful enthusiasm for odd bacteria.

Doudna recognized herself in Haurwitz. CRISPR was risky because it was so new, and that was what made Haurwitz want to jump in.

"She loved the fact that it was a novel field, even though some students would be afraid of that," Doudna says. "So I told her, 'Go for it.'"

Haurwitz did.

After Wiedenheft had worked out the structure of Cas1, he decided to do the same for the five other CRISPR-associated proteins in the bacteria he was working with. Four of the other Cas proteins were easy. But one called Cas6 was tough to crack, so he enlisted Haurwitz. They figured out this particular problem child, and soon they were able to make Cas6 in the lab.

The next step was to determine what Cas6 did and how. Haurwitz used the two things the Doudna Lab was known for—biochemistry, to figure out Cas6's function, and structural biology, to discover what the protein looked like. At that point neither she nor Blake had the full set of skills to do structural biology by themselves, so Haurwitz tapped on the shoulder of Martin Jinek, sitting at the next bench over, and asked if he would join the project and show them how to move forward.

Teamwork paid off, and they succeeded!

The team grew even stronger when Jennifer Doudna hired another researcher named Sam Sternberg. Like Haurwitz, he wanted to work with Doudna because of his interest in RNA. Before he took a position in Doudna's lab, Haurwitz invited Sternberg to a Passover seder at her apartment. Unlike at most other seders, a main topic of conversation was CRISPR. Haurwitz showed him a paper that she was writing about Cas enzymes, and he was hooked. He immediately told Doudna that he wanted to work on CRISPR.

Sternberg was cautious, though, and Doudna sometimes worried he didn't take on the kinds of projects she knew he was capable of. So, being a good coach, she urged him to do better. He needed to ask big questions and take on risks. She said, "If you don't try things, you're never going to have a breakthrough."[1]

Sternberg was convinced, and he asked Doudna if he could go to Columbia University in New York for a week to learn more about an interesting technique that might help them understand the behavior of CRISPR-associated enzymes.

"She not only sent me out there for a week to try it out; she ended up paying for me to spend six whole months there," Sternberg said.

His work resulted in two breakthrough papers that showed for the first time precisely how the CRISPR system's RNA-guided proteins find the right target sequences of an invading virus.[2]

Sternberg grew especially friendly with Wiedenheft, who

became a role model. They got a chance to spend an intense week working together in late 2011, when Wiedenheft was writing a review article on CRISPR for *Nature*.[3] They sat side by side at a computer for days arguing over wording and selecting the illustrations to publish. Other times, when a big experiment was underway, they would make bets on the outcome.

"What are we betting?" Blake would ask, and then he'd answer himself. "We're betting a milkshake."

Jennifer Doudna's next hire was Ross Wilson, who came from Ohio State University. He was interested in how RNA interacts with enzymes, and he considered her the world's leading expert. When she asked him to work with her, he cried for joy.

Martin Jinek had warned Ross that he would have to be a self-starter in the lab, and he soon discovered that was 100 percent accurate. But he thought that made her lab an exciting place to work.

"She definitely doesn't hover over you," says Wilson, "but when she goes over your experiments and results with you, there are times when she will lower her voice a bit, look you right in the eye, lean in, and say, 'What if you tried . . . ?'"

Then Doudna would describe a new approach, a new experiment, or even a big new idea, usually involving some new way of deploying RNA.

Most mornings when she is in her lab, Doudna schedules a steady stream of her researchers to come present their most recent results. Her questions are designed to get her researchers to look up from the details and address the big picture: Have you thought about adding RNA? Can we image that in living cells? Why are you doing this? What's the point?

Although Doudna takes a hands-off approach during the early stages of a researcher's project, as it gets close to the end, she engages intensely. That is when Doudna's competitive juices kick in. She doesn't want another lab to beat hers to a discovery.

"She might storm into the lab unexpectedly," one student said, "and without raising her voice make it clear what things need to be done and be done quickly."

Then, when her lab produced a new discovery, Doudna was always determined to get it published.

"I've discovered that the journal editors favor people who are aggressive or pushy," she says. "That's not necessarily my nature, but I have become more aggressive when I feel that journal editors are not appreciating that something we did is really important."

Women in science tend to be shy about promoting themselves. An analysis was conducted in 2019 of more than six million articles with a woman as the principal author. The study showed that women are less likely to describe their findings using terms that shine praise on the research, terms such as "novel" and "unique" and "unprecedented." Even worse, in the best journals that publish the most cutting-edge research, women are 21 percent less likely than men to use positive words to describe their work.[4]

Doudna did not fall into that trap. At one point in 2011, for example, she and Wiedenheft, along with another Berkeley colleague, completed a paper on an array of Cas enzymes called CASCADE. The authors sent the paper to one of the most prestigious journals, *Nature*, which accepted it. But the editors said it was not an important enough breakthrough to be a featured "article" in the journal, so they wanted to publish it as a "report," which is a step down in significance. Most of the team was thrilled to have the paper quickly accepted by such an important publication. But Doudna was upset. She argued strongly that their findings were a big advance and deserved special notice, and she wrote letters to *Nature* urging them to change their decision. Unfortunately, she didn't get her way, but her researchers admired her determination.

"Most people are jumping up and down if they get a yes from *Nature*," Wiedenheft says. "Jennifer was jumping up and down because she was mad that it was going to be a report, not an article."[5]

CHAPTER ELEVEN

Starting a Company

⎯⎯⎯⎯ ⧓ ⎯⎯⎯⎯

As much as Jennifer Doudna loved her life in the lab, she truly wanted to translate the basic discoveries about CRISPR into tools that could be useful in medicine. Her researcher, Rachel Haurwitz, took the idea one step further. She figured that if Cas6 could be turned into a medical tool, it could become the basis for a company.

Throughout her career, Doudna had never thought much about going into business. Money wasn't a big motivation in her life. She and Jamie and Andy lived in a nice but not fancy house in Berkeley, and she never had the desire for a bigger one. But she did like the idea of being part of a business, especially one that could have a direct positive impact on people's health. And unlike Genentech, a startup would not drag her away from her university.

Haurwitz was much more interested in making business a career. Although she was good at the lab work, she realized that she was not cut out to be an academic researcher. So she began taking courses at Berkeley's Haas School of Business. In her favorite class, her professor split students into teams of six, half business students and the other half science researchers.

Each team created a fictional biotech startup and then spent the semester perfecting how they would pitch it to financial investors. She also took a class in which she studied ways to commercialize medical products, including how to secure and license patents.

During Haurwitz's final year in her lab, Doudna asked what she wanted to do next.

"Run a biotech company," Haurwitz replied.

Doudna was surprised. Most PhD students at Berkeley aimed for an academic career. A few days later, Doudna went into the lab to find Haurwitz.

"I've been thinking that maybe we ought to start a company around using Cas6 and some of the other CRISPR enzymes as a tool," she said.

With no hesitation, Haurwitz responded that yes, of course they should.[1]

And so they founded a company in October 2011. Haurwitz and her boyfriend tossed around ideas about what to name it, and they decided on "Caribou," which was a mash-up of "Cas" and "**ribonucleotides**," which are nucleotides that have ribose as the sugar, such as in RNA. The company remained based in Doudna's academic lab for a year while Haurwitz finished her studies. After Haurwitz got her PhD in the spring of 2012, she became the president, and Doudna the chief scientific advisor, of the endeavor.

The idea was that the company would secure the patents related to the Cas6 structure and the other discoveries that would eventually come out of Doudna's lab. Caribou's initial aim was to turn Cas6 into a tool that doctors could use to detect the presence of viruses in humans.

New businesses need money to get going, and Caribou was no different. Today just the mention of the word "CRISPR" is enough to make investors start writing checks, but when Doudna and Haurwitz tried to raise startup funds, they had little luck. So instead of continuing to look to investors to give them money, they decided to secure what they could from friends and family. Both Doudna and Haurwitz put in their own money too. In time, they received a federal grant from the National Institutes of Health's small business innovation program, which was designed to help innovators turn basic research into commercial products. This grant kept Caribou alive during the early years.[2]

Then Caribou got a lucky break in the form of a grant from the Bill and Melinda Gates Foundation—a huge source of private funding for all kinds of scientific endeavors—which provided $100,000 to fund work on using Cas6 as a tool to diagnose viral infections.[3]

"We plan on creating a suite of enzymes that specifically recognize RNA sequences characteristic of viruses including HIV, hepatitis C and influenza," Doudna wrote in her proposal to the foundation.

The money from these various sources got Caribou firmly on its feet, and laid the foundation for the funding Doudna would receive from the Gates foundation in 2020—at the height of the COVID-19 pandemic—to use CRISPR systems to detect coronaviruses.

CHAPTER TWELVE

Making Connections around the World

Scientific discovery isn't confined to one lab at a time. Jennifer Doudna had built a strong network within her lab that was helping her make groundbreaking innovations that she could then take out into the world to sell. But there was still a vital piece that Doudna needed to reach her full potential.

That piece was making connections with other scientists around the world. To do that, she again turned to conferences.

While attending a conference in Puerto Rico in the spring of 2011, Doudna had an unexpected meeting with Emmanuelle Charpentier, a French biologist who was mysterious, sophisticated, and carefree. Charpentier had grown up in a leafy suburb south of Paris. Her father had overseen the neighborhood park system, and her mother had been the administrative nurse in a psychiatric hospital. One day when Charpentier was twelve, she walked past the Pasteur Institute, the Paris research center specializing in infectious diseases.

"I am going to work there when I grow up," she told her mother.[1]

Emmanuelle also was interested in the arts. She took piano lessons from a neighbor who was a concert musician and pursued ballet with the possibility that she might become a professional dancer. She continued her training well into her twenties, but when she realized she was too short to make a career of it, she refocused on science. She would discover that there were lessons from the arts that applied to science.[2]

"Methodology is important in both," she said. "You also must know the basics and master the methods. That requires persistence—repeating experiments and repeating them again, perfecting how to prepare the DNA when you clone a gene, and then doing it over and over again."

Fulfilling the prediction she made to her mother, she pursued her graduate studies at the Pasteur Institute, where she learned how bacteria can become resistant to antibiotics. She felt at home in the lab. It was a quiet temple for individual persistence and contemplation. She could also be creative and independent as she pursued a path toward her own discoveries.

Charpentier later enrolled at the Rockefeller University in Manhattan, but on the day she arrived, she found out that her advisor—and the lab and everyone in it!—was moving to the St. Jude Children's Research Hospital in Memphis. She moved as well; her adventurous mind and spirit made her ever ready to relocate to new towns and new topics. But after a bit, she wanted to shift her focus from single-celled microbes such as bacteria and learn about genes in mammals, mainly mice. So she headed back to New York, this time to a lab at New York University (NYU).

Charpentier was a woman of many cities, many labs, and few roots and commitments. After six years in the US, she relocated to Europe in 2002 to become the head of a microbiology and genetics lab at the University of Vienna in Austria. Then she moved on her own to Umeå, in northern Sweden. Umeå was no

Vienna. Four hundred miles north of Stockholm, the town's university had been built in the 1960s on land that had, for centuries, been a grazing ground for reindeer. The school was best known for its research on trees.

"Yes, it was a risky move," Charpentier agrees, "but it gave me a chance to think."

In the thirty years since she entered the Pasteur Institute in 1992, Charpentier has worked in at least ten institutions in seven cities in five countries. With no spouse or family, she sought out changing environments and adapted to them. Moving also made her feel like a bit of a foreigner most of the time, the way the young Jennifer Doudna had felt as a child in Hawaii. But Charpentier believed it was important to know how to be an outsider because it challenged her. In fact, she enjoyed the freedom of being on her own and of not depending on partnership, and she hated the phrase "work-life balance" because it implied that work was less important than what you did in your spare time. Her work in the lab *was* her life, bringing her a happiness that was as fulfilling as any other passion.

In 2009, the CRISPR crowd decided that Cas9 was the most interesting of the CRISPR-associated enzymes. Researchers also established the essential role of another part of the complex: CRISPR RNAs. As mentioned earlier, CRISPR RNAs, known as crRNAs, are the small snippets of RNA that contain some genetic coding from a virus that has attacked the bacteria in the past. This crRNA guides the Cas enzymes to fight that virus when it tries to invade again. These two elements are the core of the CRISPR system: a small snippet of RNA that works as a guide, and an enzyme that acts as scissors.

But there was one additional component of the CRISPR-Cas9 system that played an essential role—or, as it turned out, several roles. It was dubbed a "**trans-activating CRISPR RNA**," or tracrRNA, pronounced "tracer-RNA."

First, tracrRNA facilitates the making of the crRNA, the sequence of nucleotides that carries the memory of a virus. After that, the crRNA and tracrRNA link together to form a small unit. Then the Cas9 enzyme uses the tracrRNA as a handle to join the crRNA-tracrRNA complex. And, finally, the crRNA tells the complex where to go in order for the Cas9 enzyme to chop the right part of the virus.

The process of uncovering these roles of tracrRNA began in 2010, when Charpentier noticed that the molecule kept appearing in her experiments with bacteria. She couldn't figure out what it did, but she realized that it was in the vicinity of the CRISPR spacers, so she speculated that tracrRNA was somehow related to the spacers. Researchers had never quite pinned down how the crRNAs were made inside a bacterial cell, but Charpentier had a theory she wanted to test out.

Charpentier was in the process of moving to Sweden at the time, but she was obsessed with the tracrRNA and spent one night before her departure drawing up a long plan of experiments. "I am stubborn. It was important for me to follow up. I said, 'We have to go for it! I want someone to look at it.'"[3]

The problem was that there was nobody in her Vienna lab who had the time and inclination to pursue the tracrRNA. That's the drawback of being a wandering professor: you leave your students behind, and they move on to other things.

Charpentier considered doing the experiments herself, even

though she was in the midst of a move. But she finally found two people to work with her. Charpentier's team discovered that the CRISPR-Cas9 system accomplished its viral-defense mission using only three components: tracrRNA, crRNA, and the Cas9 enzyme. The researchers prepared a paper for *Nature*, which would be published in March 2011.[4] Unfortunately, the paper did not, in fact, describe the full role of the tracrRNA. There were some details Charpentier still didn't understand, and she knew she needed more time to find a convincing way to prove it experimentally.

For that, she needed a scientist like Doudna, who was scheduled to speak at the March 2011 conference of the American Society for Microbiology, which was going to be held in Puerto Rico.

"I knew we were both going to attend," Charpentier says, "and I put in my mind that I would find a chance to talk to her."

When Jennifer Doudna walked into the coffee shop of the hotel in Puerto Rico on the second afternoon of the conference, Emmanuelle Charpentier was at a table in the corner sitting by herself, as she often liked to do, looking far more elegant than anyone else. Doudna was with a friend, who pointed Charpentier out and offered to introduce her.

"That would be great," replied Doudna. "I've read her paper."[5]

Doudna found Charpentier to be charming, with just a hint of shyness, an engaging sense of humor, and great style. Doudna was struck by her intensity and immediately liked her. They chatted for a few minutes, and then Charpentier suggested they get together later for a more serious discussion.

"I've been thinking of contacting you about a collaboration," she said.

The next day they had lunch, followed by a stroll along the cobblestone streets of Old San Juan. When the discussion turned to Cas9, Charpentier became excited.

"We have to figure out exactly how it works," she urged Doudna. "What's the exact mechanism it uses to cut DNA?"

Charpentier was taken by Doudna's seriousness and attention to detail and told her she thought it would be fun to work with her. Doudna was similarly moved by Charpentier.

"Somehow, just the way she said that it would be fun to work with me made a chill run down my back," Doudna recalls.

For Doudna's part, she was excited because working with Charpentier would offer her the sort of adventure that gave her a sense of purpose. Together, she thought, they would be hunting for the key to one of life's real mysteries.

Doudna wanted to act fast, and she knew that meant assembling a team. She thought back to a recent conversation she had had with Martin Jinek, the researcher in her lab who had been working on the structures of Cas1 and Cas6. Jinek had confided to her that he was having doubts about whether he would be successful as an academic researcher and he was thinking about becoming an editor at a medical journal instead. Of course, Doudna had had her own career doubts before she'd gone to Genentech, and she was a good mentor who wanted to help. She said she would think about what to do.

Doudna knew that Jinek was leaning toward staying at her lab, and after her meeting with Charpentier, she came up with a great idea. Charpentier needed a structural biologist with the talent to make proteins in a lab, and she thought it would be a perfect project for Jinek.[6]

She told him, and he was enthusiastic. They agreed that they would connect Jinek with the scientist in Charpentier's lab who had worked on her earlier Cas9 paper. This researcher was Krzysztof Chylinski, a Polish-born molecular biologist who had stayed in Vienna when Emmanuelle had moved to Umeå.

Jinek and Chylinski soon connected, and the rest is history. Theirs was a meeting that would bring about great things, because—together—Jinek, Chylinski, Charpentier, and Doudna would soon make one of the most important advances in modern science.

CHAPTER THIRTEEN

Success through Teamwork

⌘

When Jennifer Doudna returned to Berkeley, she and Martin Jinek started a series of Skype calls with Charpentier in Sweden and Krzysztof Chylinski in Vienna. Their goal was to plot a strategy to uncover how CRISPR-Cas9 operates. The collaboration was like a model United Nations: a Berkeley professor from Hawaii, her researcher from the Czech Republic, a Parisian professor working in Sweden, and her Polish-born researcher working in Vienna.

"It became a twenty-four-hour operation," Jinek recalls. "I would do an experiment at the end of my day, I would send an email to Vienna, and Krzysztof would read it as soon as he got up in the morning." Then there would be a Skype call to decide what the next step should be. "Krzysztof would execute that experiment during the day and send me the results while I was asleep, so that when I woke up and opened my inbox, there would be an update."

At first Charpentier and Doudna would join the Skype calls only once or twice a month. But the pace picked up in July 2011, when Charpentier and Chylinski flew to Berkeley for the fast-growing annual CRISPR conference. Even though they had bonded over Skype, it was the first time that Jinek personally met

Chylinski, a tall, slender researcher with a friendly personality and an eagerness to be involved in turning basic research into a tool to advance science.[1]

In-person meetings can produce ideas in ways that conference calls and Zoom meetings can't. That had happened in Puerto Rico, and it did so again when the four researchers got together for the first time in Berkeley. There they were able to brainstorm a strategy for figuring out exactly what molecules were necessary for a CRISPR system to cut DNA.

Jinek and Chylinski were initially unable to make CRISPR-Cas9 chop up the DNA of a virus in a test tube. They were trying to make it work with just two components: the Cas9 enzyme and the crRNA. At this point they had not yet discovered that the tracrRNA must link together with the crRNA before the Cas9 enzyme can become part of the virus-fighting unit. Because the tracrRNA had already been involved in making the crRNA, the researchers believed the tracrRNA had fulfilled its function. In theory the crRNA would guide the Cas9 enzyme to the virus target, which would then get chopped up. But it didn't work. Something was missing, and it was extremely puzzling to the whole group.

This was when the tracrRNA reentered the picture. In her 2011 paper Charpentier had showed that tracrRNA was required for producing the crRNA guide. She later said that she suspected tracrRNA played an even larger, ongoing role, but that possibility was not part of the initial round of experiments the foursome did. When those experiments failed, Chylinski decided to throw tracrRNA into his test-tube mix.

It worked: the three-component complex reliably cut up the target DNA!

After that breakthrough, Doudna and Charpentier became more involved in the daily work. Clearly they were heading to an important discovery—determining the essential components of a CRISPR gene-cutting system.

After the team members returned to their respective homes, night after night Chylinski and Jinek would ping-pong results back and forth. Each would decipher a tiny bit of the puzzle. Then Charpentier and Doudna began to join the increasingly frequent strategy calls. Soon they were able to discover the precise mechanisms of each of the three essential components of the CRISPR-Cas9 complex. The crRNA contained the directions to guide the complex to a piece of DNA in the virus with a similar sequence. The tracrRNA, which had helped create this crRNA, now had the additional role of binding to the crRNA to form a unit that the Cas9 enzyme could join. Then, when this complex attached to the target DNA, Cas9 could begin slicing away.

One evening, right after a key experiment had produced positive results, Doudna was at home cooking spaghetti. The swirls in the boiling water reminded her of organisms she had studied under a microscope back in high school, when she'd first learned about DNA. She started to laugh. Her son, Andy, who was nine, asked her why she was laughing.

"We found this protein, an enzyme called Cas9," she explained. "It can be programmed to find viruses and cut them up. It's so incredible."

Andy asked how it worked. Over billions of years, she explained, bacteria evolved in this totally weird and astonishing way to protect themselves against viruses. And the process was adaptable; every time a new virus emerged, the bacteria learned how to recognize it and beat it back. Andy was fascinated.

"It was a double joy," she recalled, "a moment of fundamental discovery of something that is so cool, and being able to share it with my son and explaining it in a manner where he can get it."

Curiosity can be beautiful that way.[2]

It quickly became clear that this amazing little system was more than just cool. It also held incredible potential: the crRNA guide could be modified to target *any* DNA sequence you might wish to cut. It was programmable, and it could be used to edit genes.

In fact, Doudna, Charpentier, Jinek, and Chylinski realized that they had developed a means to rewrite the code of life.[3]

First things first, though. Their next step was to figure out if the CRISPR system could be made even simpler. If so, it might become not just another gene-editing tool but one that would be easier and less expensive than the existing gene-editing methods.

One day, Jinek walked down the hall from the Berkeley lab into Doudna's office. He had been experimenting with the crRNA that served as a guide and the tracrRNA that the Cas9 enzyme clamped on to. He and Doudna were standing at a whiteboard propped in front of her desk, and he was sketching out a diagram of the structure of the two small RNAs. Which parts of the crRNA and tracrRNA, he asked, were essential for cutting up DNA in a test tube? The good news was, it appeared that the system had some flexibility as to how long the two RNAs had to be. Each of the little RNAs could be made a little bit shorter and still function.

Doudna had a profound understanding of the structure of RNA and an almost childlike joy in figuring out the ways it worked. As she and Jinek brainstormed, it became clear to them that they could link the two RNAs together, fusing the tail of one to the head of the other in a way that would keep the combined molecule functional.

Their goal was to engineer a single RNA molecule that would have the guide information on one end and the binding handle on the other. That would create what they ended up calling a "**single-guide RNA**" (sgRNA).

Doudna and Jinek paused for a moment and looked at each other. Then Doudna said, "Wow." As she recalls, "It was one of those moments in science that just comes to you. I had this chill and these little hairs on my neck standing up. In that moment, the two of us realized that this curiosity-driven, fun project had this powerful implication that could change the direction of the project profoundly."

Doudna urged Jinek to begin work right away on fusing these two RNA molecules to work as a single guide for Cas9, so he hurried back down the hall to place an order with a company for the necessary RNA molecules. He also discussed the idea with Chylinski, and they quickly designed a series of experiments. Once they had figured out what parts of the two RNAs could be deleted and how the remaining portions could be connected, it took only three weeks to make a single-guide RNA that worked. It was immediately obvious that this single-guide RNA would make CRISPR-Cas9 an even more versatile, easy-to-use, and reprogrammable tool for gene editing.

By studying a phenomenon that evolution had taken a billion or so years to perfect in bacteria, the foursome had performed something amazing: they had turned nature's miracle into a tool for humans.

CHAPTER FOURTEEN

Dueling Papers and Presentations

———————— ⊰⊱ ————————

W hen it came time to write a scholarly paper describing CRISPR-Cas9, Doudna and her teammates used the same round-the-clock collaborative methods they had employed in their experiments. Jinek and Doudna worked during the day in California and handed things off with a late-night Skype call as dawn was breaking in Europe, and then Charpentier and Chylinski took the lead for the next twelve hours. Because the sun never set in northern Sweden during the spring, Charpentier announced that she could work any hour of the day.

"You can't really sleep much when it's light all the time," she says, "and you're never really tired in those months, so I was on duty at any time."[1]

On June 8, 2012, Doudna hit the send button on her computer to submit the manuscript to the journal *Science*.[2] When the editors received the paper, they were excited. Although many of the activities of CRISPR-Cas9 in living cells had been described before, it was the first time researchers had isolated the essential components of the system and discovered their biochemical mechanisms. At Doudna's urging, the editors fast-tracked the review process. She knew that other papers on CRISPR-Cas9—including one from a Lithuanian researcher (more on him in a moment)—were already circulating, and she wanted to make sure that her team was the first to publish. *Science* had its own competitive motivation: it didn't want to be scooped by a rival journal.

The editors formally accepted the paper on Wednesday, June 20, 2012, just as participants were gathering in Berkeley for the annual CRISPR conference. There the four authors could celebrate together in person, and they did.

People often assume that the drama of science only happens in a lab, where big discoveries are made. But sometimes the competitions in science are as thrilling as the breakthroughs. Doudna, Charpentier, Jinek, and Chylinski were about to see how true that was because another scientist was about to present his own findings about CRISPR.

Virginijus Šikšnys of Vilnius University in Lithuania is a mild-mannered biochemist with wire-rimmed glasses and a shy smile. He had become intrigued by CRISPR when he'd read the 2007 paper by the Danisco yogurt researchers Rodolphe Barrangou and Philippe Horvath, showing that CRISPR was a weapon that bacteria had acquired in their struggle to fight off viruses. By February 2012, Šikšnys had produced a paper—with Barrangou and Horvath as secondary authors—that described how, in a CRISPR system, a Cas9 enzyme was guided by a crRNA to cut up an invading virus. He sent the article off to a journal, which rejected it, so he decided to try *PNAS*, the publication of the US National Academy of Sciences.

One way to be published by *PNAS* is to have your research

paper approved by a member of the academy. So, on May 21, 2012, Barrangou decided to send an abstract of the article to the academy member who was most familiar with the field: Jennifer Doudna.

Doudna was just finishing her own paper with Charpentier, which meant there would be a potential conflict of interest if she were to review Šikšnys's paper, so she declined. But reading the abstract had been enough for her to learn that Šikšnys had discovered many of the mechanisms of how Cas9 worked.[3] Jennifer Doudna submitted her team's paper only a few weeks later, so her timing may have seemed a little suspicious to other CRISPR researchers. But the truth is, this is how science works. Doudna did not steal anything; her ideas had been in development for months. And that is how Barrangou saw it, saying that science is competitive and that he willingly sent his paper to her. Indeed, as it turned out, Doudna remained friendly with both Barrangou and Šikšnys. Their mix of competition and cooperation were part of a process they all understood.

Nonetheless, the drama surrounding the timing of the two papers was still high at the June 2012 CRISPR conference in Berkeley, and the stage was set for a face-off between the two teams that were racing to describe the CRISPR-Cas9 mechanisms. Both Šikšnys and the Doudna-Charpentier team were scheduled to present their work on the afternoon of Thursday, June 21, the day after Doudna had uploaded the final version of the *Science* article and gone out with her colleagues to celebrate. Her team's paper was scheduled to be published online on June 28.

Barrangou was one of the organizers of the Berkeley CRISPR conference and had decided, even though Šikšnys's work had not yet been accepted for publication, that Šikšnys should present first, followed immediately by the presentation of the Doudna-Charpentier team.

Just after lunch on June 21, Virginijus Šikšnys gave a slide presentation, based on his unpublished paper, in the seventy-eight-seat ground-floor auditorium of Berkeley's new Li Ka Shing Center, where the conference was being held. It quickly became apparent that there were some gaps in the Šikšnys paper and presentation. Most notably, the Lithuanian researcher made no mention of the role of tracrRNA in the gene-cutting process. Although he described the tracrRNA's role in creating the crRNA, he did not realize that it was necessary for this molecule to stick around in order to link with crRNA and provide the means for the Cas9 enzyme to bind to the crRNA-tracrRNA complex.[4]

For Doudna, this meant that Šikšnys had failed to discover the essential role played by the tracrRNA.

"If you don't know that the tracrRNA is required for DNA cutting," she later said, "there is no way you could implement it as a technology. You haven't defined what the components are to get it to work."

There was competitive tension in the air at the Li Ka Shing Center, and Doudna was dead set on making sure that Šikšnys's mistake involving the role of tracrRNA was highlighted. She was seated in the third row of the auditorium, and as soon as Šikšnys finished, she raised her hand. Does your data, she asked, show the role of the tracrRNA in the cleaving process?

At first Šikšnys did not engage on the point directly, so Doudna kept pressing him to clarify. He did not try to contradict her. Other conference attendees noticed there was a hint of debate in her voice, and they understood that her firmness meant she was trying to make a point about something her competitor had missed.

To be fair, Šikšnys deserves a lot of credit for making many of the biochemical findings at about the same time as Doudna and Charpentier. Perhaps I have put a bit too much focus on the role of the tiny tracrRNA in the cleaving process because I'm writing the book from Doudna's vantage point. But I do think that in explaining the amazing mechanisms of life, little things matter. And very little things matter *a lot*. Showing precisely the essential role of the two snippets of RNA—the tracrRNA and the crRNA—was key to understanding fully how CRISPR-Cas9 could be a gene-editing tool and how the two RNAs could be fused together to create a simple single guide to the right gene target.

Jennifer Doudna *did* have a point.

Immediately after Šikšnys finished, it was time for Doudna and Charpentier to deliver what most attendees by then knew was a set of big breakthroughs. The two sat next to each other in the audience, having decided that the presentation would be made by the researchers who had done most of the hands-on experiments, Jinek and Chylinski.

The two men tried to make their presentation fun. They had prepared the slides so that they could take turns explaining each of the experiments they had done, and they had practiced twice before their appearance. The audience was small, informal, and friendly. Nevertheless, it was very clear they were nervous, especially Jinek.

There was no need to be tense, though. Their presentation was a triumph. Sylvain Moineau, a CRISPR pioneer at Université Laval in Quebec, stood up and said, "Wow!" Others hurriedly emailed and texted their lab colleagues back home.

Even one of the collaborators on Šikšnys's paper, Barrangou, was impressed. He later said that as soon as he heard the presentation, he knew that Doudna and Charpentier had taken the field to a whole new level.

"Jennifer's paper was clearly so much better than ours," he admits. "It wasn't close. It was the tipping point that moved the CRISPR field from an interesting microbial-world feature to a technology."

That evening, Doudna took a walk into downtown Berkeley to eat at a sushi restaurant with a few fellow scientists, including the two men whose paper had just been overshadowed by hers, Rodolphe Barrangou and Virginijus Šikšnys. Rather than being upset that they had been scooped, Barrangou said he realized that they had been bested fairly. In fact, as they were heading down the hill to the restaurant, he asked Doudna whether he and Šikšnys might do well to withdraw their paper that was still pending publication. She smiled.

"No, Rodolphe, your paper will be fine," she said. "Don't withdraw it. It makes its own contribution, just like we all try to do."

At the dinner, the group shared where each of their labs might go from there. It was all very warm, with no hard feelings. In fact, everyone was excited, realizing how important CRISPR was going to be to the world.

The Doudna-Charpentier paper, published online on June 28, 2012, electrified an entire new field of biotechnology: making CRISPR work in the editing of human genes. CRISPR researchers knew there was going to be a big race to use their discoveries in human cells, so they began to double their efforts. Gene editing in humans was an idea whose time had come, and it was going to be a sprint to be the team to get there first.

PART THREE
Gene Editing

CHAPTER FIFTEEN

How Gene Editing Works

———— ∞∞∞ ————

Ever since she was a child, Jennifer Doudna had not been embarrassed to appear ambitious, but she knew how to balance that characteristic by being both honest and a team player. Doudna calls competition "the fire that stokes the engine," and it certainly stoked hers. She had learned about the importance of competition from reading *The Double Helix*, where James Watson describes how he and Francis Crick saw the work of Linus Pauling and became convinced they could accomplish more than he had. They did, and their healthy rivalry with Pauling led them to make some of humankind's greatest breakthroughs.[1]

Competition drives people to search for new discoveries. Many scientists say they are motivated by the joy that comes from understanding nature, but most will admit that they are also sparked by the rewards of being the first to make a discovery. These happy outcomes include papers published, patents granted, prizes won, and colleagues and friends impressed. Like any other human, scientists want credit for their accomplishments, pay-off for their labor, and prize ribbons placed around their necks. That's why they work late into the night and dream about the big things they can do.

For Jennifer Doudna and a few other scientists, that dream was learning how to edit human genes, a revolutionary process that involves inserting, deleting, or otherwise changing an organism's DNA.

The road to gene editing began, in part, in 1972 when professor Paul Berg of Stanford University discovered a way to take a bit of the DNA of a virus found in monkeys and splice, or connect, it to the DNA of a totally different virus. Presto! He had manufactured "recombinant DNA." That same year, Herbert Boyer and Stanley Cohen met at a conference in Hawaii and decided to work together. After experiments in 1973, they discovered a more efficient way to make these artificial genes and then clone millions of copies of them.

It took over fifteen years before scientists successfully began to deliver engineered DNA into the cells of humans. This was not gene *editing*, which is an attempt to change the DNA of the patient. Instead it was gene *therapy*, which involves giving the patient's cells some engineered DNA to counteract the faulty gene that causes whatever disease the patient suffers from. Think of it in these terms: If your genome is a flower garden, gene editing is like planting entirely new seeds. Gene therapy, on the other hand, is like removing weeds and adding fertilizer so the flowers that are already there can grow stronger.

The first successful attempt at gene therapy happened in 1990 on a four-year-old girl with a genetic condition that crippled her immune system and made her more likely to develop infections. Doctors removed cells from her body, gave those cells a functioning gene that would help her fight infections, and reintroduced the cells into her body. Her immune system improved dramatically, and she began to live a healthy life.

This success made the field of gene therapy seem promising at first, but there were issues within a few years. One of the most notable happened in 1999 in Philadelphia.

Jesse Gelsinger was a sweet, handsome eighteen-year-old who suffered from a mild form of a liver disease caused by a simple genetic mutation. His liver had problems ridding his body of ammonia, which is a byproduct of the breakdown of proteins. The disease often kills victims as babies, but Gelsinger's milder form meant that he could survive by eating a very-low-protein diet and taking thirty-two pills a day.

A team at the University of Pennsylvania was testing a genetic therapy for the disease. The doctors put genes that didn't have the problematic mutation into a virus that served as a delivery mechanism, and injected the viruses into an artery that led to Jesse's liver. It was unlikely that the therapy would help Gelsinger right away because the experiment was designed to see how the therapy could be used to save babies. But the research offered him hope that someday he would be able to eat hot dogs and not take handfuls of pills every day.

"What's the worst that can happen to me?" he said to a friend as he was leaving for the Philadelphia hospital. "I die, and it's for the babies."[2]

Unlike the seventeen other humans in the trial, Gelsinger had a massive immune response caused by the virus that transported the therapeutic gene, which resulted in a high fever followed by the breakdown of his kidneys, lungs, and other organs. In four days, he was dead.

This wasn't the only setback for gene therapy. In the early 2000s a gene therapy procedure for another disease triggered a cancer-causing gene that led to five patients developing leukemia. Tragedies such as these froze most of the gene therapy clinical trials for at least a decade.

While the field of gene therapy stalled out, some medical researchers began looking for ways to fix genetic problems at their source. Their goal was to *edit* the flawed sequences of DNA in the relevant cells of the patient, a procedure known as gene editing.

In the 1980s, Harvard professor Jack Szostak—who was Jennifer Doudna's doctoral thesis advisor—discovered that one of the keys to editing a gene was to cause a break in both strands of the DNA double helix. This is known as a double-strand break. When there's a break in a single strand of DNA, the remaining intact strand can be used as a template to repair the broken strand. But when both strands are broken, neither side can be used to repair the other.

In this situation the DNA can repair itself in one of two ways. In the first process, the cell removes the broken pieces of both DNA strands, and then the remaining, corresponding ends of each strand are stitched together, without any attempt to replicate the missing sequences. Unfortunately, this can be a sloppy process resulting in unwanted deletions of genetic material. In the second, more precise type of repair, the damaged DNA finds a suitable template for itself nearby, in a molecule with an almost identical DNA sequence. The original DNA molecule copies from the template the section that matches the sequence of DNA that was broken. This copied section is inserted into where the double-strand break occurred.

Let's back up a little so you can understand the necessary steps that had to occur for gene editing to happen. First, scientists had to find the right enzyme that could cut a double-strand break in DNA. Then they had to locate a guide that would navigate the enzyme to the precise target in the cell's DNA where they wanted to make that cut. By 2000, researchers had found a tool to do this.[3] But as soon as techniques using this tool were being perfected, CRISPR came along. It had a cutting enzyme, which was Cas9, and a guide that led the enzyme to cut a targeted spot on a DNA double helix.

In the earlier techniques, a protein was used as the guide. In the CRISPR system, the guide was not a protein but a snippet of RNA—and it had a big advantage. With the other technology, you had to construct a new protein guide every time you wanted to target a different genetic sequence to cut. This was difficult and time-consuming. But with CRISPR you only had to play around with the genetic sequence of the RNA guide. A good student could do it quickly in a lab.

Today using CRISPR in a lab looks something like this: First a researcher can cook up some Cas9 protein with a guide RNA that is designed to eliminate a certain gene. To do this, the Cas9 is made using the genetic sequence taken from a piece of DNA, and anyone who can grow bacteria in a lab can produce large quantities of it. However, if you don't want to create the Cas9 from scratch, you can buy it on the web for less than a hundred dollars.

The Cas9 is kept in vials that are refrigerated. Then you use pipettes to combine the Cas9 with the RNA guide for whatever you want to edit (for example, a bacterium containing a gene that makes the bacteria resistant to antibiotics). After incubating the mixture for ten minutes, you add a dye that will help illuminate the results. Once the gene editing is complete, a process called **electrophoresis**—which is a technique used to separate DNA molecules of different sizes—shows if and where the molecules were cut by Cas9.

As easy as pie!

But in the early years of developing this CRISPR procedure, there was one unanswered question. The CRISPR systems worked in bacteria and archaea, which are single-celled organisms that have no nucleus. Would CRISPR work in cells that *do* have a nucleus, especially in multicell organisms such as plants, animals, you, and me?

Jennifer Doudna and her lab were determined to find out.

CHAPTER SIXTEEN

The Gene-Editing Race

⊰⊱

The paper Jennifer Doudna and Emmanuelle Charpentier published in *Science* in June 2012 set off a feverish competition in many labs around the world to prove that CRISPR-Cas9 could work in human cells. It was a hectic race, and whoever won it was sure to collect patents, prizes, and more.

Unfortunately, Doudna entered the contest with a huge disadvantage: she had never experimented with human cells. Her lab's biochemists had the same issue. While they were highly skilled at working with bacteria in test tubes, they were not experts in human cells.

"I had a lab full of biochemists and people doing crystallography and that sort of thing," she says. "Whether it was creating cultured human cells or even those of nematode worms, that was not the kind of science my lab was expert in."

So it was proof of her willingness to take risks—as well as proof of her fierce competitiveness—that she jumped into what she knew would be a crowded field of researchers wanting to transform their discoveries about CRISPR-Cas9 into a breakthrough that would work in human cells.

Doudna knew she had to be smart, careful, and, most of all,

fast. So she pushed her primary researcher, Martin Jinek, to work more aggressively.

"You need to make this your absolute priority," she repeatedly told him. "Because if Cas9 is a robust technology for human genome editing, then the world changes."[1]

Jinek was worried that the work would be difficult, though. He had not been trained as a genome editor, unlike the scientists in some of the labs that had pioneered the method. At first Doudna, Jinek, and the other scientists in the lab had many setbacks and frustrations. Their quest to make CRISPR-Cas9 work in human cells was an uphill battle, especially because they were learning as they went along. But as the fall of 2012 began, Doudna got a lucky break. A new graduate student named Alexandra East, who had experience doing gene editing with human cells, joined the lab.

Today we know that editing DNA in a human cell is much more challenging than doing it in a bacteria in a test tube. Not only are there 3.2 billion base pairs in the human genome (compared to only a few million in bacteria and other single-celled organisms!), but it's also tough to make your editing tools get past the cell's outer plasma membrane and then the inner nuclear membrane to the location of the DNA. But it can be done.

East was skilled in a lab, so she was successful at growing the necessary human cells and beginning to test ways to get Cas9 into the nucleus. When she began compiling the data from her experiments, though, she was not sure that they showed evidence that gene editing had occurred. Sometimes biology experiments do not have clear results, and that was the case with the work East had done. But Doudna had a great eye for understanding evidence and results, and she knew right away that the experiments had been successful.

"When she showed me the data, it was immediately clear to me that she had beautiful evidence of genome editing by Cas9 in the human cells," Doudna says. "This is a classic difference between a student who is in training and someone like me who's been doing this for a while. I knew what I was looking for, and when I saw the data she had, it just clicked and I thought, 'Yes, she's got it.' Whereas she was unsure and thought she might have to do the experiments again, I was saying, 'Oh my gosh, this is huge! This is so exciting!'"[2]

Doudna knew it was important to publish her findings as soon as possible, so she pushed East to firm up her data through repeated experiments. At the same time, she urged Jinek to work on ways to turn the guide RNA that they had devised in test tubes into a guide that could get Cas9 to the right target in a human cell. But their work wasn't always easy or successful. For instance, they discovered that the guide RNA that Jinek had engineered was not quite long enough to operate efficiently on human DNA, and they had to keep trying.

Doudna and her lab had almost reached the finish line, but they weren't there yet. In order to complete the race to show that gene editing in humans was possible, they would need a guide RNA that worked, and there would need to be solid, reliable data. Then and only then could the team publish their findings and claim victory.

Unfortunately for Doudna, two other scientists were right behind her. And if she didn't act fast, one of them was going to pass her by.

CHAPTER SEVENTEEN

Doudna's First Competitor

The first person Jennifer Doudna faced off with in the race to edit human genes was an accomplished young biochemist named Feng Zhang.

Zhang was born in 1981 in Shijiazhuang, China, to a mother who taught computer science and a father who was a university administrator. His hometown was an industrial city of around 10 million people southwest of Beijing, and its streets were draped with banners celebrating Chinese history, innovation, and the importance of studying science. These messages made an impression on Zhang right away.

"I grew up playing with robot kits and fascinated by anything to do with science," he recalls.[1]

In the early 1990s his mother was hired as a visiting scholar at the University of Dubuque, a small Iowa university on the banks of the Mississippi River. After she arrived, she visited a local school, where she marveled at the computer lab and began to imagine it through the eyes of her son. She thought Zhang would love being in such a lab and school, so when she secured a new job in Des Moines—about two hundred miles away—she decided to bring Zhang over from China.

His father soon followed, but he never learned English well, so Zhang's mother became the driving force in the family. She pioneered the family's path in America, made friends at work, and volunteered to set up computers at local charities. Because of her, and her blossoming friendship with members of the community, the family always had invitations to neighbors' houses for Thanksgiving and other holidays.

"My mother always told me to keep my head down and not be arrogant," Zhang says. But she also instilled in him an ambition to be inventive and active. "She pushed me to make things, even on a computer, rather than play with things that other people had made."

At first Zhang seemed likely to follow the path of so many supersmart kids in the 1990s and become a computer geek. When he got his first computer at age twelve, he learned to take it apart and use the components to build other computers. So his mother decided to send him to computer camp and, just to make sure he was wired for success, to debate camp as well.

Instead of pursuing computer science, however, Zhang shifted his interests from digital tech to biotech. Computer code was something his parents and their generation did, not young people like him. He was different, and he wanted to be at the cutting edge of science. To Zhang, that meant studying the genetic code.

Zhang's path to biology began with his Des Moines middle school's Gifted and Talented Program, which included a Saturday enrichment class in molecular biology.[2]

"Until then, I didn't know much about biology and didn't find it interesting, because in seventh grade all they did was give you a tray with a frog and tell you to dissect it and identify the heart," he recalls. "It was all memorization and not very challenging."

In the Saturday enrichment class, the focus was on DNA and how RNA carried out its instructions, with an emphasis on the role played in this process by enzymes.

The students did a lot of hands-on experiments, including one that transformed bacteria to make them resistant to antibiotics. They also watched the 1993 movie *Jurassic Park*, in which scientists bring dinosaurs back from extinction by combining their DNA with that of frogs.

"I was excited to discover that animals could be a programmable system," he says. "That meant human genetic coding could be programmable as well."

Zhang's Saturday teacher helped him get selected to spend his afternoons and free time at the gene therapy lab of Methodist Hospital in Des Moines. As a high school student, he worked under an intense but very personable molecular biologist named John Levy, who explained over tea each day the work he was doing and assigned Zhang to increasingly more sophisticated experiments. On some days Zhang would arrive right after school and work until eight in the evening. His mom would wait for him in her car in the parking lot.

His first major experiment involved a fundamental tool in molecular biology: a gene from jellyfish that produces green fluorescent protein, which glows when exposed to ultraviolet light and thus can be used as a marker in cell experiments. Levy first made sure Zhang understood the protein's fundamental natural purpose. Sketching on a piece of paper as he sipped tea, Levy explained why a jellyfish might need that fluorescent protein as it moved up and down layers of the ocean during different phases of its life cycle.

Levy "held my hand," Zhang recalls, "as I did my first experiment." It involved putting the gene for green fluorescent protein into human melanoma (skin cancer) cells. It was a simple but exciting example of genetic engineering. He had inserted a gene from one organism (a jellyfish) into the cells of another (a human), and he could see the proof of his success when the bluish-green glow radiated from the manipulated cells. He was so excited that he began to shout, "It's glowing!"

He had reengineered a human gene.

Using $50,000 he won from a science competition, Zhang enrolled at Harvard after high school, where he landed in the same class as Facebook founder Mark Zuckerberg. Majoring in both chemistry and physics, Zhang did research with a crystallographer who was a master at determining the structure of complex molecules. Then he went to Stanford for graduate school and worked with other scientists to develop ways to make the workings of the brain and its nerve cells, known as neurons, more visible. Zhang focused on inserting light-sensitive proteins into the neurons—an echo of his high school work placing green fluorescent protein into skin cancer cells. His method was to use viruses as a delivery mechanism. For one demonstration, he inserted these proteins, which become activated when light hits them, into the part of a mouse brain that controls its movement. By using light pulses, the researchers could trigger the neurons and cause the mouse to walk in circles.[3]

But Zhang faced a challenge. It was difficult to insert the gene for the light-sensitive proteins into the exact right location of the DNA of the brain cell. This wasn't just a problem he faced; the entire field of genetic engineering was being held back by the lack of simple tools for cutting and pasting desired genes into strands of DNA inside a cell. So after he got his doctorate in 2009, Zhang took a position at Harvard and began researching the gene-editing tools that were available at the time.

Zhang worked in the most exciting lab at Harvard Medical School, which was run by a professor who was respected for embracing new ideas, sometimes wildly, and who fostered a friendly atmosphere that encouraged exploration. This professor was a longtime friend of Doudna's, named George Church. With his bushy beard and big smile, Church was a celebrity in the field of biology. He became for Zhang, as he did for almost all his students, a loving and beloved mentor—until the day when Church believed that Zhang betrayed him.

CHAPTER EIGHTEEN

Doudna's Second Competitor

———— ❦ ————

Tall and gangly, George Church looks like a gentle giant and a mad scientist. The truth is that he is both of those things. Always calm and friendly, he has a wild-man beard and a full head of hair, but his appearance and attitude hide how serious and accomplished he is in his career.[1]

Born in 1954, Church grew up on Florida's gulf coast near Tampa. His mother was married three times, so George had many last names and attended many different schools, which made him feel, he says, "like a real outsider."

Feeling isolated and different wasn't the only thing he had in common with his future friend and competitor Jennifer Doudna. When he was young, Church was also fascinated by science. His mother let him roam alone in the marshes and on the mudflats near Tampa Bay, hunting for snakes and insects. He would crawl through the high swamp grass collecting specimens. One day he found an odd caterpillar that looked like a "submarine with legs" and he put it in his jar. The next day he discovered, to his astonishment, that it had transformed into a dragonfly.

"That helped set me on my path to be a biologist," he says.

When he came home in the evening with mud on his boots,

he would dive into the books his mother gave him. Because he was mildly dyslexic, he had trouble reading but could absorb information from pictures.

"It made me a more visual person. I could imagine 3-D objects, and by visualizing the structure, I could understand how things worked."

One of George Church's stepfathers was a doctor, and he let his stepson dig into his medicine bag and use what was inside to perform experiments. At age thirteen, Church borrowed some of the thyroid hormones his stepfather had on hand and put them into the water of a group of tadpoles, leaving another group in untreated water. The first group grew faster. It was Church's first true biology experiment.

Church was bored in his small-town high school, and his mom and stepfather decided to send him to boarding school in Andover, Massachusetts. There he taught himself computer coding and maxed out on all the chemistry courses. Then he was given a key to the chemistry lab so he could explore on his own. Among his many triumphs was making Venus flytrap plants grow huge by spiking their water with hormones.

He went on to Duke University, where he earned two undergraduate degrees in two years and then skipped ahead into a PhD program. There he stumbled. He became so involved in the lab research of his advisor, which included using crystallography to figure out the three-dimensional structure of different RNA molecules, that he stopped going to classes. After failing two of them, he got a letter from the dean coldly informing him, "You are no longer a candidate for the Doctor of Philosophy degree in the department of Biochemistry at Duke University." He kept the letter as a source of pride, the way others keep their framed diplomas.

He had already been a coauthor of five important papers and was able to talk his way into Harvard Medical School.

"It's a mystery why Harvard would accept me after flunking out of Duke," he said. "Usually it's the other way around."[2]

Church became a quirky popular celebrity in 2008, when the *New York Times* interviewed him about the possibility of using his genetic engineering tools to re-create the extinct woolly mammoth from frozen hairs found in the area near the North Pole. Not surprisingly, the idea appealed to Church because it reminded him of his days making tadpoles grow with hormones.[3]

During the 1980s, Church had worked to design new gene-sequencing methods. And he had become successful not only as a researcher but as a founder of companies to commercialize the work coming out of his lab. Later he'd focused on finding new tools for gene editing. So when Doudna and Charpentier's *Science* article describing CRISPR-Cas9 went online in June 2012, Church decided to try to get CRISPR to work in humans. First, though, he did the polite thing and sent Doudna and Charpentier an email.

Science can be a competition, but it's usually a friendly competition, so Doudna wrote back to acknowledge Church's plan to play off her team's work. She admired Church's unconventional style and thinking and liked that he was not afraid of being different. She also knew they were both interested in the structure of RNA. After their initial emails, Church followed up with some phone conversations, and Doudna told him that she was likewise working on trying to get CRISPR to work in human cells. This exchange was characteristic of the way Church did science—cooperatively and openly rather than secretively.

But there was one person Church did not think of contacting: Feng Zhang. The reason was that Church had no idea that his former researcher was working on CRISPR.

"If I had known Feng was working on it, I would have asked him about it," Church says. "But he was very secretive when he suddenly hopped on CRISPR."[4]

CHAPTER NINETEEN

The Race Heats Up

After completing his postdoctoral work in Church's Harvard Medical School lab in Boston, Zhang had moved across the Charles River to the Broad Institute in Cambridge. Broad's mission is to advance the treatment of diseases using the knowledge uncovered by the Human Genome Project, and Zhang was excited to be working there. He had spent years in George Church's lab working on gene editing, but it had been difficult, time-consuming work, using the tools available then. At the Broad Institute, Zhang began looking for a better way.

That better way would turn out to be CRISPR. A few weeks after his arrival at the Broad Institute, Zhang attended a seminar by a Harvard microbiologist who was studying a species of bacteria. The researcher happened to mention that the bacteria contained CRISPR sequences with enzymes that could cut the DNA of invading viruses. Zhang had barely heard of CRISPR, but ever since his seventh-grade enrichment class, he had learned to perk up at the mention of enzymes. He was particularly interested in the enzymes that cut DNA.

So he did what any of us would do: he Googled "CRISPR."

The next day he flew to Miami for a conference, but instead

of sitting through all the talks, he stayed in his hotel room reading the dozen or so major scientific papers on CRISPR that he found online. In particular he was struck by the one published that previous November by the two yogurt researchers at Danisco, Rodolphe Barrangou and Philippe Horvath, which showed that the CRISPR-Cas systems can cut a double-stranded DNA at a specific target.[1]

"The minute I read that paper, I thought this was pretty amazing," Zhang says.

Zhang had a friend named Le Cong who was still a graduate student in Church's lab. Immediately after reading the CRISPR papers in his Miami hotel room, Zhang emailed Cong and suggested that they work together to see if CRISPR could become a gene-editing tool in humans. Cong agreed, and a couple of days later, Zhang sent another email. Cong still worked in Church's lab, and Zhang wanted to make sure that Cong kept the idea secret, even from his advisor.

"Hey let's keep this confidential," Zhang wrote.[2]

Cong did.

Soon, Zhang and Cong began using the whiteboard in Zhang's office to list what they would have to do to get CRISPR-Cas systems to penetrate into the nucleus of human cells. They began pulling late-nighters in the lab, eating noodles and dreaming of great discoveries.[3] Zhang seemed to sense from the outset that the race to turn CRISPR into a human gene–editing tool would turn out to be very competitive, so he continued to keep his plans secret. He did not talk to other colleagues about it or mention CRISPR in a video he made at the end of 2011 that described the research projects he had been working on. But he began to document each of his experiments and discoveries in a notebook.

In this competition to get CRISPR to edit human genes, Zhang and Doudna came into the arena from different routes. Zhang had never worked on CRISPR. Instead his specialty was gene editing, and for him CRISPR was simply another method to get to the same goal. For her part, Doudna and her team had never worked on gene editing in living cells. Their focus for five years had been on figuring out the components of CRISPR. As a result, Zhang would end up having some difficulty in sorting out the essential molecules in a CRISPR-Cas9 system, while Doudna's struggle would be figuring out how to get the system into the nucleus of a human cell.

By early 2012—before Doudna and Charpentier went online in June with their *Science* paper showing the essential three components of the CRISPR-Cas9 system—Zhang had made no documented progress. He and a group of colleagues from the Broad Institute filed an application for funding to pursue gene-editing experiments, but he made no claim that he had already accomplished any of the major steps to this goal.[4]

Zhang was eager for that to change, so he enlisted the help of Luciano Marraffini, a microbiologist originally from Argentina who had received his PhD from the University of Chicago. Marraffini loved studying bacteria, and as a doctoral student he had become interested in the newly discovered phenomenon of CRISPR. Like most of the CRISPR research community, Marraffini hadn't heard of Zhang, so when Zhang emailed him, Marraffini did a Google search to learn who Zhang was. About an hour later, he emailed Zhang back, and they agreed to talk by phone the next day.

Marraffini got the impression that Zhang was stuck and was trying out a variety of Cas proteins. He was testing not only Cas9 but all the different CRISPR systems, including Cas1, Cas2, Cas3, and Cas10, and nothing was working. Marraffini quickly pushed him to focus on Cas9.

"I was very sure of Cas9," Marraffini says. "I was an expert in the field. I realized the other enzymes were going to be too difficult."

For a while they collaborated by splitting up tasks. Zhang would come up with ideas that he hoped would work in humans. Then Marraffini, who specialized in microbes, would test to see if the idea worked in bacteria, an easier experiment. Marraffini believed that they had a fruitful collaboration going, based on mutual respect, that could lead to being coauthors on a ground-breaking paper and co-inventors on what might be a lucrative set of patents.

The work that Zhang did in early 2012 with Marraffini would not lead to any published results that year. In fact, there is evidence that by June 2012, when Doudna and Charpentier's *Science* paper was published, Zhang still had a long way to go. One of Zhang's notebook pages records experiments from the spring of 2012, and he claims that these experiments document that the CRISPR-Cas9 system made edits in human cells. But as is often the case with scientific experiments, those data were open to interpretation. They did not clearly prove that Zhang had succeeded in editing the cells, because some of the results indicated otherwise.[5]

CHAPTER TWENTY

Photo Finish

⸻⸺✼⸻⸺

Some great inventions and discoveries—such as Einstein's theories of relativity, which explain gravity and the speed of light—are made by one person or a small group of people. Others—such as the invention of the computer microchip—are accomplished by many people at around the same time. These group innovations happen because scientists share their knowledge, learn from one another's findings, and then apply those advances in their own work. The purpose of science is to move humanity toward better, healthier lives, so spreading groundbreaking news and findings benefits *all* of society, not just those in white coats working in a lab.

Using CRISPR to edit human DNA was one of those life-changing breakthroughs that different groups spread across the world discovered at around the same time. After Doudna and Charpentier published their famous paper in June 2012, their research team pushed hard to pin down the results of their experiments so they could win the race to publish on the use of CRISPR-Cas9 in humans. And while Doudna knew that her old friend George Church was working on CRISPR too, she had barely heard of Feng Zhang.

When Zhang began to test the idea of using a single-guide RNA, he discovered that the version described in the Doudna-Charpentier paper worked poorly in human cells. So he made a longer version of the single-guide RNA that contained a sharp turn. That made the guide more efficient.[1] Zhang's modification also showed one difference between doing something in a test tube, like Doudna's team had, and doing it in human cells.

"Jennifer was probably convinced by the biochemical results that the RNA didn't need that extra chunk," Zhang says. "She thought the short single guide that Jinek had engineered was sufficient, because it worked in a test tube. I knew that biochemistry does not always predict what will actually happen in living cells."

Zhang also did other things to improve the CRISPR-Cas9 system and optimize it so that it would work in human cells, and on October 5, 2012, he was satisfied with his results. He wrote them up in a paper that he sent to the editors of *Science*, and they accepted it on December 12. After describing the team's experiments and results, the paper concluded with a significant final sentence: "The ability to carry out multiplex genome editing in mammalian cells enables powerful applications across basic science, biotechnology, and medicine."[2]

Finally someone had proven that CRISPR could work in human cells!

Apparently George Church—who had trained Feng Zhang—had just discovered this too.

For twenty-five years Church had been working on various methods to engineer genes. But until the late fall of 2012, he hadn't been told—or at least he thought he hadn't been told—by Zhang or by Zhang's lead coauthor, Le Cong, that they had been working for more than a year on turning CRISPR into a human gene–editing tool. It was not until November of that year, when Church went to the Broad Institute to give a talk, that he found out that Zhang had submitted a paper to *Science* on using CRISPR-Cas9 in human cells. This news came as a huge shock because Church had just submitted a paper to the same journal on the same topic.

Church was furious and felt betrayed. He had previously published papers on gene editing with Zhang, and he hadn't realized that his former colleague now considered him a rival rather than a collaborator.

"I guess Feng didn't get the full culture of my lab," Church says. "Or maybe he just felt the stakes were so high, so he didn't tell me."

Zhang has a different story, and he insists that he did, in fact, tell Church that he was working on CRISPR. In August 2012, Zhang and Church drove together to the San Francisco airport from a conference, and Zhang claims that while he was telling his former colleague about his research, Church may have fallen asleep. Even if that happened, though, it does not—at least in Church's opinion—get Zhang off the hook for failing to communicate his plans. After all, surely Zhang would have noticed that he was getting no response from Church, and he would have tried to tell him again when he woke up.

There are certain ethics that govern science, and, in fact, Church taught a class on ethics at Harvard. He never thought that Zhang's actions were morally wrong. He believed they were within the norms of science. They weren't, however, within the norms that Church tried to cultivate in his own lab. He wanted collaboration and openness rather than secrecy. He knew that maintaining a steady flow of dialogue and not keeping secrets would prevent battles or confusion in the future.

Luckily, it wasn't long before Church and Zhang made peace. They realized that their discoveries were for the good of science and society rather than for their individual glory, so they reconciled.

"When one of our grandchildren was born, Feng sent us a colorful play-mat with the alphabet on it," Church says. "He also invites me to his workshops each year. We all move on."

Zhang feels the same. "We hug when we see each other," he said.[3]

Church and Zhang ended up in a virtual tie in showing how CRISPR-Cas9 could be engineered for use in human cells. Church submitted his paper to *Science* on October 26, three weeks after Zhang had sent his. Once the comments and changes to the papers were dealt with, the articles were both accepted by the journal on the same date, December 12, and were published online simultaneously on January 3, 2013.

Church had also drawn on the Doudna-Charpentier paper of June 2012, and, like Zhang, he had synthesized a single-guide RNA. His version was longer than the one Zhang had devised and ended up working even better.

Though their papers differed somewhat, both came to the same historic conclusion: the research teams' results had established an RNA-guided editing tool.[4]

While Church's and Zhang's papers had been under consideration at *Science*, Doudna and her team hadn't known that Church had just submitted a paper to *Science*, and she was unaware of Feng Zhang's submission. Then she got a phone call from a colleague.

"I hope you're sitting down," the caller said. "CRISPR is turning out to be absolutely spectacular in George Church's hands."[5]

Doudna already knew from the email Church had sent her that he was working on CRISPR, and when she heard about his progress in making it work in humans, she gave him a call. He was gracious and explained the experiments he had done and the paper he had submitted. By then Church had learned about Zhang's work, and he told Doudna that it was slated for publication as well.

Church agreed to send Doudna a copy of his manuscript as soon as the editors at *Science* accepted it. When she received it in early December, she was instantly deflated. Jinek was still doing experiments in her lab, and the data they had were not as extensive as those of Church.

"Should I still go ahead and try to publish my work anyway?" she asked Church. He said yes. "He was very supportive of our work and of us publishing," she says. "I thought he behaved as a great colleague." Whatever experimental data she produced, Church told Doudna, would add to the accumulation of evidence, especially on how best to tailor the RNA guide.

"I felt it was important to keep pushing with our experiments, even if others were already doing the same work," Doudna said, "because that would show how easy it was to use Cas9 for human genome editing. It showed that you didn't have to have special expertise to use the technology, and I felt that that was important for people to know."

Publishing their work would also help Doudna stake a

claim that she had demonstrated, at approximately the same time as competing labs had, that CRISPR-Cas9 could work in human cells. But this meant she needed to get her paper published quickly. So Doudna called a colleague at Berkeley who had recently started an open-access electronic journal, *eLife*, that published papers after less review time than traditional journals such as *Science* and *Nature*.

"I talked to him, described the data, and sent him a title," Doudna says. "He said it sounded interesting and he would get it reviewed quickly."

However, Jinek was a perfectionist, and he thought the data from his experiments wasn't ready or good enough. But Doudna insisted they push ahead to publish.

"Martin," she said, "we have to publish this, even if it's not quite the story we wish we could tell. We have to put out the best story that we can, with the data that we have, because we don't have any more time. These other papers are coming out and we have to publish."

They came to an agreement: Jinek would pull together his data and figures for the experiments, but Doudna would have to write the paper.

At the time, she was working on revising a second edition of a textbook on molecular biology she had written with two colleagues.[6] The team hadn't been entirely happy with the first edition, so they rented a house in Carmel, in California, to have a two-day gathering on how to revise the book. As a result, Doudna found herself in mid-December in Carmel, where it was freezing cold, in a house that had no working heat. The owners said they would call a repair person, but they couldn't get anyone out there right away.

So Doudna and her coauthors huddled around the fireplace as they worked late into the night revising their textbook.

After everyone else went to bed at eleven p.m., Doudna stayed up to prepare her CRISPR paper for *eLife*.

"I was exhausted and cold and I realized that I had to write the paper then or it wouldn't get written," she says. "So I sat up for three hours in bed, pinching myself to stay awake, and typed out the text of a draft."

She sent it off to Jinek, who kept coming back with suggestions. She eventually cut him off and declared the paper finished. On December 15 she emailed it to *eLife*.

Every morning after that she would check the *Science* magazine website to see if either the Church or Zhang paper had been published. Neither had, and she crossed her fingers that her paper would be published first. When the person who was reviewing Doudna's paper finally got back with comments, he asked for a few additional experiments. She replied that doing the suggested experiments would "require analyses of close to a hundred clones," which would "be better performed as part of a larger study."[7] She prevailed, and on January 3, 2013, *eLife* accepted her paper.

But she couldn't celebrate. The evening before, she had received, out of the blue, a happy-new-year email that would not give her a happy new year:

> *From: Feng Zhang*
> *Sent: Wednesday, January 02, 2013 7:36 PM*
> *To: Jennifer Doudna*
> *Subject: CRISPR*
> *Attachments: CRISPR manuscript.pdf*

Dear Dr. Doudna,

Greetings from Boston and happy new year!

I am an assistant professor at MIT and have been working on developing applications based on the CRISPR system. I met you briefly during my graduate school interview at Berkeley back in 2004 and have been very inspired by your work since then. Our group in collaboration with Luciano Marraffini at Rockefeller recently completed a set of studies applying the type II CRISPR system to carry out genome editing of mammalian cells. The study was recently accepted by Science and it will be publishing online tomorrow. I have attached a copy of our paper for your review. The Cas9 system is very powerful and I would love to talk with you sometime. I am sure we have a lot of synergy and perhaps there are things that would be good to collaborate on in the future!

Very best wishes, Feng
Feng Zhang, Ph.D.
Core Member, Broad Institute of MIT and Harvard

On the same day that Doudna's paper appeared in *eLife*, January 29, 2013, a fourth paper was published online showing that CRISPR-Cas9 worked in human cells. It was by a South Korean researcher, Jin-Soo Kim, who had been corresponding with Doudna and credited her June 2012 paper for laying the ground for his own work. Then, a fifth paper published that day, by J. Keith Joung of Harvard, showed that CRISPR-Cas9 could genetically engineer the embryos of zebra fish.

Even though Doudna had been beaten by a few weeks by Zhang and Church, the fact that five different papers on CRISPR-Cas9 editing in animal cells all appeared in January 2013 reinforced the argument that this discovery was meant to happen after Doudna and Charpentier had shown that CRISPR could work in a test tube. The idea of using an easily programmed RNA molecule to target specific genes and change them was, for humanity, a momentous step into a new age. For Jennifer Doudna it was also a step toward creating the life-changing scientific applications she had been longing to pioneer for years.

Commercializing CRISPR

These days, science stands for very little unless it can be used in the real world. Often those real-world applications involve new technologies that can help improve people's health—and there need to be companies to market and sell these groundbreaking products. This is why the excitement over the potential of CRISPR caused all the major players to begin joining forces in the quest to create businesses that would commercialize CRISPR for medical applications.

In December 2012, a few weeks before the multiple papers on CRISPR gene editing were due to be published, Doudna arranged for one of her business associates, Andy May, to meet with George Church at his Harvard lab. An Oxford-educated molecular biologist, May was the scientific advisor at Caribou Biosciences, the biotech company that Doudna had started with Rachel Haurwitz in 2011. He wanted to explore the business potential for using CRISPR-based gene editing as a medical technology.

After the meeting with Church, May called Doudna. When she answered, he said, "Are you sitting down?"

"Yes," she replied. "I'm driving."

"Well, I hope you don't drive off the road," he said, "because I had this incredible meeting with George, who says this will be the most amazing discovery. He's changing his entire gene-editing focus to CRISPR."[1]

Soon Doudna and May decided to launch a company with Church and, if they could persuade them to join, some of the other CRISPR pioneers, like Rachel Haurwitz. So in January 2013, Haurwitz accompanied May back to Boston for another meeting with Church.

Church's bushy beard and eccentric personality continued to make him a scientific celebrity, and that was most certainly the case on the day of the meeting. In an earlier interview with a German magazine, he had offhandedly wondered out loud about the possibility of bringing a Neanderthal back to life by implanting its DNA into the egg of a volunteer surrogate mother. Not surprisingly, his phone was ringing nonstop as he sat down with Haurwitz and May.[2] But he finally focused on his meeting, and within an hour they had a plan. They would try to enlist Emmanuelle Charpentier and Feng Zhang, along with a few investors, into a large company to commercialize CRISPR.

In the hope of getting all the main players to come together, a brunch gathering was scheduled in February 2013 at the Blue Room, a restaurant in Cambridge. Invited to the brunch were Doudna, Charpentier, Church, and Zhang. At the last minute Zhang canceled, but Church urged that they go ahead without him.

"We need to start a company because there is so much we can do with this," Church said. "It's so powerful."

"How big do you think it is?" Doudna asked him.

"Well, Jennifer, all that I can tell you is that there is a tidal wave coming," he replied.[3]

Doudna very much wanted to work with Emmanuelle Charpentier, even though they had been drifting apart scientifically. Over a few weeks Doudna spent many hours on the phone with her trying to convince her to come along as a cofounder of the business with George. But Charpentier really did not want to work with some of the scientists in Boston. Doudna thought it was possible that Charpentier didn't trust them.

For a while in 2013, it seemed as if Doudna and Zhang, despite their rivalry, might become business allies or partners. After he missed the February 2013 brunch at the Blue Room, Zhang sent Doudna an email suggesting they get together to talk. He came out to San Francisco for a conference that spring and met Doudna at the Claremont hotel in Berkeley. His thinking was that Berkeley's ideas and potential patents would be put into a pool with the Broad Institute's, which would make it easy for scientists to use the CRISPR-Cas9 system. Zhang thought Doudna liked the idea, but the truth was that Doudna was worried—just like Charpentier had been.

"I just didn't get a good feeling from Feng," she recalls.

In the end she decided not to work with Zhang. Instead she gave an exclusive license of her work on CRISPR—which Berkeley managed in coordination with Charpentier—to her existing firm, Caribou Biosciences.

Nonetheless, Doudna was still open to becoming a partner in a CRISPR-focused company that would license both her potential patents and those of the Broad. So throughout the spring and summer of 2013, she traveled many times to Boston to meet with investors and scientists—including Church and Zhang—who were trying to put together companies.

On one trip in early June, Doudna went jogging in the evening along the Charles River by Harvard, remembering her days there studying RNA. Back then she'd never thought that her research would lead to commercial ventures. But everything had changed, and if she wanted CRISPR to have a direct impact on people, she knew that forming companies would be the best way to do that.

As the negotiations with the other scientists and investors dragged on through the summer, the stress of figuring out how to start a business began to wear her down. So did flying between San Francisco and Boston every few weeks. Particularly difficult was having to choose between working with Charpentier—who had started her own company called CRISPR Therapeutics—or with Church and Zhang.

"I couldn't tell what the right decision was," she admits.

Until then, Doudna had rarely gotten sick. But in the summer of 2013, she found herself being hit with waves of pain and fever. Her joints locked up in the morning, and sometimes she could barely move. She went to a few doctors, who speculated that she might have a rare virus or perhaps an autoimmune condition. The problems receded after a month, but then they recurred on a trip to Disneyland with her son late in the summer.

"It was just the two of us, and each morning I'd wake up in our hotel and everything was hurting," she said.

The stress of the business situation and all the travel, she realized, was affecting her physically.[4]

Luckily, she was able to reach an agreement with Zhang and Church by the end of the summer. They got more than $40 million in startup funding and added two top Harvard biologists who had been working on CRISPR. In September 2013, Gengine Inc. was founded with what George Church called "a dream team." Two months later the company changed its name to Editas Medicine.

"We have the ability to essentially target any gene," said the president of the company. "And we have in our crosshairs any diseases with a genetic component. We can go in and fix the error."[5]

Things went well at first, but after only a few months, Doudna's discomfort and stress began to resurface. She sensed that her partners, especially Zhang, were doing things behind her back, and her qualms worsened at a January 2014 medical conference in California. Zhang came out from Boston with some of the management team from Editas, and they invited Doudna to a couple of meetings with potential investors. She got bad vibes as soon as she walked into the first meeting.

"I could immediately tell from Feng's behavior and body language that something had changed," she says. "He wasn't collegial anymore."

As she stood back and watched, the men at the meeting clustered around Zhang and began to treat him like he was the boss. He was introduced as "the inventor" of CRISPR gene editing, with little mention of the foundation Doudna had laid, or Church's findings. Over the course of the meeting, Doudna was talked to like she was a secondary player, one of the scientific advisors. It was clear she was being cut out.

"There were things involving the intellectual property and I wasn't being kept informed. There was something afoot."

And then Doudna learned that Zhang and the Broad Institute had filed a patent application for the use of CRISPR-Cas9 as an editing tool, without telling her. The situation made her physically ill—on top of the exhaustion she'd endured from having to travel back and forth between the East and West Coasts.

Enough was enough. She decided to quit Editas Medicine.

She talked to a lawyer about how to get out of the agreement she had signed. It took a little time, but by June they had drafted an email to the Chief Executive Officer (CEO) of Editas, announcing that she would be leaving. When she hit send, she wondered how many minutes it would be before her phone would ring.

It was less than five minutes before she heard from the Editas CEO.

"No, no, you can't go, you can't leave," he said. "What's wrong? Why are you doing this?"

"You know what you did to me," she replied. "I'm done. I'm not going to work with people I can't trust, people who stab you in the back. You stabbed me in the back."

The Editas CEO immediately denied being involved in Zhang's patent filings. Doudna had a right to be mad, but he maintained that he hadn't done anything against her.

"Look," Doudna replied, "you may be right, or you may be wrong, but either way I can't be part of this company anymore. I'm done."

Doudna had never been so angry. All the founders of the company took notice, and all of them—including Zhang—sent her emails that day asking her to reconsider. They offered to make things right by doing whatever was possible to heal the division. But she refused.

"I'm done," she emailed back.

Immediately she felt better, like a big weight had been lifted off her shoulders.

Doudna had a phone call with George Church soon after. When she explained the situation to him, he suggested that, if she wanted, he would consider quitting as well. Then he decided he didn't want to. He realized that he needed to stay calm, because he wanted to see the company succeed. He also didn't want to reward the Editas team's bad behavior. If he resigned, those who stayed at Editas would receive even more profits from the company.

After a few months Doudna decided that she wanted to work more with her trusted partner and former student Rachel Haurwitz, with whom Doudna had started Caribou Biosciences in 2011. Caribou had created a spin-off company called Intellia Therapeutics, whose mission was to create and sell CRISPR-Cas9 tools. The group included academic scientists that Doudna liked, trusted, and respected. They were all brilliant but had an even more important trait: they were honest and straightforward.[6]

As a result, the pioneers of CRISPR-Cas9 ended up in three competing companies: CRISPR Therapeutics, founded by Charpentier and others; Editas Medicine, which included Zhang and Church, and Doudna until she resigned; and Intellia Therapeutics, founded by Doudna, Haurwitz, and others.

Patents

When a discovery is made or a product is developed, the person who spearheads the innovation often seeks a patent. Because patents allow an inventor to utilize their creation exclusively (at least for a little bit), they provide protection and reward ingenuity. But you can't just say you have a right to a patent and automatically get it. You must apply for one through the federal government. The idea of patents is so important to the US that it appears in the Constitution.

Unfortunately, exclusive ownership of an invention is a concept that can be difficult to navigate in court. This exact issue was raised concerning one particular type of doorknob. In 1850 a case called *Hotchkiss v. Greenwood* reached the United States Supreme Court because two parties disagreed whether a porcelain doorknob—as opposed to a wood one—could be considered a "new" invention, and therefore something that could be granted a patent.

Deciding on patents has proved to be even more complicated when it involves biological processes. If you think about it, a phenomenon that happens in nature isn't really a "new" idea. Bacteria have been fighting off viruses using CRISPR for millions of years, for example. But since the discovery of a process *is* new to the human who finds it, biological patents are nonetheless granted. For example, in 1873 the French biologist Louis Pasteur was awarded the first known patent for a microorganism. He had developed a method for killing germs and sterilizing food using extreme heat, a discovery that led to pasteurized milk, juice, and wine.

A century later, scientists began patenting biotechnology, including a method to manufacture new genes using recombinant DNA. The money from these patents that flowed to the inventors and their universities quickly made biotech patents popular. Then, in 1980, a major milestone occurred for the growing biotech industry. The US Supreme Court ruled in favor of a genetic engineer who had derived a strain of bacteria capable of eating crude oil, which made it useful in cleaning up oil spills. His patent application had been rejected by the US patent office on the theory that you could not patent a living thing. But the Supreme Court ruled, in a 5–4 decision, that "a live, human-made micro-organism is patentable" if it is "a product of human ingenuity."[1]

Jennifer Doudna did not know much about patents, and that was partly because little of her previous work had had practical application. So when she and Charpentier had been finishing their June 2012 paper, Doudna had reached out to the woman at Berkeley in charge of intellectual property, who'd set her up with a lawyer.

For research professors in the United States, the patents to their inventions are usually assigned to their academic institution—which in Doudna's case was Berkeley—with the inventors having a lot of say over how the invention will be used, and the inventors take a portion of the fees. In Sweden, where

Charpentier was then based, the patent goes directly to the inventor. So the patent application in the United States was filed jointly by Berkeley, Charpentier personally, and the University of Vienna—where Charpentier's researcher, Chylinski, was based.

The 168-page application, which included diagrams and experimental data, described CRISPR-Cas9 and made more than 124 claims for ways that the system could be used. All of the data in the application were from experiments done with bacteria. However, the text mentioned delivery methods that could work in human cells, and it made the claim that the patent should cover the use of CRISPR as a gene-editing tool in all forms of life.

After that uncomfortable meeting with Zhang and the management team from Editas, Doudna was hit with a surprising piece of news related to patents, one that made her understand why she'd had an uneasy feeling that Zhang had been keeping her in the dark. On April 15, 2014, she received an email from a reporter asking for her reaction to the news that Zhang and the Broad had just been granted a patent for the use of CRISPR-Cas9 as an editing tool. Doudna and Charpentier's patent application was still pending, but Zhang and the Broad, who had put in their own application in December 2012, had paid to have their decision fast-tracked.

Suddenly it became clear to Doudna that she was being denied acknowledgment for her role in history, and her right to any commercial use of CRISPR-Cas9. She called Andy May, her business associate, and was absolutely livid when he answered.

"How did this happen?" she yelled. "How did we get beaten?²"

The fact that Doudna's application was still sitting at the patent office raised a question: What happens if you apply for a patent and, before the decision gets made, another person is granted a similar patent? Under US law, you have a year to request an "interference" hearing. So in April 2015, Doudna filed a claim that Zhang's patents should be negated because they interfered with the patent applications that she had previously submitted.[3]

It took a full year for all the briefs, declarations, and motions to be filed, after which a hearing was held in December 2016 before a three-judge panel at the Patent and Trademark Office in Alexandria, Virginia. With its simple tables, the hearing room looks like a sleepy county traffic court. But on the day of the trial, a hundred journalists, lawyers, investors, and biotech fans began lining up at 5:45 a.m. to get seats.[4]

The three-judge panel ended up siding with Zhang and the Broad Institute.[5] Doudna's team appealed, and nineteen months later Zhang prevailed again.[6] The court said that because all the data in Doudna's patent application related to bacteria, and Zhang's application specifically described a process for using CRISPR in *human* cells, his patent did not interfere with Doudna and Charpentier's application.

But as happens with many complex intellectual property cases, these rulings did not end the case or give Zhang a total victory. Because there was "no interference" between the two sets of applications, they could be considered separately, which meant that it was still possible that the Doudna-Charpentier application would be granted as well.

That is exactly what happened, and in early 2019, the US patent office granted fifteen patents based on the applications that Doudna and Charpentier had filed in 2012. Zhang fought back in court, and by late 2020 the case was still dragging along.

CHAPTER TWENTY-THREE

When Friends Drift Apart

Since Jennifer Doudna and Emmanuelle Charpentier's important paper had been published in June 2012, Doudna had tried hard to maintain a professional and personal relationship with Charpentier. For example, when Doudna and her lab crystallized Cas9 and determined its exact structure in late 2013, Doudna asked Charpentier if she wanted to be a coauthor on the journal article that described these findings. Charpentier felt that this was a project she had brought to the Doudna Lab, so she responded that she would like that. The two also worked together on a different article. Doudna wrote a draft, and Charpentier made some edits.

Nevertheless, they began drifting apart. Rather than join Doudna in the quest to find ways to use CRISPR-Cas9 in humans, Charpentier told her that she planned to focus on fruit flies and bacteria. She liked basic research more than looking for applications.[1]

But there was another underlying reason for the strain. From Doudna's perspective, she was an equal co-discoverer of the CRISPR-Cas9 system, but Charpentier viewed CRISPR-Cas9 as her own project. She believed that she had brought Doudna into the research late in the game. At times Charpentier spoke of it as "my work" and referred to Doudna as if she were a secondary collaborator. The public didn't see it that way, though. Doudna was becoming a celebrity, giving interviews and making plans to pursue new CRISPR-Cas9 studies.

Doudna never quite understood Charpentier's feelings of ownership and couldn't figure out how to deal with the coolness that was evident beneath her polite manner. She kept suggesting ways they could work together, and Charpentier would reply, "That sounds great." But then nothing would happen.

"I wanted to continue collaborating, and Emmanuelle clearly didn't," Doudna says with sadness in her voice. "She never came out and said that to me. We just drifted apart."

Part of their problem was the different levels of comfort each had with publicity. When they met at awards ceremonies or conferences, their interactions could be awkward, especially at photo sessions, where it seemed like Charpentier was in the background and the focus was on Doudna. Charpentier seemed unhappy with all the publicity Doudna got, but she never quite felt comfortable with getting publicity herself. Doudna didn't understand this. Although she was flattered by attention, she was not, in fact, someone who made an effort to become famous. She made a point of trying to share the limelight and prizes with Charpentier.

One bigger issue that came between them is something that happens in many situations in life: almost every person tends to remember their own role as being a little more important than the way others see it. We can clearly recount the brilliance of our own contributions to a conversation; we're less clear when recalling what others say or do. As Charpentier views the CRISPR narrative, she was the one who first worked on Cas9, identified its components, and then brought Doudna into the project. After they published the 2012 paper, Charpentier also occasionally suggested that she had known back in 2011, before she'd started collaborating with Doudna, that the tracrRNA had an important role in assisting Cas9. This annoyed Doudna, who believes the relationship between tracrRNA and Cas9 became clear only after Doudna and Charpentier started working together.

Their rift grew bigger in 2017 when Doudna published a book on her CRISPR work. The book was not full of bragging, but it highlighted Doudna as a central character more than Charpentier thought was appropriate.

Nevertheless, the two won a large and glamorous prize called the Breakthrough Prize in Life Sciences in November 2014, a few months after Zhang beat them to the first patents. It carried a $3 million award for each recipient. They also won the Gairdner award in biomedical science, given by a Canadian foundation. Instead of being able to honor only two researchers in each field, like the Breakthrough Prize had, the Gairdner honored five. The foundation chose Doudna, Charpentier, Zhang, and the two Danisco yogurt researchers, Horvath and Barrangou, naming their contributions to the development of CRISPR.

Doudna was upset by the exclusion of her friend Church, so she donated her prize money, about $100,000, to a project George Church had set up with his wife. The truth was that she knew that great discoveries like CRISPR aren't confined to one, two, or even five people. She wanted to share the limelight, even if at times it seemed to others that she did not.

PART FOUR
CRISPR in Action

CHAPTER TWENTY-FOUR

Creating Happy, Healthy Babies

In the spring of 2014, when the battle to win CRISPR patents and launch gene-editing companies was heating up, Jennifer Doudna had a nightmare. In it, a prominent researcher asked her to meet someone who wanted to learn about gene editing. When she went into the room, she was shocked. Sitting in front of her, with pen and paper ready to take notes, was Adolf Hitler with the face of a pig.

"I want to understand the uses and implications of this amazing technology you've developed," he said.

Doudna was jolted awake by the nightmare, and as she lay in the dark, her heart racing, she couldn't escape the terrifying warning the dream had offered up to her. After that, she began to have trouble sleeping at night.

Gene-editing technology had enormous power to do good, but the thought of using it to make alterations in humans that would be inherited by all future generations was scary.

"Have we created a toolbox for future Frankensteins?" she asked herself. Or perhaps even worse, would it be a tool for future Hitlers? "Emmanuelle and I, and our collaborators, had imagined that CRISPR technology could save lives by helping to cure genetic disease," she later wrote. "Yet as I thought about it now, I could scarcely begin to conceive of all of the ways in which our hard work might be perverted."[1]

Around that time, Doudna was confronted with an example of how people with good intentions could pave the way for those perversions to happen. Sam Sternberg, one of the researchers on Doudna's close-knit CRISPR team, received an email in March 2014 from an aspiring young entrepreneur in San Francisco named Lauren Buchman, who had gotten Sternberg's name from a friend. Lauren wanted to meet up for a coffee to discuss her new company. It was called Happy Healthy Baby.[2]

"We've seen a potential of Cas9 to aid in preventing genetic diseases in children conceived through IVF in the future," she wrote in her email. In vitro fertilization (IVF) is a procedure in which fertilization happens in a lab. "Ensuring that this is done with the highest level of scientific and ethical standards is first and foremost to us," she added.

Sternberg was surprised but not totally shocked by Buchman's email. By that time CRISPR-Cas9 had already been used to edit embryos implanted in monkeys, so he knew that editing human embryos was just around the corner. He was interested in digging a bit deeper into what Buchman's motivations were and how she was thinking about developing this concept, so he agreed to meet her at a Mexican restaurant in Berkeley.

When Sternberg and Buchman met, she told him that she had already registered the domain name HealthyBabies.com. She wasn't a scientist, but she knew that fertility clinics could screen for harmful genes before choosing an embryo to implant. She also knew that finding good embryos and implanting them success-fully could be difficult.

"You may end up producing only one or two embryos," she pointed out, "so preimplantation genetic screening is not always easy."

When she heard about CRISPR, she got excited. The idea that humans could treat something in cells, in a lab, seemed so promising and wonderful. She needed an expert on board, though, and she asked Sternberg if he wanted to be a cofounder of the company.

Sternberg was shocked. First, he had no experience edit-ing human cells. Second, he didn't know the first thing about implanting embryos. But perhaps most unsettling was the fact that the entire process of editing human cells was still confined to a lab, with none of its applications having been tested in the real world. Gene editing had not cured any diseases or prevented any genetic conditions. Like Jennifer Doudna, Sternberg knew that CRISPR gene editing in human cells was like the Wild West—a huge, promising frontier, but filled with uncertainty and danger.

Lauren Buchman worried about this too, so she wanted to use CRISPR technology ethically and in a positive manner. She had consulted with investors and biotech entrepreneurs about her business plan, and some of them had pitched her on weird ideas that had freaked her out.

"The more I heard, the more I thought 'I have to do this,'" she says, "because if I don't, these fringe folks with no regard for the impact or the ethics will take over the field."

Sternberg listened, but he left the dinner at the Mexican restaurant before dessert. He had no interest in being a cofounder, though he was intrigued enough to agree to visit the company's lab.

During his visit, Sternberg watched a promotional video for Happy Healthy Baby, filled with animation and stock footage of lab experiments, in which Buchman, sitting in a sunny room with big glass windows, explains the idea of gene-editing babies. When the video was over, he told her that he didn't see any chance that CRISPR would be approved for use on human babies in the United States for at least ten years. She replied that the clinics did not have to be in the United States. There would likely be other countries where the procedure would be allowed, and people who could afford gene-edited babies would be willing to travel.

Sternberg still said no, but George Church agreed to serve as an unpaid science advisor. One of his suggestions was that Buchman work with sperm cells rather than embryos because ethicists might find gene-edited sperm cells less controversial or troubling.[3] She took his advice to heart but didn't follow through with it. In fact, Buchman eventually abandoned her venture.

"I dug into the use cases, market regulations, and ethics, and it became obvious that I was too early to be working on this," she says. "The science wasn't ready, and society wasn't ready."

As a result of her Hitler dream and Sternberg's Happy Healthy Baby story, Doudna decided in the spring of 2014 to become more engaged in the policy discussions about how CRISPR gene-editing tools should be used. At first she considered writing an op-ed for a newspaper, but that did not seem adequate to the challenge. So she thought back to a process that had been used forty years before. In February 1975 scientists had held a conference to come up with the "prudent path forward" guidelines for work on recombinant DNA. She decided that the invention of CRISPR gene-editing tools warranted bringing together a similar group.

The organizers of the 1975 conference agreed to participate, and the meeting was set for January 2015 at a resort in Napa Valley about an hour north of San Francisco. Eighteen other top researchers were invited, including Martin Jinek and Sam Sternberg from Doudna's lab. The focus would be on the ethics of making inheritable genetic edits.

CHAPTER TWENTY-FIVE

The Ethics of Genetic Engineering

B efore we dive into what Jennifer Doudna and other scientists discussed at the Napa conference, it's important to understand how society has wrestled with the ethics of genetic engineering throughout time.

For most of modern history, the idea of creating engineered humans was the stuff of science fiction novels or movies. But in the 1960s, researchers began to crack the genetic code by figuring out the role played by some of the sequences of our DNA. And the discovery of how to cut and paste DNA from different organisms launched the field of genetic engineering.

The first reaction to these breakthroughs, especially among scientists, was excitement and optimism. Some scientists even argued that society should embrace these new genetic technologies and engineer healthier, smarter, stronger children because that would be better for humanity as a whole.

"No parents will have a right to burden society with a malformed or a mentally incompetent child," one scientist said.

But these were extreme views, and it became the mission of many scientists to find a middle ground rather than let the issue become politically polarized.

In the summer of 1972, scientist Paul Berg, who had just published his paper on recombinant DNA, led a seminar on new biotechnologies. The graduate students who attended peppered him with questions about the ethical dangers of genetic engineering, especially the modification of humans. They asked basic but hard-to-answer questions such as: What if we could genetically engineer height or eye color? What about intelligence? Would we do that? Should we?

The discussion led to biologists coming together at several different conferences to talk about the dangers of recombinant DNA, and then issuing a letter calling for a stop to the creation of recombinant DNA until safety guidelines could be formulated.[1] The concern was that recombinant DNA technology made it far too simple to combine DNA from different organisms and create new genes. Some scientists also worried that in the hands of biohackers, recombinant DNA could be used to create new microbes that could threaten the planet.

By February 1975 these types of discussions were so central to biochemistry that even legends like James Watson had gotten involved. Watson could be controversial, and he said he believed that his colleagues were overreacting and that researchers should do "whatever they wanted."

However, lawyers warned against scientists doing "whatever they wanted" in their labs. If anyone in a lab unintentionally became infected with recombinant DNA, the university involved would likely be held responsible—and even shut down. So scientists came out with a statement setting forth safeguards and restrictions on experiments. The statement had two goals: guarding against the hazards that could come from creating new forms of genes, and protecting against the threat that politicians might ban genetic engineering altogether. These restrictions on experiments were soon accepted by universities and funding agencies worldwide.

Unfortunately, the restrictions were also notable for what the scientists did *not* address. That big ethical question was, How far should we go if and when methods for engineering our genes turn out to be safe?

Several years later, in 1981, President Jimmy Carter appointed a presidential commission to study this issue. The group published a 106-page report in 1982 that added very little to the conversation except two important concerns. One was that corporations might become too involved in scientific research at universities because they would see how profitable groundbreaking discoveries could be. This might change the research community from a place where ideas were exchanged freely to a place where players focused on achieving competitive advantage and protecting trade secrets. The second concern was that genetic engineering would increase inequality. New biotech procedures would be expensive, so people who were born into privilege would likely get the most benefits. That could widen—and genetically encode—existing inequalities.

After the development of recombinant DNA in the 1970s, the next big bioengineering advance—and set of ethical issues— came in the 1990s. It resulted from the combination of two innovations: in vitro fertilization (the first IVF baby, Louise Brown, was born in 1978) and genetic sequencing technology. Combining these two tools led to a procedure known as **preimplantation genetic diagnosis.**[2] This procedure allows parents to identify gene defects before an embryo is implanted in a woman's body. For example, it lets parents choose the gender of their child and avoid having a child who carries a genetic disease or some other attribute the parents find undesirable.

Preimplantation genetic diagnosis was first used in 1989, and it was still being debated in 1998 at a conference at UCLA. While a professor delivered a speech about the need to distinguish between treating diseases, which he proclaimed to be moral, and providing children with genetic enhancements, which he said wasn't, James Watson began to snort and stir.

"No one really has the guts to say it," Watson interrupted, "but if we could make better human beings by knowing how to add genes, why shouldn't we do it?"[3]

The title of the gathering was "Engineering the Human Germline," and it focused on the ethics of making genetic edits that would be inherited. Instead of curing a disease like sickle cell anemia in one person, you could cure something inheritable, so that the negative trait wouldn't be passed on. Watson, whose son suffered from severe mental illness, thought removing inheritable genetic defects was a great idea. He believed that the human gene pool shouldn't be treated as sacred, because evolution could be cruel. Why didn't we try to improve the gene pool so that people didn't suffer, like his son did?

For the most part, Watson was preaching to the choir. The opinions at the UCLA conference ranged from enthusiasm to unbridled enthusiasm for gene editing. The attendees believed that people in the world would want to select the best traits for their children.

"For the first time we as a species have the ability to

self-evolve," one scientist told the group. "I mean, this is an incredible concept."

In fact, the scientists at the conference wanted the US government to keep away from genetic engineering entirely, and they urged officials to not pass any regulations or laws.

The American eagerness for genetic engineering was a sharp contrast to the attitude in Europe, where policymakers and various commissions had increasingly turned against it, both in agriculture and in humans. The most notable expression came from a meeting convened by the Council of Europe in Oviedo, Spain, in 1997. It barred genetic engineering in humans except "for preventive, diagnostic or therapeutic reasons and only where it does not aim to change the genetic make-up of a person's descendants." Twenty-nine European countries incorporated the principles of the Oviedo Convention into their laws, with Britain and Germany being notable holdouts. Even where the principles were not ratified, they helped shape what is still a consensus in Europe against genetic engineering.[4]

Guidelines, Regulations, and the Government

———— ◁◁◁ ————

By 2014, interest in genetic engineering had come roaring back, and Doudna was determined that the January 2015 conference in Napa Valley should tackle the moral questions surrounding it once and for all. These moral questions included: Should decisions about the gene editing of babies be left mainly to parents? To what extent would creating gene-edited babies—and giving up the idea that our genetic gifts were the result of a random natural process—make us less sympathetic to differences in others? Was there a danger in decreasing the diversity of the human species? And if the technology was available to make healthier and better babies, would it be ethically wrong *not* to use it?[1]

The researchers at the conference agreed that the use of CRISPR tools for *non-inheritable* gene editing in **somatic cells** was a good thing. Somatic cells make up the tissues, organs, and other parts of an individual and are distinct from **germ cells**, which are egg and sperm cells. Editing the somatic cells in a person does not affect that person's offspring, and the thinking was that this type of gene editing could lead to beneficial drugs and treatments.

But what about **germline editing** (also called "heritable genome editing")—that is, changing the DNA in egg and sperm cells, which would mean that the alteration becomes inheritable? For example, in germline editing you can alter a person's DNA so that they don't pass on the genes for the genetic heart condition that killed their grandfather. A lot of attendees felt that it would be bad to completely ban the practice of germline editing. They wanted to leave the door open to it and find a path forward rather than putting on the brakes.

As the scientists explored the ethics of gene editing, one of the participants brought up the social justice argument. Gene editing would be very expensive, so would only the wealthy have access to it? One scientist agreed that was a problem, but he argued it was not a cause for banning the technology entirely. He pointed to computers, which at first had been too expensive for most people. Then they'd become cheaper over time. The fact that they'd initially been priced so high had not been an argument against moving forward and trying to make computers mainstream.

In the end, the scientists at the convention decided to call for a temporary halt on germline editing in humans, at least until the technology's safety and social issues could be further understood and discussed. Ideally they wanted those conversations to happen among a full range of scientists and officials around the world.

Doudna drafted an initial version of the conference report, which she circulated to the other participants. After incorporating their suggestions, she submitted it in March to *Science*.[2] When the report was published, it got major national attention. The *New York Times* ran a story on page one, with a picture of Doudna at her Berkeley desk.[3]

She couldn't celebrate the publicity properly, though, because she couldn't get a rumor she'd heard during the conference out of her head. Supposedly—for the first time—a group of Chinese scientists had used CRISPR-Cas9 to edit genes in a human embryo. These embryos had had no possibility of growing into real babies if they'd been implanted inside a woman's body, but in theory the scientists had been able to create changes that could pass from one generation to the next. Doudna knew this was a scary first step into territory the world was not quite ready for.

Later on, she and much of the scientific establishment read an article that described what had actually happened in China. Researchers at a university in Guangzhou—a city of almost fifteen million people located northwest of Hong Kong—had isolated eighty-six zygotes, which are fertilized egg cells that have not yet developed into embryos. Then the scientists had used CRISPR-Cas9 to cut out a mutated gene the zygotes contained that causes beta-thalassemia, a life-threatening blood disorder.[4] Although the embryos had never been intended to grow into babies—nor would they have been biologically able to—this study marked the first time CRISPR-Cas9 had been used to make potential edits in the human germline.

After Doudna read the article in her Berkeley office, she stared out at San Francisco Bay feeling, she later recalled, "awestruck and a bit queasy." Other scientists around the world were probably conducting similar experiments with the technology that she and Charpentier had created. That could lead, she realized, to some very unintended consequences.

The Napa conference and the Chinese embryo-editing experiments soon captured the interest of government officials.

Senator Elizabeth Warren hosted a congressional briefing about the subject, and Doudna went to Washington to testify with her friend and fellow CRISPR pioneer George Church. The event was so popular that it was standing room only, with more than one hundred fifty senators, representatives, staffers, and agency personnel crammed into the room. Doudna recounted the history of CRISPR, emphasizing that it had begun as pure "curiosity-driven" research about how bacteria fight off viruses.[5]

In a subsequent article for *Nature*, George Church said he believed that research, even in editing the human germline, should continue—but that it should be safe.[6] Together they reinforced the case that scientists were dealing with the issues seriously and did not require new government regulations.

Following their Napa Valley meeting, Doudna and a colleague had also urged the US National Academy of Sciences and its sister organizations around the world to convene a globally representative group in order to discuss how to regulate human germline editing. More than five hundred scientists, policymakers, and bioethicists gathered in Washington for three days at the beginning of December 2015 for the first International Summit on Human Gene Editing. Unfortunately, very few patients or parents of sick children attended.[7]

Because there were so many participants and journalists, the meeting consisted mainly of prepared presentations rather than real debate. The most important conclusion was almost identical to what had been decided at the small Napa meeting at the beginning of the year. Human germline editing should be strongly discouraged until strict conditions were met, but the word "ban" was avoided.

Following the international summit, organizers from the US National Academies of Sciences, Engineering, and Medicine created a twenty-two-person committee of experts to undertake a yearlong study on whether germline DNA edits should be stopped for the time being. In their final report, issued in February 2017, the group provided a list of criteria that should be met before germline editing should be allowed.[8] The criteria included an "absence of reasonable alternatives," which would mean that no other practical options were available for treating the genetic condition. The group also recommended that germline editing be restricted to the prevention of a serious disease or condition. Notably, this US report left out one key restriction that had been in the 2015 international summit report—the need for a "broad societal consensus" before heritable genome editing would be permitted. The 2017 paper called only for "broad ongoing participation and input by the public."

Doudna felt that the US report had found a sensible middle ground in the debate. Others who were engaged in genetic research and biotechnology viewed the report as a yellow traffic light. They weren't being forced to stop. They were instead being allowed to proceed with caution.[9]

Members of Congress took seriously the warning to tread lightly, so they put some restrictions in place. First they passed a provision barring the Food and Drug Administration from considering any treatment "in which a human embryo is intentionally created or modified to include a heritable genetic modification."

President Barack Obama's science advisor, John Holdren, even declared, "The Administration believes that altering the human germline for clinical purposes is a line that should not be crossed at this time," and the director of the National Institutes of Health (NIH), Francis Collins, announced, "NIH will not fund any use of gene-editing technologies in human embryos."[10]

But despite their stern warnings, the government did not put in place any absolute and clear laws against germline editing.

Still, lawmakers clearly had CRISPR firmly in their sights, and Doudna knew that was because they understood that CRISPR could be used by terrorists or foreign adversaries as a weapon of war.

Doudna had raised concerns about CRISPR technology getting into the wrong hands when she'd attended a 2014 conference and heard a researcher speak. He had described how someone could engineer a virus to carry CRISPR components and then inject the virus into a mouse, where CRISPR would edit a gene that would cause the mouse to develop lung cancer. When Doudna had heard this, a chill had passed through her body. She knew that a tweak or a mistake in the lab could easily make the gene edit work in human lungs. Fearing that CRISPR could turn into a weapon used in biological warfare, she joined an effort funded by the US Defense Department to find ways to protect against the misuse of CRISPR.[11]

In 2016, James Clapper, the head of the US Office of the Director of National Intelligence, issued the agency's annual Worldwide Threat Assessment. For the first time in history, it included "genome editing" as a potential weapon of mass destruction. As a result, the Pentagon's research unit launched a program called Safe Genes to support ways to defend against genetically engineered weapons. The unit soon dispensed $65 million worth of grants, making the military the largest single source of money for CRISPR research.[12] These grants funded topics such as how to use CRISPR to protect humans against the nuclear radiation that would result from a nuclear attack.

Around the world other governments were funding research into CRISPR, and many put in place restrictions similar to the US's. China was no different. Because it's a Communist country, few things happen without strict oversight from the government, and this is especially true with science, an area that the government takes a special interest in. In 2015 there were no clear laws specifically outlawing the heritable genome editing of human embryos, but there were multiple regulations and guidelines that prevented—or were believed to prevent—it. At the December 2015 International Summit on Human Gene Editing, Duanqing Pei, a respected young stem cell researcher who was the director general of Guangzhou Institutes of Biomedicine and Health, assured the conference members that germline gene editing of embryos would *not* happen in China.

His strong words were why Pei and his like-minded friends from around the world were so shocked when they arrived in Hong Kong in November 2018 for the Second International Summit on Human Genome Editing. There they discovered that—despite all their proclamations, agreements, and carefully crafted reports setting limits on germline editing—a Chinese scientist had suddenly and unexpectedly thrust the world of gene editing into a new era.

PART FIVE
CRISPR Babies

He Jiankui

———— ❦ ————

He Jiankui was born in 1984 in Xinhua, one of the poorest areas in a rural part of southeast central China. His parents were struggling rice farmers, and the average family income in his area was a hundred dollars a year. His parents were so poor that they could not afford to buy him textbooks, so Jiankui walked from the rice fields to a village bookstore to read them there.

"I picked leeches from my legs every day in the summer," he recalled. "I will never forget my roots."[1]

Jiankui's childhood instilled in him a hunger for success and fame. So, like Feng Zhang, he paid attention to the posters and banners at his school, urging him to push forward the frontier of science. Young Jiankui built a physics laboratory at home, where he relentlessly conducted experiments. After doing well in high school, he was tapped to go to the University of Science and Technology of China in Hefei, 575 miles to the east of his village, and there he majored in physics.

During his last year in college, he applied to four graduate schools in the United States and was accepted by only one of them: Rice University in Houston. After he enrolled and started classes, he became a star at creating computer simulations of biological systems. Jiankui and his advisor even devised a successful mathematical model for predicting what strains of flu would emerge each year, and in September 2010 the two coauthored a paper on CRISPR that showed how the spacer sequences matching viral DNA are formed.[2] Popular, friendly, and a good networker, Jiankui became president of Rice's Chinese Students and Scholars Association and an avid soccer player.[3]

He got his PhD in physics, but he decided that the future was in biology, so he went to Stanford for postdoctoral work in a bioengineering lab. Colleagues there remember him as funny and energetic, with a passion for business. Believing that he could make the process of gene sequencing commercially successful in China, Jiankui soon headed back home and decided to start a company. After he accepted a job at a university outside Hong Kong, he founded a lab.

Chinese officials had designated genetic engineering as critical to the country's economic future and its competition with the United States, so when Jiankui formed his new company to build gene-sequencing machines in July 2012, he received an initial round of $156,000 in funding. Over the next six years, Jiankui's company received about $5.7 million in funding from government sources. By 2017, the company's gene sequencer was on the market, and the company, of which Jiankui owned a one-third stake, was valued at $313 million.

With his charming personality and thirst for fame, Jiankui became a minor scientific celebrity in China, where the state-run media was eagerly looking for innovators to advertise as role models. The broadcast network CCTV ran a series in late 2017 featuring some of the country's young science entrepreneurs. As inspiring patriotic music played, Jiankui was shown talking about his company's gene sequencer, which the narrator said works better and faster than American versions.

"Somebody said we shocked the world with our machine," a smiling Jiankui declared to the camera. "Yes, they're right! I did that—He Jiankui! That's me who did that!"[4]

Jiankui initially used his gene-sequencing technology to diagnose genetic conditions in early-stage human embryos. But he had already begun to discuss the possibility of not only reading human genomes but also editing them. His goal, he said, was to sequence a human genome for a hundred dollars, then move on to fixing any problems.

"I support gene editing for the treatment and prevention of disease," Jiankui wrote in a post on the social media site WeChat, "but not for enhancement or improving I.Q., which is not beneficial to society."[5]

Earlier, in January 2017, Jiankui had sent Jennifer Doudna an email saying that he was working on the technology to improve the effectiveness and safety of gene editing of human embryos in China. As he had done with other top CRISPR researchers, he asked to meet with her when he next came to the United States.

The email arrived when Doudna was helping to organize a small workshop on "the challenge and opportunity of gene editing." It had been two years since her Napa Valley conference, and the John Templeton Foundation, which supports the study of big ethical questions that impact society, had provided funding for a series of discussions on CRISPR. Doudna had invited twenty scientists and ethicists to a kickoff workshop in Berkeley, but few were from overseas. She saw an opportunity for the eager scientist from China to change that.[6]

"We would be delighted to have your participation," she wrote back to Jiankui.

Not surprisingly, he was equally delighted to accept.

The workshop opened with a public lecture by George Church in which he spoke of the possible benefits of germline editing. As he described his ideas, Church showed a slide outlining simple gene variations that offer beneficial effects, including a variant of the CCR5 gene that would make a person less likely to be infected by HIV, the virus that causes AIDS.[7]

Jiankui's turn to present came on the second day of the meeting, and his talk was titled "Safety of Human Gene Embryo Editing." Most of what he said was unmemorable, but there was one interesting part: his description of his work editing the CCR5 gene, which was the one that Church had mentioned in his lecture as a potential candidate for future germline editing. Jiankui told the crowd how he had edited the gene—which produces a protein that allows the AIDS virus to enter cells—in mice, monkeys, and nonviable (meaning unable to grow) human embryos discarded from fertility clinics. Jiankui's gene edits were meant to disable the production of the CCR5 protein.

Other Chinese researchers had already used CRISPR to edit CCR5 genes in nonviable embryos, so nobody at the conference thought much of Jiankui's talk. Nobody paid extra attention to He Jiankui outside of his presentation either. Doudna did notice how eager he was to meet people and be accepted by everyone, but she didn't think he was doing any important science.

What struck her and others, however, was that with everyone

he spoke to, Jiankui did not seem interested in the moral issues involved with making heritable genome edits to embryos.[8]

This was no coincidence. The fact of the matter was that Jiankui was making plans to edit genes in viable human embryos with the intent of creating genetically altered babies. In other words, he was going to be the first scientist to make germline edits in embryos that would actually develop and be born—something that Chinese authorities had approved but that was frowned upon throughout the rest of the world.

Jiankui submitted a medical ethics application to Har-MoniCare Shenzhen Women and Children's Hospital, writing in his application that he planned to use CRISPR-Cas9 to edit embryos. He would then transfer the edited embryos to women, in the hopes that the women would become pregnant. His goal was to allow couples who suffered from AIDS to have babies who would be protected from HIV, as would all their descendants.

Because there were simpler ways to prevent AIDS infections—such as screening embryos before they were implanted to be sure they were healthy—the procedure was not medically necessary. Nor would it correct a genetic disorder since AIDS was not a genetic disease. So Jiankui's plan did not meet the guidelines that had been agreed to at multiple international meetings. But it did offer Jiankui the possibility, or at least he thought so, of achieving a major historical breakthrough and enhancing the glory of Chinese science.

"This is going to be a great science and medicine achievement," he wrote in his application, comparing his proposal to "the IVF technology which was awarded the Nobel Prize in 2010." Every single person on the hospital's ethics committee gave their consent.[9]

There are approximately 1.25 million HIV-positive people in China, a number that is still growing rapidly, and victims are often discriminated against. Working with an AIDS advocacy group based in Beijing, China's second-largest city, Jiankui wanted to recruit twenty volunteer couples in which the husband was HIV positive and the wife was HIV negative. More than two hundred couples showed interest.

Two of the selected couples came to Jiankui's lab in Shenzhen one Saturday in June 2017 and, in a meeting that was videotaped, were informed about the proposed clinical trial and asked if they wished to participate. The two couples agreed, as did five more recruited at other sessions. Altogether the research team produced thirty-one embryos, sixteen of which Jiankui was able to edit. Eleven were implanted into the female volunteers unsuccessfully, but by the late spring of 2018 he was able to implant twin embryos into one mother and a single embryo into another.[10]

When Jiankui had been visiting the States, he had confided his plans to Matthew Porteus, an accomplished and respected stem cell researcher at Stanford medical school. When Porteus had heard what Jiankui was planning, Porteus's jaw had dropped.

"There's no medical need," he insisted. "It violates all the guidelines. You're jeopardizing the entire field of genetic engineering."

Porteus demanded to know if Jiankui had run it by any important Chinese officials other than the ethics committee.

No, Jiankui said.

"You need to talk to these people, the officials in China, before you proceed any further," Porteus warned with rising anger.

At that point Jiankui became very quiet, his face flushed, and then he walked out of the office.

"I don't think he was expecting such a negative reaction," Porteus says.

As the Chinese pregnancies progressed in mid-2018, Jiankui knew that his announcement would be earthshaking news, and he wanted to capitalize on it. The goal of his experiment, after all, was not merely to protect babies from developing AIDS. The prospect of achieving fame was also a motivation. He hired Ryan Ferrell, a respected American public relations executive he had worked with on another project, who found Jiankui's plans to be so exciting that he left his agency and relocated temporarily to Shenzhen.[11] Ferrell gave an Associated Press (AP) team exclusive access to Jiankui. They were even allowed to videotape a nonviable human embryo being injected with CRISPR in Jiankui's lab.

With Ferrell's guidance, Jiankui also prepared videos that featured him in his lab speaking directly to the camera. In the first one, he outlined a few ethical principles he personally held to be true.

"If we can protect a little girl or boy from certain disease, if we can help more loving couples start families, gene surgery is a wholesome development," he said.

He also made a distinction between curing disease and making enhancements to a person's abilities or appearance, saying that gene surgery should be used only for treating serious disease. It should not be used for increasing IQ, improving sports performance, or changing skin color.[12]

In the second video, Jiankui explained why he felt it was wrong for parents *not* to protect their children if nature and science give us the tools to do so. The third video explained why he had chosen HIV as his first target, and the fourth video, which was in Chinese and delivered by one of his postdoctoral students, explained the scientific details of how the CRISPR edits had been made.[13] The research team held off making the fifth video until they could announce the live births of the two babies.

The public relations campaign and release of the YouTube videos were planned for January 2019, when the babies were due to be born. But one evening in early November 2018, Jiankui got a call saying that the mother had gone into labor early. He dashed to the Shenzhen airport to fly to the city where the mother lived, taking some of the students from his lab. The woman ended up giving birth, after a caesarean section, to two apparently healthy girls, whom Jiankui nicknamed Nana and Lulu in order to protect their privacy.

The baby girls were born so early that Jiankui had not yet submitted the official description of his clinical trial to Chinese authorities. On November 8, after the birth, he finally turned it in. He had written everything in Chinese, and for two weeks the news went unnoticed in the West.[14]

Jiankui also finished an academic article he had been working on, and while it was never published, Jiankui defended the ethical value of what he had done.

"We anticipate that human embryo genome editing will bring new hope to millions of families seeking healthy babies free from inherited or acquired life-threatening diseases."

Unfortunately, buried in Jiankui's unpublished paper were some disturbing pieces of information. One bit of the paper described how, in the embryo that became Lulu, only one of the two relevant chromosomes had been properly modified. This meant that her system would still produce some of the CCR5 protein. In addition, there was evidence that some unwanted edits had been made in the embryos. There had also been enough cell division in both embryos before the CRISPR editing that some of the resulting cells in the babies were unedited. Despite these errors, Jiankui said, the parents had chosen to have both embryos implanted.

In the first few days after the babies were born, Jiankui and his publicist planned to keep everything under wraps until January, when—they hoped—*Nature* would publish the team's scholarly paper. But the secret was too explosive to hold on to. Just before Jiankui was scheduled to arrive at the Second International Summit on Human Genome Editing, which was going to be held in Hong Kong, news of his CRISPR babies leaked. A story was published online, so that same day Jiankui decided to release on YouTube the videos he had previously made, along with a final one in which he made his momentous announcement. Speaking calmly but proudly to the camera, he declared:

> Two beautiful little Chinese girls named Lulu and Nana came crying into the world as healthy as any other babies a few weeks ago. The girls are home now with their mom, Grace, and their dad, Mark. Grace started her pregnancy by regular IVF with one difference. Right after we sent her husband's sperm into her egg, we also sent in a little bit of protein and instructions for a gene surgery. When Lulu and Nana

were just a single cell, this surgery removed the doorway through which HIV enters to infect people. . . . When Mark saw his daughters for the first time, he said that he never thought he could be a father. Now he has found a reason to live, a reason to walk, a purpose. You see, Mark has HIV. . . . As a father of two girls, I can't think of a gift more beautiful and wholesome for the society than giving another couple a chance to start a loving family.[15]

The Hong Kong Summit

⬦⬦⬦⬦⬦

On November 23, two days before He Jiankui's news broke, Doudna received an email from him. The subject line was dramatic: "Babies Born." She was puzzled, then shocked, and then alarmed.

"At first I thought it was fake, or maybe he was crazy," she says. "The idea that you would use 'Babies Born' as a subject line for something like this didn't seem real."[1]

Jiankui had included in his email the draft of the manuscript he had submitted to *Nature*. When Doudna opened the attachment, she knew the situation was all too real. She also realized that the news would become even more dramatic because of its timing. In three days, five hundred scientists and policymakers were due to converge in Hong Kong for the Second International Summit on Human Genome Editing. Doudna was one of the core organizers, and He Jiankui was scheduled to be a speaker.

Upon getting Jiankui's shocking "Babies Born" email, Doudna decided that she would change her flight and arrive a day earlier than planned so that she could gather with some of the other organizers and decide what to do. When she landed at dawn on the morning of Monday, November 26, and turned her phone on,

Doudna saw that Jiankui had been desperately trying to reach her by email. One of his many messages said he was driving to Hong Kong from Shenzhen, and he wanted to meet as soon as possible.

"I have to talk to you right now," he emailed. "Things have really gotten out of control."[2]

She did not reply because she wanted to meet first with the other conference organizers. Soon after she checked into her hotel, though, a bellman knocked at her door with a message from Jiankui. It said to call him right away. Doudna did, and she agreed to meet with him in the hotel lobby—but only after she quickly brought together some of the organizers in a fourth-floor conference room.

No one on the steering committee other than Doudna had seen the scientific paper that Jiankui had submitted to *Nature*. So Doudna showed them the copy he had emailed to her. The organizers immediately decided that he should stay on the speaker list. In fact, they would give him a solo spot on the program and ask him to address the science and methods he'd used to make the CRISPR babies.

After fifteen minutes Doudna went down to the lobby to meet Jiankui. She took with her Robin Lovell-Badge, the British scientist who would be chairing Jiankui's session. The three of them sat on a couch, and Doudna and Lovell-Badge told Jiankui that they wanted his presentation to explain exactly how and why he had proceeded with his experiment. Jiankui confused them by insisting that he wanted to stick with his original slide presentation and not discuss the CRISPR babies.

Lovell-Badge turned almost white as he listened, and Doudna politely pointed out that Jiankui was being ridiculous. He had triggered the most explosive scientific controversy in years, and there was no way he could avoid discussing it. Her words seemed to surprise Jiankui. But after pressing their case even harder, Doudna and Lovell-Badge convinced the Chinese scientist to have an early dinner with some members of the organizing committee to discuss the issue.[3]

The dinner was tense. When Jiankui arrived, he was defensive, even a bit defiant, about what he had done. He pulled out his laptop to show his data and the DNA sequencing he had performed on the embryos. The other scientists peppered him with questions: Had there been oversight on his consent process? Why did he believe that germline embryo editing had been medically necessary? Had he read the guidelines that the international academies of medicine had adopted?

"I feel I complied with all those criteria," Jiankui answered.

His university and hospital had known all about what he was doing and had approved, he insisted. But when Doudna walked through the reasons why germline editing was not "medically necessary" to prevent HIV infection, Jiankui got very emotional.

"Jennifer, you don't understand China," he said. "There's an incredible stigma about being HIV positive, and I wanted to give these people a chance at a normal life and help them have kids when they otherwise might not have."[4]

The dinner table conversation became increasingly stressful, and after an hour Jiankui shifted to being angry. He stood up abruptly and tossed some bills onto the table. He had been receiving death threats, he said, and now he was going to move to a hotel where the press couldn't find him. Doudna chased after him, begging him to appear at the conference to present his work.

He paused and finally agreed, but he wanted security. He was afraid.

After Jiankui left the hotel restaurant, the organizers stayed at the table discussing how to handle the situation. One scientist looked at his smartphone and reported that a group of more than one hundred Chinese scientists had put out a statement condemning Jiankui. Doudna and her dinner partners realized that they, as the conference organizers, should put out a statement as well. But they did not want to make it too strong for fear that it would provoke Jiankui to cancel his talk.

"We put out a very short statement that was quite bland and got criticism for that," Doudna says, "but we wanted to ensure that he would show up."

Truth be told, Doudna later admitted, their motives were not merely scientific. The global buzz was huge, all eyes were on Hong Kong, and it would be quite a letdown if Jiankui drove back to Shenzhen and they all missed the chance to be part of a historic moment.

As Doudna and her colleagues were eating, Jiankui's extensive publicity plan was unfolding: the YouTube videos were released, the AP story he had cooperated with went viral, and a piece Jiankui had written about ethical principles for gene editing was published online by the *CRISPR Journal* editors (though they later retracted it).

On Wednesday, November 28, 2018, it was finally time for He Jiankui to present.[5] Robin Lovell-Badge, the moderator, came to the podium looking nervous. He later told Doudna that he had not slept at all the night before. He instructed the audience to be polite, as if he were afraid that the attendees might rush the stage.

"Can you please allow him to speak without interruptions?" he pleaded. Then he waved his hand and added, "I have the right to cancel the session if there is too much noise or interruption."

But the only sounds were from the clicking cameras of the dozens of photographers standing in the back.

Lovell-Badge explained that Jiankui had been scheduled to speak before the news of his CRISPR babies had come out and that no one had known that the story was going to break over the previous couple of days. In fact, Jiankui had earlier sent Lovell-Badge the slides he was going to show in his session, and they did not include any of the work he now planned to talk about. Then, looking around nervously, the British scientist invited Jiankui to the stage to present his work.[6]

At first no one appeared onstage. The audience seemed to be holding its breath, wondering whether Jiankui would actually show up. Then, from directly behind Lovell-Badge, who was standing on the right side of the stage, a young Asian man appeared in a dark suit. There was scattered, tentative applause and a bit of confusion. The man fiddled with a laptop to get the right slide up, then adjusted the microphone. The audience members began to laugh nervously as they realized that it was the audiovisual technician.

"Look, I don't know where he is," Lovell-Badge said, waving his notebook.

For an eerie thirty-five seconds, which in cases like this is a *very* long time, there was silence in the room and no movement. Finally, somewhat tentatively, a slight man wearing a striped shirt and carrying a bulging tan briefcase stepped out from the far side of the stage. In the somewhat formal atmosphere of Hong Kong

(Lovell-Badge was wearing a suit), this man didn't fit in, with his wide-open collar and no jacket or tie. Lovell-Badge looked relieved, though, and waved Jiankui over. When Jiankui got to the podium, the moderator whispered into his ear: "Please not too long. We need time to ask you questions."

As Jiankui started to speak, a barrage of clicks and flashes from the paparazzi cameras drowned him out and seemed to startle him. The sound of the cameras was so loud that the audience couldn't hear what was happening onstage, so one of the conference organizers paused the meeting for a moment and got the press to stop.

Jiankui glanced around shyly, his smooth face making him look even younger than his thirty-four years.

"I must apologize that my results leaked unexpectedly, taking away the chance for peer review before being presented to this conference," he began, and then he started to read slowly from his speech.

With little emotion, he described the many HIV infections in China, the deaths and discrimination that resulted, and how a CCR5 gene mutation could prevent the infection of babies born to HIV-positive parents. After twenty minutes of showing slides and discussing his process, it was time for questions. Although some of the questions weren't confrontational, others were. One scientist went right to the point. After describing the international guidelines that were supposed to be met before any germline editing of humans, he declared, "That has not happened." He called Jiankui's actions "irresponsible," secretive, and not "medically necessary."

A prominent biochemist from Harvard spoke next and challenged Jiankui about why he felt embryo editing was warranted in this case, since there were simpler, safer methods for ensuring that embryos were not infected with HIV. Speaking softly, Jiankui responded that he was not just trying to help the twin girls but wanted to find a way to protect millions of children from being infected with HIV even after they were born. The gene editing he had performed had the potential to provide children with a level of immunity to HIV.

"There's a consensus to not allow genome editing on germline cells," a professor from Peking University pointed out. "Why did you choose to cross this red line? And why did you conduct these [procedures] in secret?"

When Lovell-Badge took it upon himself to rephrase the question, he asked only about the secrecy part, which Jiankui avoided by describing how he had consulted with a lot of researchers in the United States. He never directly addressed the fact that he had violated internationally agreed-upon guidelines.

The final question was submitted by a journalist: "If this was going to be your baby, would you have gone ahead with this?"

Jiankui answered, "If it was my baby in this situation, I would have tried it."

Then Jiankui picked up his briefcase, exited the stage, and was driven back to Shenzhen.[7]

Sitting in the audience, Doudna began to sweat.

"I was feeling a combination of nervous energy and being sick to my stomach," she recalls.

Here was the amazing gene-editing tool, CRISPR-Cas9, that she had co-invented, being used to produce—for the first time in history—a genetically designed human being. And it had been done before the safety issues had been clinically tested, the ethical issues had been resolved, or a social consensus had formed over whether this was the way for science—and for humans—to evolve.

Later that evening Doudna went to the bar of the hotel and huddled with a few of her exhausted fellow organizers. One of the organizers believed—more than the others—that there had been a failure by the scientific community to do enough self-regulation.

"One thing is clear," this scientist said. "If this guy really did what he claims to have done, this is actually not very hard to do."

That terrified everyone, and they decided that they had to issue a statement.[8]

Doudna and seven other scientists took over a small meeting room and began hammering out a draft. They spent many hours going over it line by line and discussing what the point of each sentence was. All of them wanted to express strong disapproval for what Jiankui had done and yet avoid using the word "moratorium," which would require the research community to stop gene editing altogether for a while. They didn't want to do anything that might hamper the progress of gene-editing research.

Doudna was tugged in two directions. She was appalled at what Jiankui had done. Yet she had come to believe, and hope, that CRISPR-Cas9 would prove to be a powerful tool for human well-being, including through germline edits someday. During the discussion of the draft statement, her sentiments became the consensus at the table, and the scientists decided, once again, to find middle ground in the debate.[9] They agreed that there was a need for more specific guidelines on when germline gene editing should be done, but it was also important to avoid language that would lead to CRISPR gene editing being banned.

"The sense at the meeting was that the technology had advanced to the stage where we need to have a clear pathway to clinical use of gene editing in embryos," Doudna says.

In other words, instead of trying to stop any further uses of CRISPR to make gene-edited babies, she wanted to pave the way to making it safer to do so.

The statement that the organizers crafted was very restrained.

"At this summit we heard an unexpected and deeply disturbing claim that human embryos had been edited and implanted, resulting in a pregnancy and the birth of twins," they wrote. "The procedure was irresponsible and failed to conform with international norms."

But there was no call for a ban or moratorium. Instead their words simply emphasized that the safety risks were too great to permit germline editing "at this time." It then proceeded to stress, "Germline genome editing could become acceptable in the future if these risks are addressed and if a number of additional criteria are met."

The germline was no longer a red line.[10]

CHAPTER TWENTY-NINE

Acceptance

⟨⟨⟨∞⟩⟩⟩

Some people in the world weren't upset by what He Jiankui had done. One of these people was a biohacker named Josiah Zayner.

Biohacking is also known as "do it yourself (DIY) biology." It is biological experimentation done to improve the qualities or abilities of living things, especially by individuals and groups working outside the traditional medical or scientific communities. Examples of biohacking include creating synthetic insulin and—as Zayner once did—injecting yourself with a CRISPR-edited gene to try to get bigger muscles. One of the goals of some biohackers is to make biological advances available to all people, sidestepping the things that restricts these advances, such as patents, drug companies, governmental laws, and regulations.

Josiah Zayner was so excited when he heard about the CRISPR babies that he stayed up all night watching a livestream of He Jiankui's announcement in Hong Kong. It was, he felt, not just a scientific achievement but a milestone for the human race.

"In all of human history," he said, "we didn't get to decide what genes we have, right? Now we do."

He also thought another great thing about germline gene

editing was that it could remove a disease or genetic abnormality permanently from the human race.

"Not just cure it in a patient," he said, "but completely remove miserable death-sentence diseases like muscular dystrophy from the future of humanity, forever."

Zayner and other biohackers like him even support using CRISPR to make enhancements in sperm, eggs, and embryos. Their thinking is that if babies can be born less likely to grow up and become obese, or can have genes that make them stronger or smarter, there should be nothing to prevent making those improvements.

It wasn't only biohackers and people on the extreme edge of scientific thought that felt this way, though. When Jennifer Doudna returned home from Hong Kong, she found that her teenage son could not understand why there was so much fuss about Jiankui's gene editing. It made her wonder whether future generations will see this as such a big deal and if history will treat germline editing like IVF, which was very controversial when it first happened. She remembered that her parents had been shocked when the first baby had been born through IVF in 1978, and they'd talked about how growing embryos in a lab was unnatural and wrong. But when her parents had then seen their friends have children through IVF after struggling for years to get pregnant, they'd been delighted that the technology existed.[1]

As it turned out, the political and public reaction to the CRISPR babies was in line with Doudna's son's. Two weeks after returning from Hong Kong, Doudna attended a meeting on Capitol Hill with eight senators to discuss gene editing. Such meetings are usually a forum for politicians to express their shock and dismay about something they don't fully understand and then call for more laws and regulations. Quite the opposite occurred at the Senate briefing. All the senators who attended were encouraging of the general idea of editing as an important technology. Doudna was surprised that none of them demanded more regulations. They just wanted to figure out, "Where do we go from here?"

They also expressed concerns about the high cost of treatments using CRISPR technologies and how these costs would bankrupt the healthcare system. Because of this discussion, Doudna decided that making sickle-cell treatments affordable should become a mission of her Innovative Genomics Institute, a research group that had begun in 2014 as a partnership between the University of California–Berkeley and the University of California–San Francisco.

When she arrived back at Berkeley after the Senate hearing, she convened a series of meetings of her team to discuss how to make wide access to sickle-cell treatments a new core part of their mission.[2] To do that, she reached out to the Bill and Melinda Gates Foundation and the National Institutes of Health (NIH). Soon Doudna and the Innovative Genomics Institute announced a partnership for a sickle-cell initiative using $200 million in funding provided by the Gates foundation and the NIH.[3]

The initiative is still underway, and if it is successful, it will not only cure a lot of people of a dreadful disease. It will also advance the cause of health justice. Most sickle-cell patients in the world are Africans or African Americans. These are populations that have been historically underserved by the medical establishment. Even though the genetic cause of sickle cell disease has been understood for longer than any similar disorder, new treatments have lagged behind. For example, the fight against cystic fibrosis, which affects primarily white Americans and Europeans, has received eight times more funding from government, charities, and foundations. The great promise of gene editing is that it will transform medicine for marginalized communities.

At the Capitol Hill meeting, Doudna also explained to the senators what regulations against germline editing were already in place, specifically those to restrict the use of gene editing in embryos. Satisfied with this answer, the senators turned their attention to trying to understand the value CRISPR might have in medicine and agriculture. Rather than focus on the just-born Chinese CRISPR babies, they asked detailed questions about how, in addition to possibly curing sickle cell anemia, CRISPR might work to cure other debilitating genetic diseases such as Huntington's disease and Tay-Sachs disease.

Two international commissions were also created to deal with the issue of germline editing. Doudna feared that having two different groups might lead to conflicting messages, thus allowing future He Jiankuis to make their own interpretations of the guidelines. But the commissions divided up responsibilities well. One focused on science, and the other looked at how to create a process to regulate the technology around the world.

Unfortunately, as the two commissions were getting to work in mid-2019, a public dispute erupted in the scientific community that pitted Doudna against the head of the Broad Institute, where Feng Zhang was a core member. The hard-charging Eric Lander, president and founding director of the Broad, disagreed with Doudna over the use of the word "moratorium." Most scientific committees over the years had avoided this word, thinking it too restrictive. Other researchers wondered why it was needed in this situation, since the conditions that had been specified to permit embryo gene editing—that it be safe and "medically necessary"— could not be met for the time being. But some scientists argued that Jiankui's actions showed the need for a clearer and brighter stoplight. Among them were Lander, Zhang, and Doudna's scientific collaborator Emmanuelle Charpentier.

Lander set about rounding up support for an article to be published in *Nature* titled "Adopt a Moratorium on Heritable Genome Editing." Zhang of course signed up, as did Charpentier.

"We call for a global moratorium on all clinical uses of human germline editing—that is, changing heritable DNA (in sperm, eggs or embryos) to make genetically modified children," the article began.[4]

Lander and the others felt they had to make the clearest possible statement that germline editing was a path science was not ready to go down, not now, and potentially not ever. They emphasized that the issue should not be left to individual choice and the free market.

Doudna opposed a moratorium because it felt unrealistic. After all, germline editing had already been done with the Chinese babies, so calling for a moratorium wouldn't stop germline editing. It would only drive the technology underground. In the end Doudna's view prevailed. In September 2020, a two-hundred-page report was issued by one of the two international science commissions formed after Jiankui's shocking announcement. The report did not call for a moratorium, nor mention that word. Instead it said that heritable human genome editing "might, in the future, provide a reproductive option" for couples with genetic diseases. The report noted that making inheritable gene edits was not yet safe and usually not medically necessary, but the commission came down in favor of "defining a responsible pathway for clinical use" of heritable human genome editing. In other words, the commission wanted to pursue a careful path forward. This was the same sentiment endorsed years earlier at the January 2015 Napa Valley conference that Doudna had organized.[5]

As for He Jiankui, instead of being acclaimed a national hero, as he had dreamed of, he was put on trial at the end of 2019 in a Shenzhen court. He was allowed to have his own attorneys and to speak in his own defense, so the trial seemed fair. But he eventually pled guilty to the charge of "illegal medical practice" and was sentenced to three years in prison, fined the Chinese equivalent of $430,000, and banned for life from working in reproductive science.[6]

The official Chinese news report on the trial also confirmed that a third CRISPR baby engineered by Jiankui had been born to a second woman. There were no details about the baby nor about the current status of Lulu and Nana, the original CRISPR-edited twins.

When Doudna was asked by the *Wall Street Journal* to comment on the conviction, she was careful to criticize Jiankui's work but not to condemn germline gene editing. The scientific community would have to sort out the safety and ethical issues.

"To me, the big question is not will this ever be done again," she said. "I think the answer is yes. The question is when, and the question is how."[7]

PART SIX
The Moral Questions

CHAPTER THIRTY

Regulating Gene Editing

———— ∞∞∞ ————

Before hard-and-fast rules can be made about what's right and wrong in terms of gene editing, scientists—including Jennifer Doudna—have to look hard at the genetic diseases that exist and see what questions come up when they're treated.

If ever there was a case for editing a human gene, it would be to get rid of the mutation that produces the cruel and painful killer known as Huntington's disease. Caused by an abnormal repetition of base pairs in a DNA sequence, the disease causes brain cells to die. As this happens, victims start to twitch uncontrollably, usually as they reach middle age. They cannot focus. They lose their jobs. Eventually they are unable to walk, then talk, then swallow. Sometimes dementia sets in. Huntington's causes a slow and painful death. And it is devastating for the families—especially the kids, who watch their parent's decline and then face the fact that there is a 50 percent chance of inheriting the condition.[1]

Huntington's is a dominant disease, meaning that if the child has even one copy of the mutation, he or she will develop it. Symptoms usually show up only after a person's childbearing years, so the disease's victims often have children before they know they have the genetic disease. Therefore, the gene and the illness are not weeded out by natural selection.

Fixing Huntington's is not a complex gene edit. So why not edit the disease out of the germline of afflicted families—and out of our species once and for all? One argument is that it would be better, where possible, to find an alternative approach to germline gene editing. In most cases—except when both parents have the disease—it might be possible to assure healthy children by using preimplantation genetic diagnosis. A couple who knows they carry the gene could decide to have a baby through IVF in order to screen their embryos for the disease. If the parents can produce enough fertilized eggs, the ones with Huntington's can be eliminated. Unfortunately, preimplantation screening may not be as straightforward as it sounds because producing a lot of viable eggs isn't always easy. A woman may produce only two or three, and because Huntington's is dominant, that means it's possible all these eggs would contain the mutated gene.

In making a gene edit to eliminate Huntington's, nothing is changed except the bad mutation. You won't also change the gene for eye color, for example. Given the fact that this gene edit is so targeted, should it be allowed, especially in cases where preimplantation genetic screening is difficult? Even if we decide to severely restrict germline editing, it seems logical to try to eliminate Huntington's from the human race.

Sickle cell anemia is an interesting next case to consider because it raises two complexities, one medical and the other moral. Like Huntington's, sickle cell is caused by a simple mutation. By 2020, trials were underway for sickle-cell therapies involving gene editing, such as the trial described in this book's introduction involving the Mississippi woman Victoria Gray. The treatment Gray underwent is extraordinarily expensive, so it's not possible for the scores of people afflicted globally with the disease to receive this treatment. Fixing the sickle-cell mutation in the germline by editing eggs, sperm, or early-stage embryos would be a cheaper cure that could eventually eliminate the disease from our species. So, does that kind of germline editing fall into the same category as Huntington's?

Unfortunately, determining that is not a simple issue. People who get a copy of the sickle-cell gene from only one parent usually do not develop the disease, but they do develop immunity to most forms of malaria. In other words, the gene was (and in some places still is) useful, especially in sub-Saharan Africa, where malaria is a huge problem.

Let's suppose that researchers show that editing out the sickle-cell mutation is safe. Would there then be any reason to prohibit patients from having the gene edited out when they conceive children? This is also a tough question to answer.

The next question is, Should we edit out disabilities so that no one suffers from them? Initially this seems like a good idea, but we have to ask: Don't the courage and bravery of those who struggle through disabilities add something to the world?

That then raises the question of what characteristics should be labeled "disabilities." Sharon Duchesneau and Candy McCullough are a lesbian couple who wanted a sperm donor so they could conceive a child. Both women are deaf. They consider their deafness to be part of who they are rather than a disability that needs to be cured, and they wanted a child who would be part of their cultural identity. So they advertised for a sperm donor who was congenitally deaf (meaning that a person is born deaf or will become deaf from a condition that's present at birth). They found one, and now they have a deaf child.

After a story about the couple appeared in the *Washington Post*, Duchesneau and McCullough were criticized by some people who said the women had given their child a "disability."[2] But they were applauded in the deaf community. Which was the right response? Should they be criticized for making sure their child had a "disability," or should they be praised for preserving a subculture that contributes to the diversity and perhaps even the empathy of society? Would it be different if, instead of using a deaf sperm donor, the couple had used preimplantation genetic diagnosis to select an embryo that had a genetic mutation for deafness? What if the embryo were typical, but they edited it to be deaf? Would that be okay?

The ethical questions go on and on.

Now let's do some thought experiments to see if we might want to cross the line between gene editing that is done to treat health conditions and gene editing that is done to enhance the traits of our children. For example, the MSTN gene produces a protein that stops the growth of muscles when they reach a certain level. Suppressing the gene allows muscles to grow past that point. Researchers have already performed this sort of gene editing to produce "mighty mice" and cattle with "double muscling."

Athletic directors and coaches may be interested in suppressing the MSTN gene, and parents who want champion children may feel the same way. If we move ahead with this gene editing, we might produce a whole new breed of athletes with bigger bones and stronger muscles. Is this a problem? If so, for whom? And what does a genetically engineered athlete do to the "purity" of athletics? We negatively judge athletes who "cheat" by using drugs to enlarge their muscles. But what do we do if an athlete's bigger muscles come from genes they were born with? Does it matter if those genes were paid for by their parents rather than produced by a random natural lottery?

One way to think through the fairness of using gene editing for physical enhancements is by looking at height. Let's start with the case of children who suffer from genetic mutations that inhibit their growth. Should it be permissible to genetically edit out these defects so that the kids will grow to an average height? Most of us would think so.

Now let's take the case of parents who just happen to be short. Should they be permitted to edit the genes of their children so the kids will grow to average height? If not, what's the moral difference between these two cases? Suppose there was a genetic edit that could add eight inches to a kid's height. Would it be proper to use it on a boy who would otherwise be under five feet tall, to turn him into someone of average height? What about using the edit on a boy who would otherwise be average height, to make him six feet tall?

Perhaps some enhancements will gain broad social acceptance. But then what about super-enhancements? Should we ever engineer traits and capacities that exceed what any human has ever had? The golfer Tiger Woods had laser surgery to improve his eyesight to be even better than 20/20. Do we want future kids to have super-eyesight? What about adding the capacity to see infrared light or some new color?

These kinds of human improvements are already happening. For example, the military is working with Jennifer Doudna's lab to study how to create genetically enhanced soldiers. We might someday have superior soldiers with night vision. We may also someday be able to enhance human genes so that cells are more resistant to radiation if there is a nuclear attack.

Two decades after the completion of the Human Genome Project, we still have little understanding of how human behavior is influenced by genetic dispositions. But eventually we may isolate genes that contribute to the development of mental health conditions including schizophrenia, bipolar disorder, and severe depression.

Many of the difficult questions about gene editing involve not just how to decide the issue but *who* should decide. As is the case with so many policy issues, the desires of an individual might conflict with the good of the community.

One reason to be open to some limit on individual choice is that gene editing could make inequality in our society even worse than it already is. It is natural to want what is best for our children, but many of these advantages—private tutors, special camps, personal coaches, specialized classes—are advantages of privilege.

Allowing parents to buy the best genes for their kids would greatly further social inequality. Many societies have spent centuries dismantling systems in which people were given power based solely on the family they were born into. And most cultures have now embraced a basic principle of democracy: we believe in equal opportunity. This understanding could be destroyed if we develop a system where the people who have money can give their children genetic advantages.

This does not mean that gene editing is inherently bad. But it does argue against allowing it to be commercialized so that the rich can buy the best genes and embed them into their families.

Restricting individual choice would be difficult to enforce, though. Scientists want to pioneer procedures and make discoveries. If a nation imposes too many restrictions, its scientists will move elsewhere, and its wealthy parents will seek clinics in some other country.

Nonetheless, it's possible to aim for some social agreement on gene editing rather than simply leaving the issue totally to individual choice. There are other practices we cannot fully control, such as shoplifting, that are kept to a minimum by a combination of laws and social pressure. The Food and Drug Administration, for example, regulates new drugs and procedures. Even though some people find ways to get drugs for things other than what they are prescribed for, or people travel to places for unconventional treatments, FDA restrictions are pretty effective.

Our challenge is to figure out what the norms for gene editing should be. Then we can find the regulations and social sanctions that will cause most people to follow them.[3]

Doudna's Ethical Journey

———— ✦✦✦ ————

Victoria Gray isn't the only person whose health was transformed when CRISPR's gene-editing tools were put into action. Since 2016, CRISPR has been used to fight all sorts of diseases that have plagued humanity and caused an untold number of deaths.

For example, CRISPR applications have already been used in the fight against cancer. The first cancer patient to be treated using CRISPR lived in Chengdu, a city of twenty million in the central Chinese province of Sichuan, and he suffered from lung cancer. In October 2016 a team took some of the patient's blood and isolated his T cells, which are a type of white blood cell that helps the body fight off infection and disease. The doctors used CRISPR-Cas9 to disable a gene that helps stop a cell's immune response. When the patient's T cells were placed back into his body, they became more effective at killing the cancer cells. Within a year China had seven clinical trials that incorporated this technique.[1]

CRISPR is also being used as a detection tool to identify certain types of cancer. Mammoth Biosciences, a company Doudna founded with two of her graduate students, now designs diagnostic tools based on CRISPR that can help recognize a tumor's DNA sequences. When the tumor is correctly categorized, doctors can then tailor precision treatments for each patient.

Another application of CRISPR gene editing that was underway by 2020 involves curing a form of congenital blindness. In this case the procedure was performed in vivo—inside the patient's body—because eye cells cannot be extracted and returned the way blood and bone marrow cells can. The goal was to treat a genetic condition called Leber congenital amaurosis, which is a rare disorder that causes childhood blindness. For those with the condition, the gene that makes the eye's light-receptor cells has a mutation. This mutation causes a critical protein to be shortened, so that the light that hits the cells isn't converted into nerve signals.[2]

The treatment was first used in March 2020 at the Casey Eye Institute in Portland, Oregon. In an hour-long procedure, doctors used a tiny hair-width tube to inject three drops of fluid containing CRISPR-Cas9 just beneath the patient's retina, which is the specialized tissue at the back of the eye that detects light and color. If the cells are edited as planned, the fix will be permanent.

At the beginning of 2020, there were two dozen other clinical trials in the pipeline for various uses of CRISPR-Cas9. They included potential treatments for hereditary angioedema (a disease that causes severe swelling), a type of cancer called acute myeloid leukemia, extremely high cholesterol, and male-pattern baldness.[3]

One thorny issue that scientists who work with CRISPR have had to wrestle with involves what to do when the patients who might benefit from gene editing are children. To Jennifer

Doudna, the idea of editing a child's genes always felt unnatural and scary.[4] Children cannot consent to their own medical treatment, so they are at the mercy of their parents to make decisions about their health. In Doudna's mind, decisions like what kind of medicine to give a child for an illness seem much less significant than permanently altering their genetic makeup.

Then she began to hear stories from people who had been affected by genetic diseases and were desperate for science to help. The stories about kids were especially touching to her as a mother. For example, one woman sent a note with beautiful pictures of her new baby boy, bald and cute, which reminded Doudna of when her own son, Andy, had been born. The baby had just been diagnosed with a genetic neurodegenerative disease. His nerve cells would soon start dying, and eventually he would be unable to walk, speak, then swallow or eat. He would sadly die an early and painful death. The note was a wrenching plea for help.

"How could you not want to make progress on coming up with ways to prevent such a thing?" Doudna asks. "My heart broke."

She decided that if gene editing could prevent painful diseases in the future, it would be immoral not to follow that path. She wrote the mother back and promised that she and other researchers were working diligently to find therapies and preventions for such genetic conditions. Unfortunately, Doudna also had to tell the mother that it would be years before something like gene editing would be potentially useful to prevent conditions like the one her child had.

After appearing at the World Economic Forum in Davos,

Switzerland, in January 2016, Doudna was pulled aside by another woman on the panel, who described how her sister had been born with a degenerative disease, meaning it caused progressive damage to her organs or tissues. This woman confessed that it affected not only her sister but the lives and finances of her whole family.

"She said if we could have done gene editing to avoid that, everyone in her family would be absolutely in favor of it," Doudna recalls. "She was very emotional about the cruelty of those who would prevent germline editing, and she was on the verge of tears. I found it so touching."

Later that year a man came to see her at Berkeley. His father and grandfather had died of Huntington's disease. Three of his sisters had been diagnosed with it and faced a slow, agonizing death. Doudna refrained from asking the man if he was also afflicted. But his visit convinced her that if germline editing became a safe and effective way to eliminate Huntington's, she was in favor. She felt that once you've seen the face of someone with a genetic disease—especially one like Huntington's—it's hard to justify refraining from gene editing.

The change in her thinking made her more sympathetic to the viewpoint that many gene-editing decisions should be left to individual choice rather than to the government and ethics panels. As a parent, she thought that other parents should have the ability to make choices about their health or their family's health as these new technologies come along. However, because there are still huge risks that may be unknown, she feels that CRISPR should be used only when it is medically necessary and there are no good alternatives.

"That's why I had a problem with He Jiankui's use of CRISPR to attempt to achieve immunity to HIV. There were other ways of doing that. It wasn't medically necessary."

By limiting gene edits to those that are truly "medically necessary," Doudna believes that we can make it less likely that parents would seek to "enhance" their children, which she feels is morally and socially wrong. She acknowledges that the line between medical treatment and enhancement is blurry, but it is not totally meaningless. For example, we know the difference between correcting a very harmful genetic disease and changing someone's genes to make them smarter, more attractive, or faster. Doudna feels that as long as scientists stick to correcting genetic mutations by restoring the "normal" version of the gene—not inventing some completely new enhancement not seen in the average human genome—they are probably on the safe side.

Doudna is also confident that the good that can come from CRISPR will eventually outweigh the dangers. Soon we may be able to safely edit genes to make our children less susceptible to coronaviruses, which is one of the most profound developments humans have ever achieved. For the first time in the evolution of life on this planet, we as a species have developed the capacity to change our own genetic makeup, and that is a massive leap ahead for science *and* for humanity.

"We've never seen anything like this before," Doudna says. "We now have the power to control our genetic future, which is awesome and terrifying."

PART SEVEN

CRISPR *and* COVID-19

The Front Lines

———— ⟨⟨⟨⟨⟩⟩⟩⟩ ————

At the end of February 2020, Jennifer Doudna was scheduled to travel from Berkeley to Houston for a seminar. Life in the United States had not yet been disrupted by the looming coronavirus pandemic, and there had been no officially reported US deaths from COVID-19. But red flags were flying. There were already 2,835 deaths in China, and the US economy was beginning to become shaky. The stock market's Dow index had dropped more than a thousand points on February 27.

"I was nervous," Doudna recalls. "I talked with Jamie about whether or not to go. But at the time everyone I knew was carrying on as usual, and so I went to Houston."

She took with her a supply of hand wipes. When she returned home to Berkeley, she began thinking about what she and her colleagues should be doing to fight the virus's spread. Having turned CRISPR into a gene-editing tool, she and her team had a strong grasp on the molecular mechanisms that could be used by humans to detect and destroy viruses. She was also a master of collaboration, and if there was any way to battle the coronavirus, it would require putting together teams that spanned many specialties and disciplines.

Fortunately, she had a base from which she could build such an effort. As the executive director of the Innovative Genomics Institute (IGI), she understood that one of IGI's core principles is to foster collaboration between different fields. To do that, its spacious five-story modern building on the northwest corner of the Berkeley campus houses plant scientists, microbial researchers, and biomedical specialists.[1] Doudna had spent the previous year talking to a biochemist whose office was next to hers about launching a project at IGI that would become a model for teamwork across academic specialties. One idea for this plan came from her son, Andy, who'd had a summer internship at a local biotech company. His day there had begun with a check-in at which leaders from different divisions shared what they were doing to further the company's projects. Hearing this, Doudna laughed and told Andy she couldn't imagine running an academic lab that way.

"Why not?" he asked.

She explained that academic researchers get comfortable in their areas of expertise and too protective of their independence. But she agreed that this had to change, so she began having conversations with Andy and Jamie about teams, innovation, and how to create a work environment that stimulates creativity.

She developed some ideas at home and took them to work, where she kicked them around with her colleague. She said she wanted to combine the best features of a corporate team culture with academic independence, and she wondered if it would be possible to find a project that would bring together researchers from a variety of labs around a single goal. She and her colleague nicknamed the idea "Wigits," for "Workshop for IGI Team Science," and they joked that they would join hands and build widgets together. When they floated the idea at one of the institute's Friday happy hours, it met with enthusiasm from some of the students but not from most of the professors. With no source of funding and little faculty enthusiasm, the idea soon hit a dead end.[2]

Then the new coronavirus came along.

At two a.m. on Thursday, March 12, Doudna lay in bed wide awake. Despite the fact that Berkeley had just shut down its campus because of the pandemic, she had driven her son to the train station that afternoon so he could go to Fresno for a robot-building competition. Unable to fall asleep, she woke up Jamie and insisted that they retrieve Andy before the start of the match, when more than twelve hundred kids and teachers would be gathering in an indoor convention center. The two of them pulled on their clothes, got into the car, found an open gas station, and started the three-hour drive. When they arrived in Fresno, Andy was not happy to see them, but they convinced him to pack up and come home. As they pulled out of the parking lot, Andy got a text from the team:

Robotics match canceled! All kids to leave immediately![3]

This was the moment when Doudna realized that her world—and the world of science—had changed.

The next day she gathered up her Berkeley colleagues and other scientists in the Bay area to discuss what roles they might play. A dozen of them made their way across the abandoned Berkeley campus and converged on the building that housed her lab. The chairs in the ground-floor conference room were clustered together, so the first thing they did was move them six feet apart. Then they turned on a video system so that fifty other researchers from nearby universities could join by Zoom. As she stood in front of the room to rally them, Doudna displayed an intensity that she usually covered up with calm.

"This is not something that academics typically do," she told them. "We need to step up."[4]

The rapidly spreading new coronavirus had by then been given an official name: severe acute respiratory syndrome coronavirus 2, or SARS-CoV-2. It was called that because its symptoms were similar to those of the SARS coronavirus that had spread out of China in 2003, infecting more than eight thousand people worldwide. The disease caused by the new virus was named COVID-19.

Like all other viruses, SARS-CoV-2 is just a tiny bit of genetic material inside a protein shell. When it makes its way into an organism's cell, it can hijack that cell's genetic material in order to replicate itself. The genetic material of coronaviruses is RNA.

RNA was Doudna's specialty.

In SARS-CoV-2, the RNA is about 29,900 base letters long, compared to more than three billion base pairs in human DNA. The viral sequence is the code for making only about twenty-nine proteins.[5] One of the proteins sits on the outside of the virus shell and looks like a spike. This gives the virus, when viewed through an electron microscope, the appearance of a crown, which in Latin is *corona*. This spike is like a key that can fit into specific receptors on the surface of human cells.

For the SARS-CoV-2 coronavirus, one of the human receptors is a protein known as ACE2. It plays a role similar to the one played for HIV by the CCR5 protein, which He Jiankui had edited out of his CRISPR twins. Because the ACE2 protein has functions other than just being a receptor, though, it's probably not a good idea to try to edit it out of our species.

On January 9, 2020, Chinese researchers publicly posted the full genetic sequence of the SARS-CoV-2 coronavirus. Using cryo-electron microscopy, which fires electrons at proteins that have been frozen in a liquid, structural biologists were able to create models of the virus's spike proteins. With the sequencing information and structural data in hand, molecular biologists began racing to find treatments and vaccines that would block the ability of the virus to latch on to human cells.[6]

The March 13 meeting that Doudna mobilized drew far more participants than she'd expected. But she quickly discovered that there was an advantage to being part of large organizations such as UC Berkeley and IGI. There were teams of people who could help with things like writing proposals, sending out group emails, arranging Zoom meetings, and coordinating equipment.

First Berkeley's legal team came up with a policy for sharing discoveries freely with other coronavirus researchers while protecting the underlying intellectual property. In short, no one would have to pay to license any information from Doudna's lab because the project was about saving lives, not making money. The university would still file for patent protection of anything that was discovered, but then they would make the discovery available to people for the purpose of fighting the coronavirus.

By the time of the group's second meeting on March 18, Doudna had a slide listing ten projects she and the other scientists had decided to pursue, with the names of the team leaders. Each expert paired up with someone who could perform the same functions, so that if any of them got sick from the virus, there would be someone to step in and continue the work.

Some of the planned tasks made use of the latest CRISPR technology, including finding a way to send a CRISPR-based system into a patient's lungs to target and destroy the virus's genetic material. When these ideas had first started rolling in, one of the professors had spoken up. He'd insisted that the group had to deal with the urgent need for public COVID-19 testing before they could sit at their lab benches and develop biotechnologies for the future.

Doudna knew he was right, so the first team she launched was given the mission of claiming a space on the ground floor of the building where they were meeting and converting it into a state-of-the-art, high-speed, automated coronavirus testing lab.

"I'd like everyone to get started soon," she said. "Really soon."

"Don't worry," one of the participants assured her. "Nobody's got any travel plans."

Testing

───❧───

There was an urgent need for widespread testing because the work the government had done thus far had been miserable.

The first official guidance to local health officials in the United States about testing for the new coronavirus had come in a conference call on January 15, 2020, led by Stephen Lindstrom, a microbiologist at the Centers for Disease Control and Prevention (CDC). He'd announced that the CDC had developed a test for the new coronavirus but that the center could not make the test available to state health departments until the Food and Drug Administration (FDA) approved it. That would be soon, Lindstrom promised, but until then doctors would have to send samples to the CDC in Atlanta for testing. The next day a Seattle doctor sent the CDC a nose-swab sample from a thirty-five-year-old man who had come down with flu-like symptoms. The man had just returned from a visit to Wuhan, China, where the COVID-19 virus had first started to spread. He became the first person in the United States to test positive for SARS-CoV-2.[1]

On January 31, Health and Human Services Secretary Alex Azar, whose department oversees the FDA, declared a public health emergency. The declaration gave the FDA the right to speed up approvals for coronavirus tests. But it had a weird unintended consequence. In normal circumstances, hospitals and university labs can create their own tests to use at their facilities, as long as they do not market them. But a declaration of a public health emergency imposes the requirement that such tests not be used until they get an "emergency use authorization." The intent is to avoid the use of unproven tests during a health crisis.

As a result, Azar's declaration triggered new restrictions on academic labs and hospitals. That would have been fine if the CDC's test had been widely available. But the FDA had still not approved it.

The approval finally came on February 4, and the next day the CDC began sending test kits to state and local labs. The way the test works, or was supposed to work, is that a long swab is inserted into the back of a patient's nasal passage. The lab uses some of the chemical mixtures in the test kit to extract any RNA that is in the mucus. The RNA is then turned into DNA through a process called **reverse transcription**. After this transformation, the DNA strands are amplified into millions (or billions) of copies using a well-known process called a **polymerase chain reaction** (PCR), done using a machine the size of a microwave that raises and lowers the temperature of the mixture. If the genetic material of the coronavirus is present in the mucus, the PCR process amplifies it so that it can be detected.

PCR is such an easy test that most college biology students learn how to do it. When state health officials received the test kits from the CDC, they set about verifying that they worked by trying them on patient samples that were already known to be positive or negative. When officials ran the tests on samples known to contain the virus, they got a positive result. That was good. Unfortunately, when officials ran the test on purified water, they also got a positive result. This was not good, and it indicated that one of the chemical compounds in the CDC test kits was defective.[2]

Adding to the disgrace was the fact that the World Health Organization had delivered 250,000 diagnostic tests that worked just fine to countries around the world. The United States could have gotten some of those tests or replicated them, but officials refused to.

The University of Washington, near the site of one of the first COVID outbreaks in the United States, rushed in to help with this testing disaster. At the beginning of January, after seeing the reports from China, Alex Greninger, the young assistant director of the virology lab at the university's medical center, talked to his boss about developing their own test.

"We're probably going to be wasting some money on this," his boss said. "[The virus is] probably not going to come over here. But you've got to be ready."[3]

Greninger soon had a working test, which under normal circumstances they could have used in their own hospital system. But when Health and Human Services Secretary Azar issued his emergency declaration, that made regulations stricter. So Greninger took close to one hundred hours to fill out all the forms for an emergency use authorization, which he submitted to the FDA. He got a response from the FDA on February 20 informing him that, in addition to sending his application electronically, he had to mail a printed copy along with a copy burned onto a compact disc (remember those?) to FDA headquarters in Maryland.

A few days later the FDA responded by requiring him to do more trials to see if the test he was using inadvertently detected the MERS (Middle East respiratory syndrome) and SARS coronaviruses, even though those viruses had been dormant for years and he had no samples of those viruses to test. When he called the CDC to see if he could get a sample of the old SARS virus, the center refused.

"That's when I thought, 'Huh, maybe the FDA and the CDC haven't talked about this at all,'" Greninger said. "I realized, Oh, wow, this is going to take a while."[4]

Others had similar problems. The Mayo Clinic had created a crisis team to deal with the pandemic. Of its fifteen members, five were tasked to deal full-time with the FDA's paperwork requirements. By late February, there were dozens of hospitals and academic labs, including at Stanford and the Broad Institute of MIT and Harvard, that had developed testing capabilities, but none had managed to win FDA authorization.

At that point Anthony Fauci, the National Institutes of Health infectious disease chief, stepped in. On February 27 he spoke to Health and Human Services Secretary Azar's chief of staff, Brian Harrison, and urged the FDA to allow universities, hospitals, and private testing services to start using their own tests while waiting for emergency use authorizations. Harrison held a conference call with the FDA, CDC, and other agencies and told them, using strong language, that before the end of the meeting they had to come up with a plan to resolve the lack of testing options.[5] The FDA finally relented on Saturday, February 29, and announced that it would allow nongovernment labs to use their own tests as they waited to get emergency use authorizations. That Monday, Greninger's lab tested thirty patients. Within a few weeks, it would be testing more than twenty-five hundred a day.

Eric Lander's Broad Institute also jumped into the fray. Deborah Hung, the codirector of the Broad's infectious diseases program, also worked as a physician at Brigham and Women's Hospital in Boston. On the evening of March 9, when confirmed cases of COVID in Massachusetts had risen to forty-one, it struck her how bad the virus was going to be. She called her colleague Stacey Gabriel, the senior director of the Broad Institute's genomics sequencing facility, which is a few blocks from the Broad headquarters in a former warehouse that stored beer and popcorn for Fenway Park. Could Gabriel turn the lab into a facility for testing for the coronavirus? Gabriel said yes. The lab went into full operation on March 24, receiving samples from hospitals across the Boston area.[6]

CHAPTER THIRTY-FOUR

The Berkeley Lab

———— ✦✦✦ ————

After Doudna and her colleagues at the Innovative Genomics Institute decided at their March 13 meeting to focus on building their own coronavirus testing lab, they sent out a tweet:

> Innovative Genomics Institute @igisci: We are working as hard as possible to establish clinical #COVID19 testing capability at @UCBerkeley campus. We will update this page often to ask for reagents, equipment, and volunteers.

Within two days more than eight hundred sixty people had responded, and the volunteer list had to be cut off.

The team that Doudna put together reflected the diversity of her lab and of the biotech field in general. To command the operation, she turned to Fyodor Urnov, a gene-editing wizard who had been leading IGI's efforts to develop affordable methods to cure sickle cell anemia.

Urnov was born in Russia and is among those researchers who are comfortable with having one foot in academia and the other in industry.[1] For sixteen years, even while teaching at Berkeley, he was a team leader at Sangamo Therapeutics, which translates scientific discoveries into medical treatments. One of his two scientific field marshals was Jennifer Hamilton, who grew up in Seattle and studied biochemistry and genetics at the University of Washington. After completing her doctorate at Mount Sinai medical center in New York, where she turned viruses and virus-like particles into mechanisms for delivering medical treatments, Hamilton moved to Berkeley and joined Doudna's lab. When the coronavirus crisis hit in early March, Hamilton told Doudna that she wanted to work to fight the pandemic, just like people at her University of Washington alma mater were. So Doudna tapped her to lead the technical development of the UC Berkeley lab.

Working side by side with Hamilton to get the testing lab running was Enrique Lin Shiao. Born and raised in Costa Rica, he is the son of Taiwanese immigrants who left everything behind to raise their family in a very new place. An expert in the relationship between DNA and disease progression, he, like Feng Zhang, was an American success story from when the nation was a magnet for diverse global talent.

As a postdoc researcher in Doudna's lab, Lin Shiao worked on ways to make new gene-editing tools that could cut and paste long DNA sequences. While sheltering at home in March 2020, he was scrolling through his Twitter feed and saw the tweet from his IGI colleagues seeking volunteers for the planned testing lab.

"They were asking for experience in RNA extraction and PCR, which are techniques I routinely perform in the lab," he says. "The next day I got an email from Jennifer asking if I would be interested in co-leading the technical efforts, and I immediately agreed."[2]

The IGI was fortunate that there was a 2,500-square-foot space on the building's ground floor that was being converted into a gene-editing lab.[3] Doudna's team began moving in new machines and boxes filled with chemicals to turn the space into a coronavirus testing facility. This kind of lab-building project would normally take months, but they did it in days.

As they moved in, they begged and borrowed supplies from labs across campus. One day, when they were ready to start an experiment, they realized that they did not have the right plates to run in one of the PCR machines. Lin Shiao and others went through all the labs in the IGI building and then in two nearby buildings until they found some.

"Since campus was largely closed, it felt like a giant scavenger hunt," Lin Shiao says. "Every day felt a bit like a roller coaster, where we discovered a new problem early in the morning, got worried, and then figured it out by the end of the day."

Hamilton's grandfather had been an engineer on the NASA Apollo rocket launches, and one day her team paused to watch a clip someone had posted online from the movie *Apollo 13*. It was the scene where the engineers must figure out how to make a "square peg fit in a round hole" in order to save the astronauts.

"Every day we've been facing challenges, but we're solving these problems as they come up because we know that time is short," Hamilton said. "This experience has made me wonder if this is what it was like for my grandfather working at NASA in the 1960s."

It was a good comparison. COVID and CRISPR were helping to make human cells the next frontier.

Doudna had to figure out what legal problems the university

might run into by testing people who weren't a part of the university community. This was a process that would normally have taken the lawyers weeks to do, so Doudna called the president of the University of California system. In twelve hours Doudna had the approval.

With federal testing still a mess and commercial labs taking more than a week to return results, there was huge demand for Berkeley's testing. The city of Berkeley's health officer, Lisa Hernandez, asked Urnov for five thousand tests, some of which would be used for the area's poor and homeless. The fire chief, David Brannigan, told Urnov that thirty of his firefighters were quarantined because they couldn't get test results. Doudna and Urnov promised to accommodate them all.

The first major challenge for the new lab was making sure that their COVID tests were accurate. Doudna brought a special eye to this task, since she had been an expert at deciphering readouts involving RNA ever since she was a graduate student. As the results came in, researchers would share them on a Zoom screen and then watch online as Doudna leaned forward and looked intensely at the images of inverted blue triangles, green triangles, and squares indicating data points. Sometimes she would just sit and stare, not moving, as the others held their breath.

"Yes, that looks good," she said during one session as she pointed a cursor to a part of an RNA detection test. Then her expression changed as she pointed to another place and muttered, "Nope, nope, nope."

Finally, early in April, she looked at the latest data that Lin Shiao had gathered and pronounced it "awesome." The tests were ready to go live.

On Monday, April 6, at eight a.m., a fire department van pulled up to the door of the IGI, and Officer Dori Tieu delivered a box filled with samples. Urnov, wearing white gloves and a blue mask, accepted the Styrofoam cooler and promised that they would have results the next morning.

As they were making the final preparations to get the lab into operation, Urnov went to get a take-out meal for his parents, who live nearby. When he arrived back at the IGI building, he saw a sheet of paper taped to the big glass door. On it was written, "Thank you, IGI. Sincerely, the people of Berkeley and the World."

CHAPTER THIRTY-FIVE

Companies for the Common Good

———— ⚬⚬⚬ ————

At the March 13 meeting that Doudna convened to address the coronavirus pandemic, Fyodor Urnov suggested that—in addition to developing a high-speed lab where they could conduct polymerase chain reaction (PCR) tests—they should try to invent a new type of test. It would use CRISPR technology to directly detect the RNA of the virus, similar to how bacteria use CRISPR to spot attacking viruses.

One participant piped up right away. "There's a paper that just came out on that—" he said.

Urnov's expression slipped into impatience because he knew the paper well, and then he interrupted. "Yes, from Janice Chen, formerly of the Doudna Lab."

There were actually two similar papers that had just come out. One was the paper by Janice Chen and a few other past members of the Doudna Lab who had formed a company to use CRISPR as a detection tool. The other paper was from Feng Zhang of the Broad Institute. Once again it appeared that Doudna and Zhang would be competing. This time, however, it was not a race to patent methods for editing human genes. In this new race the goal was to help save humanity from the novel coronavirus, and the two team's discoveries were being shared for free.

Back in 2017, Janice Chen and Lucas Harrington were PhD students working in Doudna's lab exploring newly discovered CRISPR-associated enzymes. Specifically, they were analyzing one that became known as Cas12a, and it had a special property. Like Cas9, it could be targeted to find and cut a specified sequence of DNA. But it didn't stop there. Once it sliced the double-stranded DNA target, it went into a cutting frenzy, chopping up any single-stranded DNA that was nearby.

Over breakfast one day Doudna's husband, Jamie, suggested that this property could be harnessed to create a diagnostic tool. Chen and Harrington had dreamed up the same idea. So they decided to add a "reporter" molecule to the CRISPR-Cas12 system. In this case the reporter molecule was a fluorescent signal connected to a bit of single-stranded DNA. Once the CRISPR-Cas12 system found a specified sequence of DNA and cut it, the CRISPR tool would then chop up nearby reporter molecules, which would activate the fluorescent signal. The presence of the fluorescent signal let the researchers know that Cas12 had found the target sequence. The result was a diagnostic tool that could detect whether the patient had a particular virus, bacteria, or cancer. Chen and Harrington dubbed it the "DNA endonuclease-targeted CRISPR trans reporter," a very clunky phrase crafted so that they could create the acronym "DETECTR."

When Chen, Harrington, and Doudna submitted their findings in an article to *Science* in November 2017, the editors requested that they write more about how to turn the discovery into a diagnostic test. Even the traditional scientific journals were now showing greater interest in connecting basic science to potential applications. So over Christmas break of 2017, Harrington and Chen collaborated with a researcher at UC San Francisco to show how their CRISPR-Cas12 tool could detect human papillomavirus (HPV), a sexually transmitted infection. They resubmitted their article in January 2018 with the data the editors had requested showing that DETECTR had identified HPV infections. The editors accepted the paper, and a version went online in February.

For decades it's been standard practice among scientists to end journal papers with a sentence that looks forward. Chen, Harrington, and Doudna ended their paper by saying that the CRISPR-Cas12 system "offers a new strategy to improve the speed, sensitivity and specificity of nucleic acid detection for point-of-care diagnostic applications." In other words, it might be used to create a simple test to detect virus infections quickly—at home or in a hospital.[1]

Even though Harrington and Chen had not yet gotten their doctorates, Doudna encouraged them to form a company. They agreed, and Mammoth Biosciences officially launched in April 2018, with Doudna serving as chair of its scientific advisory board.

At around the same time, far across the country, Doudna's longtime rival Feng Zhang had also been hard at work studying CRISPR. In October 2015, after sorting through the genomes of thousands of microbes, Zhang and a colleague reported on their discovery of many new CRISPR-associated enzymes. In addition to the previously known Cas9 and Cas12 enzymes that target

DNA, they had found a class of enzymes that target RNA. Those enzymes soon became known as Cas13.[2]

Cas13 had the same odd trait as Cas12: when it found its target, it went into a cutting frenzy—slicing not only its targeted RNA but also any other nearby RNA. At first Zhang assumed this was a mistake, and he asked his lab team whether they were sure the enzymes they were working with weren't contaminated. They painstakingly eliminated all possible sources of contamination, but the cutting spree kept happening. Zhang speculated that it was an evolutionary method to have the cell commit suicide if it got too infected by an invading virus, thus preventing the virus from spreading as fast.[3]

Doudna's lab then helped uncover exactly how Cas13 works. In a paper published in October 2016, Doudna and her coauthors—including her husband, Jamie—explained the different functions that Cas13 performs. Their article laid out how the chopping makes it possible to use Cas13 with fluorescent reporters (as was done with Cas12) as a detection tool for a specified RNA sequence, such as that of a coronavirus.[4]

Zhang and his colleagues at the Broad were able to create such a detection tool in April 2017, which they named "specific high-sensitivity enzymatic reporter unlocking." They named the tool this so that they could use the acronym "SHERLOCK." The acronym wasn't just a clever name to make the instrument sound like the world-famous fictional British detective. SHERLOCK actually *could* detect! In fact, Zhang showed that SHERLOCK could find and identify specific strains of the Zika and dengue viruses, both of which are spread mostly in tropical areas by infected mosquitoes.[5]

Over the next year Zhang and his team made a bigger, better version of SHERLOCK that combined Cas13 and Cas12 to identify multiple targets in one reaction. Then they were able to simplify the system and make it possible for the detection to be reported on paper strips, similar to the rectangular strips you can dip into a fish tank to determine the pH and ammonia levels of the water.

Zhang decided to start a company to commercialize SHERLOCK, just like Chen and Harrington had done when they launched Mammoth in April 2018. It took a while to get Sherlock Biosciences funded because Zhang and his cofounders did not want money to be the main goal of the company (and investors are always interested in how much money a company expects to earn). Zhang wanted the technologies to be affordable to people and governments in the developing world. So they structured their company in a way that allowed it to profit on its innovations while still working like a nonprofit in places where there was great need.

Scientific innovation does not have to be a race or a rivalry, even when the players have a history of competition like Jennifer Doudna and Feng Zhang did. Both sides knew that the technology created by their companies had enormous potential to do good. Whenever there was a new epidemic, Mammoth and Sherlock could quickly reprogram their diagnostic tools to target the virus or bacteria in question and produce testing kits. The Broad team, for example, sent a group with SHERLOCK to Nigeria in 2019 to help diagnose victims of an outbreak of Lassa fever, a sickness similar to that caused by the Ebola virus.[6]

Unfortunately, while using CRISPR as a diagnostic tool was a worthwhile pursuit in many people's minds, the public didn't find it particularly exciting. It did not get as much buzz as using CRISPR to treat diseases or edit human genes.

But then, at the beginning of 2020, the world suddenly changed. The ability to quickly detect an attacking virus became critical. And the best way to do it faster and cheaper than using the conventional PCR tests, which required a lot of mixing steps and temperature cycles, was to deploy RNA-guided enzymes that had been programmed to detect the genetic material of the virus.

In other words, scientists like Feng, Doudna, and their teams could adapt the CRISPR system that bacteria had been deploying for millions of years.

CRISPR-Based Coronavirus Tests

In early January 2020, Feng Zhang started getting emails about coronavirus written in Chinese. Some were from Chinese academics he had met, but he also got an unexpected one from an official at China's consulate in New York City.

"Even though you are American and not living in China," the email read, "this is really a problem that's important for humanity." The official quoted an old Chinese saying: *When one place is in trouble, assistance comes from all quarters.* The email then urged, "So we hope that you can think about it and see what you can do."[1]

Zhang knew little about the novel coronavirus other than what he had read in a *New York Times* article describing the situation in Wuhan, but the multiple emails made him sense how urgent the crisis was. He was especially alarmed by the fact that he'd heard directly from the Chinese consulate.

Zhang decided to reconfigure the SHERLOCK detection tool so that it could test for the new coronavirus, and he chose to do it in his Broad Institute lab rather than at Sherlock Biosciences. Unfortunately, he didn't have anyone in his lab to handle the necessary experiments, so he decided to do them himself. He also enlisted two of his former graduate students.

Zhang divided his lab into different areas to avoid contamination. After a reaction was completed, the test tube would be walked into another room and the door sealed shut before the tube was opened. He did not initially have access to samples of the coronavirus from human patients, so he made a synthetic version of it. Using the SHERLOCK process, he and his team devised a detection test that took only three steps and could be done in an hour without fancy equipment. All it required was a small device to keep the temperature constant while the genetic material from the samples was amplified through a chemical process that was simpler than PCR. The results could be read using a paper dipstick.

On February 14, well before most of the United States had focused on the fact that the coronavirus was growing into a full-fledged pandemic, Zhang's lab posted a paper describing the test and inviting any lab to use or adapt the process.[2] Sherlock Biosciences quickly began work on turning the process into a commercial testing device that could be used in hospitals and doctors' offices. When the company's CEO, Rahul Dhanda, told his team that he wanted them to focus on COVID, the researchers literally swung their chairs back to their workbenches to take on the mission.

"When we say a pivot, there was a literal pivot of chairs at the same time there was a pivot of the company towards a new goal," he remembers.

By the end of 2020, the company was working with manufacturing partners to turn out hundreds of small machines that could be used to get results in less than an hour.[3]

Around the time that Zhang began working on his coronavirus test, Janice Chen got a call from a researcher on the scientific advisory board of the company she had founded with Doudna and Lucas Harrington, Mammoth Biosciences.

"What do you think about developing a CRISPR-based diagnostic to detect the SARS-CoV-2 virus?" he asked.

She agreed that they should try. As a result, she and Harrington became part of yet another cross-country competition between Doudna's circle and Zhang's.[4]

Within two weeks, the Mammoth team was able to reconfigure its CRISPR-based DETECTR tool so that it would identify SARS-CoV-2. One benefit of collaborating with UC San Francisco, which has its own hospital, was that they could test on real human samples, drawn from thirty-six COVID patients. This was an improvement over how the Broad Institute had conducted its initial tests, by creating synthetic viruses in a lab.

The Mammoth test relied on the CRISPR-associated enzyme that Chen and Harrington had studied in Doudna's lab, Cas12, which targets DNA. That would seem to make it less effective than SHERLOCK's Cas13, which targets RNA, the genetic material of the coronavirus. However, both detection techniques need to convert the RNA of the coronavirus into DNA for the coronavirus to be amplified. In the SHERLOCK test, the DNA has to be transcribed back into RNA to be detected, which adds a small step to the process.

Like Zhang, the Mammoth team decided to make what they had devised free to the public. On February 14, while they were preparing to put a paper online with the details of their Mammoth test, Chen and Harrington saw a message pop up on the online messaging platform they were using. Someone had posted the tweet that Zhang had sent out announcing that he had just published his paper on how to use SHERLOCK for detecting the coronavirus.

"We were like, 'Oh, shoot,'" Chen recalls of that Friday afternoon.

But after a few minutes, they realized that having both their papers appear was a good thing.[5] Zhang was gracious too, though it was easy for him to be, since he had beaten the Mammoth team by a day.

"Check out the resource provided by Mammoth," he tweeted, including a link to its paper. "Glad that scientists are working together and sharing openly. #coronavirus."

That tweet reflected a welcome new trend in the CRISPR world.

The passionate competition for patents and prizes in science would probably never entirely go away. But the urgency that Doudna and Zhang and their colleagues felt about defeating the coronavirus caused them to be more open and willing to share their work. Competition was still important, and it pushed Doudna's and Zhang's teams to publish papers and make advances on the new COVID tests. But coronavirus made the rivalry less cutthroat because, more than anything else, everyone wanted solutions and an end to the damage and death the pandemic was causing.

The CRISPR-based tests developed by Mammoth and Sherlock are cheaper and faster than conventional PCR tests. They also have an advantage over antigen tests, such as the one developed by Abbott Labs that was approved in August 2020. The CRISPR-based tests can detect the presence of the RNA of a virus as soon as a person has been infected. But the antigen tests, which detect the presence of proteins that exist on the surface of the virus, are most accurate only after a patient has become highly infectious to others.

The ultimate goal of the CRISPR-based coronavirus tests was to provide a cheap, disposable, fast, and simple test that you could buy at the corner drugstore and use in the privacy of your home.

Harrington and Chen of the Mammoth team unveiled their concept for such a device in May 2020 and announced a partnership with the London-based multinational pharmaceutical company GlaxoSmithKline (maker of Excedrin and Tums) to manufacture it. It would provide accurate results in twenty minutes and require no special equipment.

Likewise, Zhang's lab that same month developed a way to simplify the SHERLOCK detection system, which originally required two steps, into a process that required just a single-step reaction. The only equipment necessary was a pot to keep the system heated at a steady 140 degrees Fahrenheit. Zhang named the system STOP, for "SHERLOCK Testing in One Pot."[6] It was simple: you put a nasal or saliva sample into a cartridge, slid the cartridge into the device, added a solution that extracted the virus RNA, and then added some freeze-dried CRISPR, which activated the reaction that delivered the test results.

Zhang named the device STOP-COVID. But the platform could be easily adapted to detect any virus.

"That's why we chose the STOP name, which can be paired with any target," he says. "We could create a STOP-flu or a STOP-HIV or have many detection targets on the same platform. The device is agnostic about what virus it's looking for."

Mammoth has the same vision of making it easy to reprogram its own tool to detect any new virus that comes along.

"The beauty of CRISPR is that once you have the platform, then it's just a matter of reconfiguring your chemistry to detect a different virus," Chen explains. "It can be used for the next pandemic or any virus. It can also be used against any bacteria or anything that has a genetic sequence, even cancer."

The development of home testing kits has a potential impact beyond the fight against COVID: bringing biology into the home. The process may be similar to how personal computers in the 1970s brought digital products and services—and an awareness of microchips and software code—into people's daily lives and consciousness. Personal computers led to smartphones and other cutting-edge products built by waves of innovators.

When Zhang was growing up, his parents emphasized that he should use his computer as a tool to build things on. After his attention turned from microchips to microbes, he wondered why biology did not have the same involvement in people's daily lives as computers did. There were no simple biology devices or platforms that people could use in their homes.

"As I was doing molecular biology experiments, I thought, 'This is so cool . . . but why hasn't it impacted people's lives in ways that a software app does?'"

As he was working on developing his at-home CRISPR tests for viruses, he realized that they could be the way to do that. Home testing kits could become the platform and operating system that will allow us to weave the wonders of molecular biology more into our daily lives. Developers and entrepreneurs may someday be able to use what they've learned from CRISPR-based home testing kits to build a variety of biomedical apps: virus detection, disease diagnosis, cancer screening, nutritional analyses, genetic tests, and more.

"We can get people in their homes to check if they have the flu or just a cold," says Zhang. "If their kids have a sore throat, they can determine if it's strep throat."

In the process, these tools might give us all a deeper appreciation for how molecular biology works.

For most people the inner workings of molecules may remain as mysterious as those of microchips, but at least all of us will be a bit more aware and respectful of the beauty and power of both.

CHAPTER THIRTY-SEVEN

Vaccines

———— ∞∞∞ ————

Vaccinations were pioneered in the 1790s by an English doctor named Edward Jenner who noticed that many milkmaids were immune to smallpox. They had all been infected by a form of pox that afflicts cows but is harmless to humans, and Jenner guessed that the cowpox had given them immunity to smallpox. So he took some pus from a cowpox blister, rubbed it into scratches he'd made in the arm of his gardener's eight-year-old son, and then later exposed the child to smallpox. (This was in the days before there were strict ethical guidelines for biological research.) The boy didn't become ill.

Vaccines work by stimulating a person's immune system. A substance that resembles a dangerous virus or another pathogen (a pathogen is any microorganism that causes disease) is delivered into a person's body. The immune system then produces antibodies, which are proteins that cells create after they are exposed to a pathogen. These antibodies will, sometimes for many years, fight off an infection if the actual virus ever attacks.

Vaccines use a variety of methods to try to stimulate the human immune system. One traditional approach is to inject a weakened and safe (called "attenuated") version of the virus into the patient. **Attenuated viruses** can be good teachers for our bodies because they look very much like the real virus. A scientist named Albert Sabin used this approach for the oral polio vaccine in the 1950s, and that's the way we now fend off measles, mumps, rubella, and chickenpox. It takes a long time to develop and cultivate these vaccines, but in 2020 some companies decided to start on this method as a long-term option for attacking the COVID-19 virus.

While Sabin was trying to create a weakened polio virus to use in the oral polio vaccine, the scientist Jonas Salk succeeded with an approach that seemed somewhat safer—using a killed virus. This type of vaccine can still teach a person's immune system how to fight off the live virus. Among the earliest COVID-19 vaccines was one using this approach, and it was developed by the Beijing-based company Sinovac Biotech.

Another traditional approach is to inject a purified subunit of the virus, such as one of the proteins that are on the virus's coat. The immune system will then remember that portion of the virus, allowing the body to mount a quicker and stronger response when it encounters the actual virus. The vaccine against hepatitis B, for example, works by introducing proteins that are on the virus's surface. The fragments of the virus are safer to inject into a patient and are easier to produce than attenuated or killed viruses, but the fragments are usually not as good at producing long-term immunity. Many companies pursued this approach in the 2020 race for a COVID vaccine by developing ways to introduce into humans the spike protein that is on the surface of the coronavirus.[1]

In scientific circles, 2020 is likely to be remembered as the time when these traditional vaccines began to be replaced by genetic vaccines. Instead of injecting a weakened or partial version of the dangerous coronavirus into humans, these new vaccines deliver a piece of genetic coding that will guide human cells to produce, on their own, components of the virus. The goal is for these components to stimulate the patient's immune system.

One method for doing this is to take a harmless virus and insert some genetic code from the dangerous virus that we want to protect against. As we all now know, viruses are very good at finding their way into human cells. That is why safe viruses can be used as a delivery system, or vector, to transport material into the cells of patients.

This approach led to one of the earliest COVID vaccine candidates, which was developed at Oxford University. Scientists took a virus that usually causes the common cold in chimpanzees and genetically changed it so that it would be impossible for the cold virus to grow in humans. They then added to this safe virus the genetic sequence of the spike protein of SARS-CoV-2, the virus that causes COVID. Similar vaccines developed by other companies in 2020—such as by Johnson & Johnson—used a safe human virus as the vector. But the Oxford team decided that using a chimpanzee virus was better, because patients who had previously had cold infections might have an immunity to a human virus being used as the delivery system.

The idea behind both the Oxford and the Johnson & Johnson vaccines was that the safe virus with the spike protein code would make its way into human cells, where it would cause the cells to make lots of these spike proteins. That in turn would stimulate the person's immune system to make antibodies. As a result, the person's immune system would be primed to respond rapidly if the real coronavirus struck.

The lead researcher at Oxford was named Sarah Gilbert.[2] Like Jennifer Doudna, she loved working in a lab more than almost anything else, and her family supported that as much as Doudna's did. In 1998, when Gilbert gave birth to triplets prematurely, her husband took time off from his job so that she could return to her career as soon as possible. In 2014 she worked on developing a vaccine for a different coronavirus that causes an illness known as Middle East respiratory syndrome (MERS). She used a neutralized chimp virus edited to contain the genetic sequence for a MERS virus spike protein. That epidemic died away before her vaccine could be deployed, but the experience gave her a head start when COVID struck.

Gilbert already knew that the chimp virus was a safe delivery system and that it had successfully delivered into humans the genetic material for the spike protein of the MERS virus. As soon as the Chinese published the genetic sequence of the new coronavirus in January 2020, Gilbert began engineering its spike protein genetic code into the chimp virus, waking each day at four a.m. so that she could get as much work in as possible.

Her triplets were now twenty-one, and all were studying biochemistry. They volunteered to be early testers of the vaccine Gilbert was formulating, and trials in monkeys conducted at a Montana primate center in March 2020 produced promising results.

Money is crucial for creating effective vaccines, and luckily, the Bill and Melinda Gates Foundation provided early funding to Sarah and Oxford's efforts. Bill Gates also pushed Oxford to team up quickly with a major company that could manufacture and distribute the vaccine if it worked. So Oxford partnered with AstraZeneca, a British-Swedish pharmaceutical company.

The methods that Johnson & Johnson and Oxford forged ahead with to create vaccines against the coronavirus weren't the only things scientists tried. There is another way to get genetic material into a human cell and cause it to produce the part of a virus that can stimulate the immune system. Scientists can make cells become vaccine-manufacturing facilities by delivering the genetic code for the component—such as DNA or RNA—into them.

Let's start with DNA vaccines. Although no DNA vaccine had ever been approved before the COVID pandemic, the concept had always seemed promising. As the pandemic raged in 2020, researchers at Inovio Pharmaceuticals and a handful of other companies created a little circle of DNA that coded for parts of the coronavirus spike protein. The idea was that if this DNA could get inside the nucleus of a cell, it could very efficiently churn out many strands of messenger RNA to go forth and oversee the production of the spike protein parts, which serve to stimulate the immune system. Some advantages were that DNA is cheap to produce in large quantities, and DNA vaccines are safer to develop than traditional vaccines that deal with live viruses.

Unfortunately, the big challenge facing a DNA vaccine is delivery. How can you get the little ring of engineered DNA not only into a human cell but into the nucleus of the cell? Injecting a lot of the DNA vaccine into a patient's arm will cause some of the DNA to get into cells, but it's not very efficient.

Some of the developers of DNA vaccines, including Inovio, tried to facilitate the delivery into human cells through a method called **electroporation**, which shoots electrical shock pulses right at the site of the injection. This process briefly opens pores in the cell membranes and allows the DNA to get in. The electric pulse guns have lots of tiny needles and are a little scary to look at, so it's easy to understand why this technique is unpopular, especially with those on the receiving end.

One of the teams that Doudna organized at the beginning of the coronavirus crisis in March 2020 focused on these delivery challenges facing DNA vaccines. That group was led by her former student Ross Wilson, and Alex Marson of the University of California–San Francisco. At one of Doudna's regular all-teams Zoom meetings, Wilson showed a slide of the Inovio electric zapper.

"They actually shoot the patient in the muscle with one of these guns," he said. "About the only visible advance they've made in ten years is now they have a little plastic thing to hide the tiny needles so they don't frighten the patient as much."

So that patients wouldn't have to face the terrifying zapper, Marson and Wilson devised a way to address the DNA vaccine delivery problem using CRISPR-Cas9. They put together a Cas9 protein, a guide RNA, and a special signal that helps the complex get into the nucleus. The result was a "shuttle" that could deliver the DNA vaccine into cells. The DNA then instructs the cells to make SARS-CoV-2 spike proteins and thus stimulate the immune system to fend off the real coronavirus.[3]

That leads us back to our favorite molecule, the biochemical star of this book: RNA.

The first two vaccines used in the United States—produced by the drug companies Moderna and Pfizer—use messenger RNA (mRNA) technology. mRNA is a piece of code that carries genetic instructions from DNA, which is bunkered inside a cell's nucleus, to the manufacturing region of the cell, where it directs what protein to make. In the case of the COVID vaccine, the mRNA instructs cells to make a version of the spike protein that is on the surface of SARS-CoV-2.

Instead of using a safe virus as a delivery vehicle, RNA vaccines are delivered inside tiny oily capsules, known as lipid nanoparticles, which are injected through a long syringe into the muscle of the upper arm. One of the main side effects of the vaccine—other than fever, tiredness, and chills—is a sore arm muscle. Many people have complained that their arms hurt for days, in fact.

An RNA vaccine has certain advantages over a DNA vaccine. Most notably, the RNA does not need to get into the nucleus of the cell, where DNA is headquartered. The RNA does its work in the outer region of cells, the **cytoplasm**, which is where proteins are constructed. So an RNA vaccine simply needs to deliver its payload into this outer region.

By December 2020, with COVID once again resurging throughout much of the world, the two RNA vaccines were the first to be authorized in the United States and became the frontline in the biotech battle to beat back the pandemic. Never before had an RNA vaccine been approved for use. Almost exactly a year after the novel coronavirus had first been identified, both Pfizer and Moderna had devised these new genetic vaccines and tested them in large clinical trials, where they'd proved more than 90 percent effective.

The fearless little RNA molecule, which introduced life on our planet and later plagued us in the form of coronaviruses, rode to our rescue. Jennifer Doudna and her colleagues had already employed RNA in a tool to edit our genes, and then had used it as a surefire method to detect coronaviruses. Now scientists had found a way to enlist RNA's most basic biological function—serving as a messenger to direct cells to make a desired protein—to turn our cells into manufacturing plants for the spike protein that would stimulate our immunity to SARS-CoV-2.

Throughout human history we have been subjected to wave after wave of viral and bacterial plagues. The first known recorded one was the Babylon flu epidemic around 1200 BC. The plague of Athens in 429 BC killed close to one hundred thousand people, the Antonine plague in the second century killed ten million, the plague of Justinian in the sixth century killed fifty million, and the Black Death of the fourteenth century took almost twenty-five million lives, close to half of Europe's population. The COVID pandemic that has killed more than five million people worldwide as of January 2022 will not be the final pandemic. However, thanks to the new RNA vaccine technology, our defenses against most future viruses are likely to be immensely faster and more effective.

The invention of easily reprogrammable RNA vaccines was a triumph of human ingenuity, but it was based on decades of curiosity-driven research into one of the most fundamental aspects of life on planet earth: how genes encoded by DNA are transcribed into snippets of RNA that tell cells what proteins to assemble. Likewise, the invention of CRISPR gene-editing technology came from understanding the way that bacteria use snippets of RNA to copy bits of the genetic material of dangerous viruses and then guide enzymes to chop up these viruses when they reappear.

Great inventions come from understanding basic science. Nature is beautiful that way.

CRISPR Cures

The development of vaccines—both the conventional sort and those employing DNA or RNA—would eventually help to fight the COVID-19 pandemic. But they are not a perfect solution. They rely on stimulating a person's immune system, and that is always a risky thing to do. In fact, most deaths from COVID-19 came from organ inflammation due to unwanted immune-system responses.[1] As vaccine makers have repeatedly discovered, the human immune system is hard to control and contains many mysteries. It contains no simple on-off switches but instead works through the interaction of complicated molecules that are not easy to regulate.[2]

The long-range solution to our fight against viruses is the same as the one bacteria found: using CRISPR to guide a scissors-like enzyme to chop up the genetic material of a virus, without having to enlist the patient's immune system. Once again the circles of scientists around Doudna and Zhang found themselves in competition as they raced to adapt CRISPR to this urgent mission.

Cameron Myhrvold (pronounced MEER-vold) is the son of Nathan Myhrvold, who was the longtime chief technology officer (CTO) at Microsoft. Cameron has his father's happy eyes, round face, bubbly laugh, and free-range curiosity. His dad was a genius and a pioneer not only in the digital realm but also in fields ranging from food science to asteroid tracking to the speed at which dinosaurs could whip their tails. Cameron shares his father's skill with computer coding, but he chose to focus more on genetic coding and the wonders of biology.

As a Princeton undergraduate, Cameron studied molecular and computational biology. Then he got his doctorate from Harvard's Systems, Synthetic, and Quantitative Biology program, which combines biology and computer science. Worried that the work he did while he was getting his PhD was so cutting-edge that it would have little practical impact in the future, he decided to take time off to hike the Colorado Trail. He thought it would help him figure out where to go scientifically.[3]

On one leg of his hike, he met a guy who asked him a lot of questions about science.

"During that conversation," Myhrvold says, "it became apparent to me that I liked working on problems that were directly relevant to human health."

That led him to work in the lab of a Harvard biologist. While studying for his doctorate at Harvard, Myhrvold had become friends with two grad students who worked with Feng Zhang on CRISPR-Cas13. Myhrvold would often kick around ideas with them when he visited Zhang's lab to use its gene-sequencing machine. Some of those ideas involved ways to use Cas13 to detect different RNA sequences.

As a postdoc, Myhrvold deepened his connection with Zhang's group by becoming part of the team that worked on Zhang's 2017 paper describing the SHERLOCK system for detecting RNA viruses. The following year he collaborated on another paper about SHERLOCK that appeared in the same April 2018 issue of *Science* as the paper from Doudna's lab describing their CRISPR-Cas12 virus-detection tool.

In addition to using CRISPR-Cas13 to detect viruses, Myhrvold became interested in turning CRISPR into a therapeutic treatment that could get rid of viruses.

"There are hundreds of viruses that can infect people, but there's only a handful that have available drugs," he says. "That's in part because viruses are so different from each other. What if we could come up with a system that we could program to treat different viruses?"[4]

Most of the viruses that cause human problems, including coronaviruses, contain RNA as their genetic material. They are precisely the type of virus for which you would want a CRISPR enzyme that targets RNA, such as Cas13. So Myhrvold came up with a way to use CRISPR-Cas13 to do for humans what it does for bacteria: identify the genetic material of a dangerous virus and chop it up. He named the proposed system CARVER, for "Cas13-assisted restriction of viral expression and readout."

In December 2016, Myhrvold performed some experiments using CARVER to target a virus that causes **meningitis** or **encephalitis**, two infections that affect the brain. His data showed that CARVER reduced the levels of the virus significantly.[5] Because of this, Myhrvold's boss was able to get a grant to study the CARVER system as a way to prevent flu and other viruses.[6] Myhrvold then did a computer analysis of more than three hundred fifty genomes from RNA viruses that infect humans, and identified what are known as "conserved sequences," meaning those that are the same in many viruses. These sequences have been preserved unchanged by evolution, and thus are not likely to mutate away anytime soon. His team engineered a huge group of guide RNAs designed to target these sequences. He then tested Cas13's ability to stop three viruses, including a type that causes severe flu. CARVER reduced the level of viral RNA in the cell cultures by up to forty times.[7]

Their paper was published online in October 2019, and a few weeks after it came out, the first cases of COVID-19 were detected in China.[8]

"It was one of these moments when you realize the stuff you've been working on for a long time might be a lot more relevant than you thought," Myhrvold says.

By late January 2020, he and his colleagues had studied the sequence of the coronavirus genome and had begun work on CRISPR-based tests for detecting it. The result was a burst of papers in the spring of 2020 for improving CRISPR-based detection technologies for viruses. These included a system known as CARMEN, designed to detect 169 viruses at one time,[9] and a process that combined SHERLOCK's detection capability with an RNA extraction method called HUDSON to create a single-step detection technique Myhrvold named SHINE.[10]

However, Myhrvold decided that his time could best be used in developing tools that could detect viruses, rather than working on treatments like CARVER, designed to destroy viruses. In the longer term we do need treatments, but diagnostics were more urgently needed in the beginning of the pandemic. That's why, in 2021, he moved his lab and his focus to Princeton University.

In the West Coast orbit of Jennifer Doudna, however,

there was a team that was pushing forward with a coronavirus treatment. Similar to the CARVER system that Myhrvold had invented, it would use CRISPR to seek and destroy viruses. The person leading that team was named Stanley Qi. Qi grew up in what he calls a small city in China—Weifang, on the coast about three hundred miles south of Beijing. Small it is not, however; it's actually home to more than 2.6 million people, which is about the same size as Chicago. The town was full of factories but no world-class university, so Qi (pronounced "tshee") went to Tsinghua University in Beijing, where he majored in math and physics. He applied to Berkeley to do graduate work in physics, but he found himself increasingly attracted to biology because it had more application for helping the world.[11]

At Berkeley he gravitated to the lab of Doudna, who became one of his two advisors. Instead of focusing on gene editing, he developed new ways to use CRISPR to interfere with the expression of genes. Immediately Qi was surprised and pleased at how Doudna spent time discussing science with him, not in a shallow way but down to the deep level and including key technical details.

His interest in viruses grew in 2019 when he was funded (as Myhrvold and Doudna were) by government grants focused on preparing against pandemics. He first dove into finding a CRISPR method to fight influenza, but then coronavirus struck. In late January 2020, Qi read a story about the situation in China, and he called together his team.

Qi's approach to battling COVID-19 was similar to that pursued by Myhrvold. He wanted to use a guided enzyme to target and then cut the RNA of the invading virus. Like Zhang and Myhrvold, he decided to use a version of Cas13. This was an enzyme known as Cas13d.

Cas13d was small and had highly specific targeting capabilities, so Qi chose it as the best enzyme to attack the coronavirus in human lung cells. In the competition to come up with good acronyms, Qi scored high. He dubbed his system PAC-MAN, which he had extracted from "prophylactic antiviral CRISPR in human cells." The name was that of the chomping character in the video game that was popular in the 1980s.

Qi and his team tested PAC-MAN on synthesized fragments of the coronavirus. In mid-February 2020 one of his doctoral students ran experiments showing that PAC-MAN had reduced the amount of the coronavirus by 90 percent. According to Qi, PAC-MAN was "a promising strategy to combat not only coronaviruses, including that causing COVID-19, but also a broad range of other viruses."[12]

The paper written by Qi's team describing their findings went online March 14, 2020, the day after Doudna's initial meeting of Bay Area researchers who had joined the coronavirus fight. Qi emailed her a link, and within an hour she had replied, inviting him to join the group and present at their second weekly online meeting.

"I told her we needed some resources to develop the PAC-MAN idea, get access to live coronavirus samples, and figure out delivery systems that might get it into the lung cells of patients," he says. "She was super-supportive."

The concept behind CARVER and PAC-MAN was a brilliant one, although in fairness it should be noted that bacteria had thought of it more than a billion years ago. The RNA-cleaving

Cas13 enzymes could chomp up coronaviruses in human cells. If CARVER and PAC-MAN could be made to work, they would act more efficiently than a vaccine that produces an immune response. By directly targeting the invading virus, these CRISPR-based technologies avoid having to rely on the body's unpredictable immune response.

The challenge was delivery. How could you get the enzyme to the right cells in a human patient and then through the membranes of those cells? That is a very difficult challenge, especially when it involves getting into lung cells, which is why CARVER and PAC-MAN were still not ready for use in humans in 2021.

The traditional way to deliver CRISPR and other genetic therapies is by using viruses, which are very good (as we well know) at worming their way into human cells. Scientists can use safe viruses, which don't cause any disease or provoke severe immune responses, to deliver genetic material into cells. Or they can create synthetic virus-like particles to do the delivery, which is the specialty of some of the researchers in Doudna's lab. Another method, electroporation, like with Inovio's electrical pulse gun, works by applying an electric field onto a cell's membrane to make it more permeable. All of these approaches have their drawbacks, though.

To work on delivery systems, Doudna put Qi in touch with Ross Wilson, her former researcher who was leading one of Doudna's coronavirus teams. Wilson is an expert on new ways to move material into the cells of patients, but he feared that delivering PAC-MAN or CARVER into cells would be difficult. Qi is nevertheless hopeful that these CRISPR-based therapies can be deployed in the next few years.

A method that is proving promising is to encase the CRISPR-Cas13 complex inside of synthetic molecules called **lipitoids,** which are about the size of a virus. So Qi has been working with the Biological Nanostructures Facility at Lawrence Berkeley National Lab, a sprawling government complex on a hill above Berkeley's campus, to create lipitoids that can deliver PAC-MAN into lung cells.[13]

One way this could work, Qi says, is by delivering PAC-MAN treatments through a nasal spray or some other form of nebulizer (a device that turns liquid medication into a mist that you can breathe in, usually through a mask). Qi's son has asthma, and he used a nebulizer before his football games to prevent asthma attacks. People use these regularly to prepare the lung to be less allergic if they are exposed to something, and the same could be done during a coronavirus pandemic; people could use a nasal spray so that PAC-MAN or another CRISPR-Cas13 treatment will protect them.

Once the delivery mechanisms are worked out, CRISPR-based systems such as PAC-MAN and CARVER will be able to treat and protect people without having to activate the body's own immune system, which can be quirky and delicate. The CRISPR systems can also be programmed to target essential sequences in the virus's genetic code, so a mutating virus won't be able to evade the enzymes. And these tools will be simple to reprogram when a new virus emerges.

This concept of reprogramming is also helpful in a larger sense. The CRISPR treatments come from working with a system that we humans found in nature.

"That gives me hope," Myhrvold says, "that when we face

other great medical challenges, we will be able to find other such technologies in nature and put them to use."

It is a reminder of the value of curiosity-driven basic research into what Leonardo da Vinci liked to refer to as the infinite wonders of nature.

"You never know," Myhrvold says, "when some obscure thing you're studying is going to have important implications for human health."

CHAPTER THIRTY-NINE

A Virtual Return to Cold Spring Harbor

⸺⋙⋘⸺

COVID-19 was practically the only thing on anyone's mind at the Cold Spring Harbor Laboratory's annual CRISPR conference in August 2020. The conference's primary topic was how CRISPR was being used to fight the coronavirus, and it featured talks by Jennifer Doudna and Feng Zhang as well as some of the other COVID warriors. Instead of gathering on the rolling campus overlooking an inlet of Long Island Sound, participants convened online, looking a bit bleary from months of interacting with boxed faces on their computer screens.

The meeting also wove in another strand of this book. It celebrated the hundredth anniversary of the birth of Rosalind Franklin, whose pioneering work on the structure of DNA had inspired Doudna, when she'd read *The Double Helix* as a young girl, to believe that women could do science. The cover of the meeting's program featured a colorized photograph of Franklin peering into a microscope.

Fyodor Urnov, who directed the COVID testing lab that Doudna had created at Berkeley, gave the opening tribute to Franklin. It was a serious look at her scientific work, including her research into the location of RNA in tobacco mosaic viruses. The only dramatic statement came at the end when Urnov showed a picture of Franklin's empty lab bench after her death.

"The best way to honor her is to remember that the structural sexism she faced remains with us today," he said, his voice choking up a bit. "Rosalind is the godmother of gene editing."

Doudna's talk began with a reminder of the natural connection between CRISPR and COVID.

"CRISPR is a fabulous way that evolution has dealt with the problem of viral infection," she said. "We can learn from it in this pandemic."

Zhang followed with an update on his STOP technology for easy-to-use portable testing machines. The great news was that he already had photographs of the latest prototypes, which had been delivered that week.

Cameron Myhrvold, speaking animatedly with both hands like his father, gave a description of how his CARMEN system could be programmed to detect multiple viruses at once. There were also presentations on the DETECTR platform, the PAC-MAN system—which could be used to not only detect coronaviruses but also destroy them—and the work being done at Doudna's lab to create better methods for amplifying genetic material so it could be detected.

While everyone at the conference believed that the pandemic was a tragedy—and possibly the most difficult thing our society had faced in decades—it also offered some gifts. One of them was the possibility that the pandemic might create greater public interest in biology. When at-home testing kits become low-cost and easy to use, Zhang said, they will make medicine more available to everyone. The most important next steps will be innovations in "microfluidics," which involves channeling tiny amounts of liquid in a device, and then connecting the information to our cell phones. That will allow us all, in the privacy of our homes, to test our saliva and blood for hundreds of medical indicators, monitor our health conditions on our phones, and share the data with doctors and researchers. Doudna added that the pandemic had accelerated the merging of science with other fields.

"The engagement of nonscientists in our work will help achieve an incredibly interesting biotechnology revolution," she predicted.

This truly was molecular biology's moment.

During the conference one audience member electronically raised his hand. An employee of the National Institutes of Health, he asked why there were so few African Americans like himself enrolled in the clinical trials for COVID vaccines. That led to a discussion of the distrust many Blacks have about medical trials. Part of the reason they feel this way is that, between 1932 and 1972, the United States Public Health Service and the CDC decided to study the effects of untreated syphilis, a sexually transmitted disease caused by a bacteria, in an effort named the Tuskegee experiment. Instead of treating the nearly four hundred African American men who had syphilis symptoms and had signed up for free medicine, the researchers gave the men placebos, or inactive pills. Many of these men died from the disease.

A few of the conference attendees asked whether it was important to have racial diversity in the COVID vaccine trials, and the consensus of the group was that yes, this was vital for medical and moral reasons. The NIH employee suggested enlisting African American churches and colleges into the effort of enrolling volunteers.

The conference presentations on how CRISPR was being deployed to fight COVID were impressive, but equally so were the reports on the discoveries that were pushing CRISPR gene-editing forward. The most important were those made by one of Doudna's co-organizers of the conference, a scientist from Harvard named David Liu.

Beginning in 2016, Liu began developing a technique known as "base editing," which can make a precise change in a single letter in DNA without cutting a break in the strands. It's like a very sharp pencil for editing. At the 2019 Cold Spring Harbor meeting, he announced a further advance called "prime editing." In this procedure, like with other CRISPR systems, the guide RNA finds the DNA that needs fixing, but the RNA also carries a copy of the edit to be made. When the RNA finds the target DNA, it makes only a tiny nick, rather than a double-strand break, and then adds the corrected DNA sequence. Afterward the cell breaks down the original, unwanted sequence because it has the tiny nick in it. Edits of up to eighty letters are possible.[1]

Dozens of the presentations at the 2020 meeting involved young researchers who had found clever new ways to use base editing and prime editing. Liu himself described his latest discovery of how to deploy base-editing tools into the energy-producing region of cells.[2] In addition, he was a coauthor of a paper that described a user-friendly web app that could help design prime-editing experiments.[3]

COVID had not slowed the CRISPR revolution.

The importance of base editing was highlighted on the cover

of the conference book. Just below the colorized picture of Rosa-lind Franklin was a beautiful 3-D image of a base editor attached to a purple RNA guide and a blue DNA target. Using some of the structural biology and imaging techniques that Franklin had pioneered, the image had been published a month earlier by the labs of Doudna and Liu.

In the dining hall on the Cold Spring Harbor campus, there is a wood-paneled lounge, known as the Blackford Bar, that man-ages to be both spacious and cozy. Old photographs line the walls, TV sets broadcast both scientific lectures and Yankees baseball games, and an outdoor deck overlooks the tranquil harbor.

There you can find, on most summer evenings, confer-ence attendees, researchers from nearby lab buildings, and the occasional groundskeeper or campus worker. During previous CRISPR conferences, it was filled with talk of big discoveries, great ideas, failed experiments, potential job openings, and all kinds of gossip.

In 2020 the conference organizers tried to re-create the scene with a room online called #virtual-bar. Its purpose, they said, was to "simulate the serendipitous introductions you would've experi-enced at the Blackford Bar."

About forty attendees showed up the first night. People intro-duced themselves carefully, like at a real party, except they were far less interactive. Then a moderator broke everyone into groups of six and sent them to breakout Zoom rooms. After twenty min-utes each breakout session ended, and people were assigned ran-domly to a different group. The format worked rather well when the conversations drilled down on specific scientific questions, and there were interesting discussions of such topics as protein synthesis techniques and the hardware being built to do automated cell editing. But there was none of the ordinary social chat that enriches real life and nurtures emotional connections. There was no Yankees game in the background nor sunset to share while sitting on the deck. But that was 2020, and most attendees took what they could get.

Cold Spring Harbor Laboratory was founded in 1890 based on a belief in the magic of in-person meetings. The formula is to attract interesting people to a beautiful location and provide them with opportunities to interact. The beauty of nature and the joy that comes from unstructured human engagement is a powerful combination. Even when they don't interact—such as when an awed young Jennifer Doudna had passed the aging icon Barbara McClintock on a path through the Cold Spring Harbor campus in 1987—people benefit from an atmosphere that is charged in a way that sparks creativity.

One of the transformations brought by the coronavirus pandemic is that more meetings in the future will be done virtually. This may open conferences to more people who might not be able to travel, but it's also a shame. New ideas are born out of chance encounters. In-person interactions are especially important in the initial brainstorming of new ideas and the forging of personal bonds. As Aristotle taught, we are a social animal, an instinct that cannot fully be satisfied online.

Nevertheless, the upside is the fact that the coronavirus has expanded how we work together and share ideas. By ushering in the Age of Zoom, the pandemic will broaden the horizons of scientific collaboration, allowing it to be even more global and crowdsourced. A walk along the cobblestone streets of Old San Juan was the catalyst for the collaboration between Doudna and Charpentier, but the technology of Skype and Dropbox allowed them and their two researchers to work together for six months in three countries to decipher CRISPR-Cas9. Because people have now become comfortable meeting in boxes on a computer screen, teamwork will be more efficient. Ideally a balance will be struck—the reward for efficient virtual meetings will be the chance to hang out together in person in places like the campus of Cold Spring Harbor.

At the end of Doudna's scientific presentation at the 2020 conference, a young researcher asked a personal question:

"What inspired you to work on CRISPR-Cas9 the very first time?"

Doudna paused for a moment, since it was not the type of question that scientific researchers usually ask after a technical presentation.

"It started as a wonderful collaboration with Emmanuelle Charpentier," she replied. "I am forever indebted to her for the work we did together."

It was an interesting answer, because a few days earlier in an interview Doudna had expressed her sorrow that she and Charpentier had drifted apart, personally as well as scientifically. Doudna had studied French in high school and college, and even at one point had considered switching her major from chemistry to French. She had always had a fantasy of herself as a French girl, and in some ways Charpentier reminded her of that.

Doudna had invited Charpentier to speak at the Cold Spring Harbor virtual conference and had asked her to give the tribute to Rosalind Franklin or speak on any other topic. Charpentier had hesitated at first, then replied that she had another meeting to attend remotely during that period. Doudna then offered to be flexible about the time and date, but Charpentier still declined.

Fortunately, Charpentier and Doudna were able to meet by Zoom for a private chat the day after the conference ended. As soon as they saw each other, they began talking and catching up, at first in the slightly awkward manner of people who have not seen each other for a while, and then, after a few minutes, more animatedly. Doudna began referring to Charpentier by her nickname, Manue, and soon they were both laughing.

Doudna talked about how tall her teenage son, Andy, had grown, shared a picture that Martin Jinek had sent of his new baby, and joked about an awards event she and Charpentier had done with the American Cancer Society in 2018, at which Joe Biden had told them that he did not plan to run for president. Doudna congratulated Charpentier on the success of her CRISPR Therapeutics company in curing sickle cell anemia in its Nashville trial.

"We published our paper in 2012, and here we are in 2020 and someone has already been cured of a disease," Doudna said.

Charpentier nodded and laughed. "We can be very happy at how fast things happened," she said.

The talk gradually turned more personal. Charpentier recalled the beginning of their collaboration, when they'd had lunch at the conference in Puerto Rico, walked the cobblestone streets together, and ended up in a bar for a drink. Many times when you meet another scientist, she said, you know that you could never work with them. But their meeting was the opposite.

"I knew we would be good collaborators," she told Doudna.

Then they swapped memories about working around the clock by Skype and Dropbox in their six-month race to decode CRISPR-Cas9. Charpentier confessed that she worried whenever she sent Doudna some writing for the paper they produced jointly.

"I thought you would have to correct my English," she said.

Doudna replied, "Your English is great, and I remember you had to correct some of my own mistakes. It was a lot of fun to write that paper together, because we have different ways of thinking about things."

Charpentier was eager to explain what had happened between them.

"We were on the road a lot because of the prize ceremonies and other things," she said. "People were overloading our schedule, and we did not have any time to enjoy the in-between. So part of the problem was the simple fact that we both became terribly busy."

She spoke fondly of the week they had spent together in Berkeley in June 2012 when they were finishing their paper.

"There is this picture of us, with me with a funny haircut, in front of your institute," Charpentier said. It was the last time they had been relaxed together, Charpentier continued. "After that, it was crazy because of the impact our paper had. We had little time for ourselves."

Charpentier's words made Doudna smile, and she opened up even more.

"I enjoyed our friendship as much as doing the science," she said. "I love your delightful manner. I always had this fantasy, ever since I studied French in school, of living in Paris. And, Manue, you embodied that for me."

The conversation ended with talk about working together again someday. Charpentier said she had a fellowship to do research in the United States. Doudna had previously made plans, which COVID ruined, to spend the spring 2021 semester on sabbatical at Columbia. They agreed that they should coordinate sabbaticals.

"Maybe in the spring of 2022 in New York," Doudna suggested.

"I would very much like that, to be there with you," Charpentier replied. "We could collaborate again."

CHAPTER FORTY

The Nobel Prize

———— ◦◦◦◦ ————

Doudna was sound asleep at 2:53 a.m. on October 9, 2020, when she was awakened by the persistent buzz of her cell phone. She was alone in a hotel room in Palo Alto, California, where she had traveled to be part of a small meeting on the biology of aging, the first such in-person event she had attended in the seven months since the onset of the coronavirus crisis. The call was from a reporter for *Nature*.

"I hate to bother you so early," she said, "but I wanted your comment on the Nobel."

"Who won?" Doudna asked, sounding slightly irritated.

"You mean you haven't heard?!" the reporter asked. "You and Emmanuelle Charpentier!"

Doudna looked at her phone and saw a bunch of missed calls. After pausing for a moment to absorb the news, she said excitedly, "Let me call you back."[1]

The awarding of the 2020 Nobel Prize in Chemistry to Doudna and Charpentier was not a complete surprise, but the recognition came with historic swiftness. Their CRISPR discovery was merely eight years old. The day before, Sir Roger Penrose had shared the Nobel in physics for a discovery about black holes he had made more than fifty years earlier. There was also a sense that this chemistry award was historic. More than just recognizing an important achievement, it seemed to herald the start of a new era.

"This year's prize is about rewriting the code of life," the secretary-general of the Royal Swedish Academy of Sciences proclaimed in making the announcement. And in the Nobel Prize press release the Academy added, "These genetic scissors have taken the life sciences into a new epoch."

Also noteworthy was that the prize went only to two people, rather than the usual three. Given the ongoing patent dispute over who first discovered CRISPR as a gene-editing tool, the third slot could have gone to Feng Zhang, although that would have left out George Church, who published similar findings at the same time. In addition, there were many other worthy candidates.

There was also the historic significance of the prize going to two women. One could sense a smile on the face of Rosalind Franklin's ghost. Although Franklin had made the images that had helped James Watson and Francis Crick discover the structure of DNA, as discussed in chapters one and two, she became just a minor character in the early history of genetics, and she died before they got their 1962 Nobel Prize. Even if she had lived, it is unlikely she would have displaced Maurice Wilkins as that year's third honoree. Until 2020, only five women, beginning with Marie Curie in 1911, had won a Nobel for chemistry, out of 184 honorees.

When Doudna called a Stockholm number that had been left on her voicemail, she got an answering machine. But after a few minutes she was able to connect and officially receive the news. After taking a few more calls, including from Martin Jinek and the persistent reporter from *Nature*, she threw her clothes into her bag and jumped into her car for the hourlong drive back to Berkeley. On the way she talked to Jamie, who said that a communications team from the university was already setting up on their patio. When she arrived home at four thirty a.m., she texted her neighbors to apologize for the commotion and camera lights.

For a few minutes she got a chance to celebrate the news over coffee with Jamie and Andy. Then she made a few remarks to the camera team on her patio before heading to Berkeley for a hastily assembled virtual global press conference. On the ride over she spoke to her colleague Jillian Banfield, who in 2006 had called her out of the blue and asked to meet at the Free Speech Movement Café on campus to discuss some clustered repeated sequences that she kept finding in the DNA of bacteria.

"I am so grateful to have you as a collaborator and friend," she told Banfield. "It's been so much fun."

Many of the questions at the press conference focused on how the awards represented a breakthrough for women.

"I'm proud of my gender!" Doudna said with a big laugh. "It's great, especially for younger women. For many women there's a feeling that, whatever they do, their work may not be as recognized as it might be if they were a man. I would like to see that change, and this is a step in the right direction."

Later she reflected on her days as a schoolgirl. "I was told more than a few times that girls don't do chemistry or girls don't do science. Fortunately, I ignored that."

As Doudna spoke, Charpentier was holding her own press conference in Berlin, where it was midafternoon. Carrying a glass of white wine, she came into the lobby of her institute, posed for photos, and then answered questions in a way that managed to be both lighthearted and earnest.

"I had been told that this might someday come," she'd said in an earlier interview, "but when I received the call, I became very moved, very emotional."

It took her back, she said, to her early childhood and deciding, while walking past the Pasteur Institute in her native Paris, that she someday would be a scientist. At her press conference, as had happened in Berkeley, the reporters turned their focus to what the award meant for women.

"The fact that Jennifer and I were awarded this prize today can provide a very strong message for young girls," she said. "It can show them that women can also be awarded prizes."

Doudna mentioned at her press conference that she was "waving across the ocean" at Charpentier. But she badly wanted to actually talk to her. She texted Charpentier repeatedly throughout the day and left messages on her cell three times.

"Please, please call me," Doudna texted at one point. "I won't take much of your time. I just want to say congratulations on the phone to you."

Charpentier finally responded with a text: "I'm really, really exhausted, but I promise I'll call you tomorrow."

She was true to her word, and the next morning they finally connected for a relaxed and rambling chat.

After her press conference, Doudna went to her lab building for a champagne celebration, followed by a Zoom party where she was toasted by a hundred or so friends. Mark Zuckerberg and Priscilla Chan, whose foundation was funding some of Doudna's work, made a virtual appearance, as did Jillian Banfield and various Berkeley deans and officials. The nicest toast came from Jack Szostak, the Harvard professor who had turned her on to the wonders of RNA back when she'd been a graduate student. Szostak, who had won a Nobel in medicine in 2009 (jointly with two women named Elizabeth H. Blackburn and Carol W. Greider), raised a glass of champagne while sitting in the backyard of his stately brick Boston town house.

"The only thing better than winning a Nobel Prize," he said, "is having one of your students win one."

Doudna and Jamie cooked Spanish omelets for dinner, and then Doudna joined her two sisters on a FaceTime call. They talked about how their late parents would have reacted.

"I really wish they could have been around," Doudna said. "Mom would have been so emotional, and Dad would have pretended not to be. Instead he would have made sure he understood the science, then asked me what I planned to do next."

CHAPTER FORTY-ONE

The Next Scientific Horizon

———— ✺ ————

By honoring a discovery about CRISPR—a virus-fighting system found in nature—in the midst of a virus pandemic, the Nobel committee reminded us how curiosity-driven basic research can end up having very practical applications. CRISPR and COVID are speeding our entry into a life-science era. Molecules are becoming the new microchips.

At the height of the COVID crisis, Doudna was asked to write a piece for *The Economist* on the social transformations happening all around her.

"Like many other aspects of life these days, science and its practice seem to be undergoing rapid and perhaps permanent changes," she wrote. "This will be for the better."[1]

The public, she predicted, will have a greater understanding of biology and the scientific method. Elected officials will better appreciate the value of funding basic science. And there will be enduring changes in how scientists collaborate, compete, and communicate.

Before the pandemic, communication and collaboration between academic researchers had become limited. Universities have created large legal teams dedicated to staking a claim to each new discovery, no matter how small, and guarding against any sharing of information that might jeopardize a patent application.

"They've turned every interaction scientists have with each other into an intellectual property transaction," says Berkeley biologist Michael Eisen. "Everything I get from or send to a colleague at another academic institution involves a complex legal agreement whose purpose is not to promote science but to protect the university's ability to profit from hypothetical inventions that might arise from scientists doing what we're supposed to do—share our work with each other."[2]

The race to beat COVID was not run by those rules. Instead, led by Doudna and Zhang, most academic labs declared that their discoveries would be made available to anyone fighting the virus. This allowed greater collaboration between researchers and even between countries. The consortium that Doudna put together of labs in the Bay Area could not have come about so quickly if they'd had to worry about intellectual property arrangements. Likewise, scientists around the world contributed to an open database of coronavirus sequences that, by the end of August 2020, had thirty-six thousand entries.[3]

The sense of urgency about COVID also neutralized the gatekeeper role played by scholarly journals such as *Science* and *Nature*. Instead of waiting months for the editors and reviewers at these journals to decide whether a paper should be published, researchers at the height of the COVID crisis were posting more than a hundred papers a day to online preprint servers, such as medRxiv and bioRxiv, that are free and open and require a minimal review process. This allowed information to be shared in real time, freely, and even to be dissected on social media. Despite the potential danger of spreading research that had not been fully vetted, the rapid and open distribution of research worked well. It sped up the process of building on each new finding and allowed the public to follow the advance of science as it happened. On some important papers involving SARS-CoV-2, publication on the preprint servers led to crowdsourced vetting and wisdom from experts around the world.[4]

Like his former researcher Feng Zhang, George Church says he had long wondered whether there would ever be a biological event that was explosive enough to bring science into our daily lives.

"COVID is it," he says.

Most of us someday will have detection devices in our homes that will allow us to check ourselves for viruses and many other health conditions. We will also have clothes or glasses or wristbands that can monitor all our biological functions, and they will be networked so that they can share information and create a global bio-weather map showing in real time the spread of biological threats. All of this has made biology an even more exciting field of study. The proof is in the data: in August 2020, applications to medical school had jumped 17 percent from the previous year.

The academic world will also change, and not just by the rise of more online classes. Instead of being closed-off and elite institutions, universities will be engaged in tackling real-world problems, from pandemics to climate change. These projects will be cross-disciplinary, breaking down the walls between labs, which have traditionally been independent kingdoms that fiercely guard their right to privacy. Fighting the coronavirus required collaboration across disciplines. In that way, it resembled the effort to develop CRISPR, which involved microbe-hunters working with geneticists, structural biologists, biochemists, and computer geeks. Fighting SARS-CoV-2 also resembled the way things operate in innovative businesses, where units work together to pursue a specific project or mission. The nature of the scientific threats we face will accelerate this trend toward project-oriented collaborations among widely different kinds of labs.

One fundamental aspect of science, though, will remain the same. It has always been a collaboration across generations, from Darwin and Mendel to Watson and Crick to Doudna and Charpentier.

"At the end of the day, the discoveries are what endure," Charpentier says. "We are just passing on this planet for a short time. We do our job, and then we leave and others pick up the work."[5]

All the scientists in this book say that their main motivation is not money, or even glory, but the chance to unlock the mysteries of nature and use those discoveries to make the world a better place. That may be one of the most important legacies of the pandemic: reminding scientists of the nobility of their mission. So, too, might our experience with COVID imprint these values on a new generation of students—like you!—who, as they dream about their careers, may be more likely to pursue scientific research now that they have seen how exciting and important it can be.

Epilogue

━━━⬥⬥⬥━━━

The Great Pandemic is starting to recede, and the earth is beginning to heal. In New Orleans you can hear music on the street and smell shrimp being boiled in the corner restaurant, and in New York City the lights of Broadway have been turned back on.

But more viral waves are likely to come, either from the current coronavirus or novel ones in the future, so we require more than just one-off vaccines. Like bacteria, humanity needs a system that can be easily adapted to fend off each new virus. CRISPR could provide that to us, as it does for bacteria. It could also someday be used to fix genetic problems, defeat cancers, enhance our children, and allow us to hack evolution so that we can steer the future of the human race in a positive direction.

In the past, people became fascinated by personal computers and the web. We made sure kids learned how to code. Now we will have to make sure future generations understand the code of life. One way to do that is for all of us to realize, as the interwoven tales of CRISPR and COVID show, how useful it is to understand the way life works. It's good that some people have strong opinions about gene engineering in humans, but it's even better if you know what a gene actually is.

Fathoming the wonders of life is more than merely useful. It is also inspiring and joyful. That is why we humans are lucky that we are endowed with curiosity.

When you see something like a baby lizard crawling around the side of a building and onto a vine, changing color slightly, think about it. What *causes* the skin to change color? Curiosity is the key trait of the people who blazed the biggest trails in the world, from Benjamin Franklin and Albert Einstein to Steve Jobs and Leonardo da Vinci. Curiosity drove James Watson and Francis Crick to understand the structure of DNA; and the Spanish graduate student Francisco Mojica, who was intrigued by clustered repeated sequences of DNA; and Jennifer Doudna, who wanted to understand what made the sleeping grass curl up when she touched it. And maybe that instinct—curiosity, pure curiosity—is what will save us.

Humanity is so diverse. For example, people may be short or tall, gay or straight or trans, fat or skinny, white or black or brown. They use sign language and speak in different languages. The supposed promise of CRISPR is that we may someday be able to pick which of these traits we want in our children and in all our descendants. We could choose for them to be red-haired or muscular or brown-eyed or not deaf or—well, pick your preferences. After more than three billion years of evolution of life on this planet, one species (ours) has developed the talent to grab control of its own genetic future. There is a sense that we have crossed the threshold into a whole new age.

Our newfound ability to make edits to our genes raises some fascinating questions. Should we edit our species to make us less susceptible to deadly viruses? What a wonderful benefit that would be! Right? Should we use gene editing to eliminate dreaded disorders, such as Huntington's, sickle cell anemia, and cystic fibrosis? That sounds good too. And what about deafness or blindness? Or being short? Or depressed? Hmmm. . . . How should we think about that?

A few decades from now, if it becomes possible and safe, should we allow parents to enhance the IQ and muscles of their kids? Should we let them decide eye color? Skin color? Height?

Whoa! Let's pause for a moment before we slide all the way down this slippery slope. What might that do to the diversity of our societies? If we are no longer subject to a random natural lottery when it comes to our endowments, will it weaken our feelings of empathy and acceptance? If these offerings at the genetic supermarket aren't free (and they won't be), will that greatly increase inequality—and indeed encode it permanently into the human race? Given these issues, should such decisions be left solely to individuals, or should society as a whole have some say? Perhaps we should develop some rules.

By "we" I mean *we*. All of us, including you and me. Figuring out if and when to edit our genes will be one of the most consequential questions of the twenty-first century.

The promise of CRISPR might be its peril. It took nature millions of years to weave together three billion base pairs of DNA in a complex and occasionally imperfect way to permit all the wondrous diversity within our species. Are we right to think we can now come along and edit that genome to eliminate what we see as imperfections? Will we lose our diversity? Our humility and empathy?

This doesn't have to be the case. If we are wise in how we use it, biotechnology can make us more able to fend off viruses, overcome genetic defects, and protect our bodies and minds. All creatures large and small use whatever tricks they can to survive, and so should we. It's natural. Bacteria came up with a pretty clever virus-fighting technique, but it took them trillions of life cycles to do so. We can't wait that long. We will have to combine our curiosity with our inventiveness to speed up the process.

After millions of centuries during which the evolution of organisms happened "naturally," we humans now have the ability to hack the code of life. Or, to confuse those who would label gene editing as "unnatural" and "playing God," let's put it another way: nature and nature's God, in their infinite wisdom, have evolved a species that is able to modify its own genome, and that species happens to be ours.

Like any other evolutionary trait, this new ability may help the species thrive and perhaps even produce successor species. Or it may not. It could be one of those evolutionary traits that, as sometimes happens, leads a species down a path that endangers its survival. Evolution can be fickle.

That's why change works best as a slow process. We may be tempted to move quickly, but if we are wise, we can pause and decide to proceed with more caution. Slopes are less slippery that way.

To guide us, we will need not only scientists but people who think long and hard about the human condition and our place on this earth. And most important, we will need people who feel comfortable in both worlds, like Jennifer Doudna. This is why it is useful for all of us to try to understand this new room that we are about to enter, one that seems mysterious but is rich with hope.

Not everything needs to be decided right away. We can begin by asking what type of world we want to leave for future generations. Then we can feel our way together, step by step, preferably hand in hand.

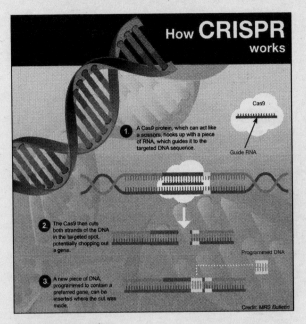

How CRISPR works
(*MRS Bulletin*)

Darwin
(George Richmond/Wikimedia/Public Domain)

Mendel
(Wikimedia/Public Domain)

Watson and Crick with their DNA model, 1953
(A. Barrington Brown/Science Photo Library)

Rosalind Franklin
(Universal History Archive/Universal Images Group/
Getty Images)

Jack Szostak
(Jim Harrison)

Francisco Mojica
(Courtesy of BBVA Foundation)

Luciano Marraffini
(Wikimedia Commons)

Jillian Banfield
(The Royal Society / CC BY-SA (https://
creativecommons.org/licenses/by-sa/3.0))

Rodolphe Barrangou
(Marc Hall/NC State courtesy of Rodolphe Barrangou)

Herbert Boyer and Robert A. Swanson
(Courtesy of Genetech)

Philippe Horvath
(Franklin Institute /YouTube)

Rachel Haurwitz
(Courtesy of Caribou Biosciences)

Emmanuelle Charpentier, Jennifer Doudna, Martin Jinek,
and Krzysztof Chylinski at Berkeley in 2012
(Berkeley Lab)

George Church
(Seth Kroll / Wyss Institute at Harvard University)

Eric Lander
(Casey Atkins, courtesy Broad Institute)

He Jiankui taking a selfie with Doudna at Cold Spring Harbor Laboratory
(Courtesy He Jiankui)

Feng Zhang and Patrick Hsu
(Justin Knight/McGovern Institute)

Stanley Qi
(Paul Sakuma)

GLOSSARY

Attenuated viruses: A safe, weakened version of a virus, often used in a vaccine to stimulate the immune system without making a subject sick.

Aerodynamics: The science of how objects move through air.

Adenine: Abbreviated "A," one of the four chemical bases that is a building block of both RNA and DNA.

Bacteriophage: A virus that attacks bacteria and archaea.

Base: A biological compound, including adenine (A), cytosine (C), guanine (G), and thymine (T), which bonds to another base to help form the structure of RNA and DNA.

Biohacking: Biological experimentation done to improve the qualities or abilities of living things, especially by individuals and groups working outside the traditional medical or scientific communities.

Clone: An exact copy, or to make an exact copy.

Coronavirus: A type of virus characterized by its studded, circular shape. Coronaviruses infect humans and may lead to upper respiratory infections.

CRISPR: Short for "clustered regularly interspaced short palindromic repeats," this is a method of editing genes in which a piece of RNA with a short "guide" sequence binds to a specific sequence of DNA.

CRISPR RNA: Short segments of RNA that can guide a scissors-like enzyme to a virus and cut up its genetic material.

Crystallographer: A scientist who studies the arrangement of atoms in solids.

Cytoplasm: The thick fluid inside cells, encased by the cell membrane, in which all cellular replication, growth, and metabolism take place.

Cytosine: Abbreviated "C," one of the four chemical bases that is a building block of both RNA and DNA.

DNA: Short for "deoxyribonucleic acid," this is the molecule inside every organism that carries its genetic instructions for growth and development.

Dominant traits: The physical manifestation of the dominant allele (or version of a gene) masking the recessive allele in the genome.

Electrophoresis: A laboratory technique used to separate DNA, RNA, or protein molecules using an electric charge.

Electroporation: A process in which an electrical field is applied to a cell in order to introduce a molecule into that cell.

Encephalitis: Inflammation of the tissues of the brain.

Enzymes: Proteins that regulate chemical reactions in an organism.

Fibrous proteins: Complex molecules that help form biological structures such as bones, muscles, hair, fingernails, tendons, and skin.

Gene: A unit of heredity located on a chromosome.

Genome: An organism's full set of genetic information.

Germline editing: The process of modifying an organism's genome within the reproductive (germ) cells, so that the change can be inherited, or passed through the germline.

Guanine: Abbreviated "G," one of the four chemical bases that is a building block of both RNA and DNA.

IVF: Short for in vitro fertilization, a process in which eggs are taken from a woman's body and combined in a lab with sperm. After fertilization occurs, the embryos are placed back into the woman's body, and if one or more implants in the woman's uterus, she becomes pregnant.

Lipitoids: Synthetic (man-made) molecules that can help deliver genetic material into cells in a lab.

Membrane proteins: Complex molecules that help relay signals within cells or to nearby cells.

Meningitis: An inflammation of the brain and spinal cord membranes caused by an infection.

Naturalist: A person who studies the natural world.

Natural selection: First described by Charles Darwin, this is the process in which organisms who have adapted better to their environment survive and pass on their traits to successive generations.

Nucleic acids: Large molecules comprised of a chain of nucleotides that store an organism's genetic information.

Nucleotides: Molecules that help form the structure of DNA and RNA, they are made up of a base (adenine, thymine, guanine, and cytosine) plus a molecule of sugar and a molecule of phosphoric acid.

Polymerase chain reaction: A laboratory method to rapidly make many copies of DNA.

Preimplantation genetic diagnosis: A screening test conducted on embryos conceived via in vitro fertilization in order to determine genetic characteristics or abnormalities.

Recessive traits: The physical manifestation of the recessive allele (or version of a gene) expressing itself in the absence of the dominant allele in the genome.

Recombinant DNA technology: A process that involves cutting pieces of DNA from two different organisms and joining them together to create new genetic combinations.

Reverse transcription: A cellular process in which an enzyme makes a copy of DNA from RNA.

Ribonucleotide: A nucleotide that contains a type of sugar called ribose.

Ribozymes: An RNA enzyme that catalyzes a chemical reaction.

RNA: Short for "ribonucleic acid," molecule in living cells that is similar to DNA, but each nucleotide has one more oxygen atom in the sugar-phosphate backbone, and one of RNA's four bases is different.

RNA interference: A biological process where small pieces of RNA can silence protein translation.

Sequence: The chain-like order of the nucleotides in DNA.

Single-guide RNA: A type of nucleic acid sequence used in gene editing to cut a specific target on DNA or RNA.

Somatic cells: Cells that make up the tissues, organs, and other parts of a living thing.

Structural biology: The study of the molecular structure of a living being.

Thermodynamics: The science that deals with the relations between heat and other forms of energy.

Thymine: Abbreviated "T," one of the four chemical bases that is a building block of both RNA and DNA.

Trans-activating CRISPR RNA: Abbreviated "tracrRNA," these are small snippets of RNA that facilitate the making of CRISPR RNA, the sequence of nucleotides that carries the memory of an invading virus.

Transposons: Repetitive DNA sequences that can change their position within a genome.

ACKNOWLEDGMENTS

I want to thank Jennifer Doudna for her willingness to put up with me. She sat for dozens of interviews, answered my incessant phone calls and emails, allowed me to spend time in her lab, gave me access to a wide variety of meetings, and even let me lurk in her Slack channels. And her husband, Jamie Cate, he put up with me as well, and he also helped.

Feng Zhang was notably gracious. Although the book focuses on his competitor, he cheerfully hosted me in his lab and gave me multiple interviews. One of the joys in reporting this book was getting to spend time in Berlin with Emmanuelle Charpentier, who was *charmante*. Although I'm not sure what that means, I know it when I see it, which I hope comes through in these pages. I likewise got a kick out of hanging around George Church, who is a charming (*charmant?*) gentleman disguised as a mad scientist.

Kevin Doxzen of the Innovative Genomics Institute and Spencer Olesky of Tulane were the scientific vetters of this book. They provided very smart comments and corrections. Max Wendell, Benjamin Bernstein, and Ryan Braun of Tulane also chipped in. All of them were wonderful, but please don't blame them for any mistakes that crept in.

I am also grateful to all of the scientists and their fans who spent time with me, provided insights, gave interviews, and checked facts: Richard Axel, David Baltimore, Jillian Banfield, Cori Bargmann, Rodolphe Barrangou, Joe Bondy-Denomy, Dana Carroll, Janice Chen, Francis Collins, Kevin Davies, Sarah Doudna, Kevin Doxzen, Victor Dzau, Eldora Ellison, Sarah Goodwin, Margaret Hamburg, Jennifer Hamilton, Lucas Harrington, Rachel

Haurwitz, Don Hemmes, Megan Hochstrasser, Patrick Hsu, Maria Jasin, Martin Jinek, Elliot Kirschner, Gavin Knott, Eric Lander, Le Cong, Enrique Lin Shiao, Richard Lipton, David Liu, Luciano Marraffini, Alex Marson, Andy May, Sylvain Moineau, Francisco Mojica, Cameron Myhrvold, Rodger Novak, Val Pakaluk, Duanqing Pei, Matthew Porteus, Stanley Qi, Antonio Regalado, Matt Ridley, Meredith Salazar, Dave Savage, Jacob Sherkow, Virginijus Šikšnys, Erik Sontheimer, Sam Sternberg, Jack Szostak, Fyodor Urnov, Elizabeth Watson, James Watson, Jonathan Weissman, Blake Wiedenheft, Ross Wilson, and Josiah Zayner.

As always, I owe deep thanks to Amanda Urban, my agent for forty years now. She manages to be caring and intellectually honest at the same time, which is very bracing. Priscilla Painton and I worked together at *Time* when we were in our salad days and were neighbors when our kids were in their pre-salad ones. Suddenly, she is now my editor. It's sweet the way the world turns. She did a diligent and smart job both restructuring this book at one point and polishing it line by line.

Science is a collaborative effort. So is producing a book. The joy of being with Simon & Schuster is that I get to work with a great team led by the irrepressible and insightful Jonathan Karp, who seemed to read this manuscript many times and kept suggesting improvements. They include Stephen Bedford, Dana Canedy, Jonathan Evans, Marie Florio, Kimberly Goldstein, Judith Hoover, Ruth Lee-Mui, Hana Park, Julia Prosser, Richard Rhorer, Elise Ringo, and Jackie Seow. Helen Manders and Peppa Mignone at Curtis Brown did a wonderful job working with international publishers. I also want to thank Lindsey Billups, my assistant, who is smart and wise and very sensible. Her help every day was invaluable.

My greatest thanks as always go to my wife, Cathy, who helped with the research, carefully read my drafts, provided sage counsel, and kept me on an even keel (or tried). Our daughter, Betsy, also read the manuscript and made smart suggestions. They are the foundations of my life.

This book was launched by Alice Mayhew, who was the editor of all of my previous books. In our first discussions, I was amazed at how well she knew the science. She was relentless in insisting that I make this book a journey of discovery. She had edited the classic of the genre, Horace Freeland Judson's *The Eighth Day of Creation*, back in 1979, and forty years later she seemed to remember every passage in it. Over the 2019 Christmas holidays, she read the first half of this book and came back with a torrent of joyful comments and insights. But she didn't live to see it finished. Nor did dear Carolyn Reidy, the CEO of Simon & Schuster, who had always been a mentor, guide, and joy to know. One of life's great pleasures was to make Alice and Carolyn smile. If you'd ever seen their smiles, you'd understand. I hope this book would have. I've dedicated it to their memory.

NOTES

Introduction

1. Rob Stein, "In a First, Doctors in U.S. Use CRISPR Tool to Treat Patient with Genetic Disorder," *Morning Edition*, NPR, July 29, 2019; Rob Stein, "A Young Mississippi Woman's Journey through a Pioneering Gene-Editing Experiment," *All Things Considered*, NPR, Dec. 25, 2019.
2. "CRISPR Therapeutics and Vertex Announce New Clinical Data," CRISPR Therapeutics, June 12, 2020.
3. Rob Stein, "A Year In, 1st Patient to Get Gene-Editing for Sickle Cell Disease Is Thriving," *Morning Edition*, NPR, June 23, 2020.
4. See chapter 8 on the yogurt makers for a fuller discussion of the iterative process that can occur between basic researchers and technological innovation.

Chapter One: Hilo

1. Author's interviews with Jennifer Doudna and Sarah Doudna. Other sources for this section include *The Life Scientific*, BBC Radio, Sept. 17, 2017; Andrew Pollack, "Jennifer Doudna, a Pioneer Who Helped Simplify Genome Editing," *New York Times*, May 11, 2015; Claudia Dreifus, "The Joy of the Discovery: An Interview with Jennifer Doudna," *New York Review of Books*, Jan. 24, 2019; Jennifer Doudna interview, National Academy of Sciences, Nov. 11, 2004; Jennifer Doudna, "Why Genome Editing Will Change Our Lives," *Financial Times*, Mar. 14, 2018; Laura Kiessling, "A Conversation with Jennifer Doudna," *ACS Chemical Biology Journal*, Feb. 16, 2018; Melissa Marino, "Biography of Jennifer A. Doudna," *PNAS*, Dec. 7, 2004.
2. Author's interviews with Lisa Twigg-Smith, Jennifer Doudna.

3. Author's interviews with Jennifer Doudna, James Watson.

4. Jennifer Doudna, "How COVID-19 Is Spurring Science to Accelerate," *The Economist*, June 5, 2020.

Chapter Two: Genes and DNA

1. This section on the history of genetics and DNA relies on Siddhartha Mukherjee, *The Gene* (Scribner, 2016); Horace Freeland Judson, *The Eighth Day of Creation* (Touchstone, 1979); Alfred Sturtevant, *A History of Genetics* (Cold Spring Harbor, 2001); Elof Axel Carlson, *Mendel's Legacy* (Cold Spring Harbor, 2004).

2. Janet Browne, *Charles Darwin*, vol. 1 (Knopf, 1995) and vol. 2 (Knopf, 2002); Charles Darwin, *The Journey of the Beagle*, originally published 1839; Darwin, *On the Origin of Species*, originally published 1859. Electronic copies of Darwin's books, letters, writings, and journals can be found at Darwin Online, darwin-online.org.uk.

3. Erwin Chargaff, "Preface to a Grammar of Biology," *Science*, May 14, 1971.

4. This section draws from my multiple interviews with James Watson over a period of years and from his book *The Double Helix*, originally published by Atheneum in 1968. I used *The Annotated and Illustrated Double Helix*, compiled by Alexander Gann and Jan Witkowski (Simon & Schuster, 2012), which includes the letters describing the DNA model and other supplemental material. This section also draws from James Watson, *Avoid Boring People* (Oxford, 2007); Brenda Maddox, *Rosalind Franklin: The Dark Lady of DNA* (HarperCollins, 2002); Judson, *The Eighth Day*; Mukherjee, *The Gene*; Sturtevant, *A History of Genetics*.

5. Rosalind Franklin, "The DNA Riddle: King's College, London, 1951–1953," Rosalind Franklin Papers, NIH National Library of Medicine, https://profiles.nlm.nih.gov/spotlight/kr/feature/dna; Nicholas Wade, "Was She or Wasn't She?," *The Scientist*, Apr.

2003; Judson, *The Eighth Day*, 99; Maddox, *Rosalind Franklin*, 163; Mukherjee, *The Gene*, 149.

Chapter Three: The Education of a Biochemist

1. Author's interviews with Jennifer Doudna.
2. Author's interviews with Jennifer Doudna.
3. Author's interviews with Jennifer Doudna; Jennifer A. Doudna and Samuel H. Sternberg, *A Crack in Creation* (Houghton Mifflin, 2017), 58; Kiessling, "A Conversation with Jennifer Doudna"; Pollack, "Jennifer Doudna."

Chapter Four: RNA

1. Jennifer Doudna, "Hammering Out the Shape of a Ribozyme," *Structure*, Dec. 15, 1994.
2. Jennifer Doudna and Thomas Cech, "The Chemical Repertoire of Natural Ribozymes," *Nature*, July 11, 2002.
3. Jack Szostak, "Enzymatic Activity of the Conserved Core of a Group I Self-Splicing Intron," *Nature*, July 3, 1986.
4. Author's interviews with Richard Lifton, Jennifer Doudna, Jack Szostak; Greengard Prize citation for Jennifer Doudna, Oct. 2, 2018; Jennifer Doudna and Jack Szostak, "RNA-Catalysed Synthesis of Complementary-Strand RNA," *Nature*, June 15, 1989; J. Doudna, S. Couture, and J. Szostak, "A Multisubunit Ribozyme That Is a Catalyst of and Template for Complementary Strand RNA Synthesis," *Science*, Mar. 29, 1991; J. Doudna, N. Usman, and J. Szostak, "Ribozyme-Catalyzed Primer Extension by Trinucleotides," *Biochemistry*, Mar. 2, 1993.
5. Author's interviews with Jack Szostak.
6. Author's interview with James Watson; James Watson et al., "Evolution of Catalytic Function," Cold Spring Harbor Symposium, vol. 52, 1987.

7. Author's interviews with Jennifer Doudna and James Watson; Jennifer Doudna . . . Jack Szostak, et al., "Genetic Dissection of an RNA Enzyme," Cold Spring Harbor Symposium, 1987, p. 173.

Chapter Five: The Twists and Folds of Structural Biology

1. Author's interview with Lisa Twigg-Smith.
2. Jamie Cate . . . Thomas Cech, Jennifer Doudna, et al., "Crystal Structure of a Group I Ribozyme Domain: Principles of RNA Packing," Science, Sept. 20, 1996. For the first major step in the Boulder research, see Jennifer Doudna and Thomas Cech, "Self-Assembly of a Group I Intron Active Site from Its Component Tertiary Structural Domains," RNA, Mar. 1995.

Chapter Six: Going West

1. Cate et al., "Crystal Structure of a Group I Ribozyme Domain."
2. Author's interviews with Jamie Cate, Jennifer Doudna.
3. Author's interviews with Jennifer Doudna, Martin Jinek, Ross Wilson; Ian MacRae, Kaihong Zhou . . . Jennifer Doudna, et al., "Structural Basis for Double-Stranded RNA Processing by Dicer," Science, Jan. 13, 2006; Ian MacRae, Kaihong Zhou, and Jennifer Doudna, "Structural Determinants of RNA Recognition and Cleavage by Dicer," Natural Structural and Molecular Biology, Oct. 1, 2007; Ross Wilson and Jennifer Doudna, "Molecular Mechanisms of RNA Interference," Annual Review of Biophysics, 2013; Martin Jinek and Jennifer Doudna, "A Three-Dimensional View of the Molecular Machinery of RNA Interference," Nature, Jan. 22, 2009.
4. Bryan Cullen, "Viruses and RNA Interference: Issues and Controversies," Journal of Virology, Nov. 2014.
5. Alesia Levanova and Minna Poranen, "RNA Interference as a Prospective Tool for the Control of Human Viral Infections," Frontiers

of Microbiology, Sept. 11, 2018; Ruth Williams, "Fighting Viruses with RNAi," *The Scientist*, Oct. 10, 2013; Yang Li . . . Shou-Wei Ding, et al., "RNA Interference Functions as an Antiviral Immunity Mechanism in Mammals," *Science*, Oct. 11, 2013; Pierre Maillard . . . Olivier Voinnet, et al., "Antiviral RNA Interference in Mammalian Cells," *Science*, Oct. 11, 2013.

Chapter Seven: In the Lab with CRISPR

1. Author's interviews with Francisco Mojica. This section also draws from Kevin Davies, "Crazy about CRISPR: An Interview with Francisco Mojica," *CRISPR Journal*, Feb. 1, 2018; Heidi Ledford, "Five Big Mysteries about CRISPR's Origins," *Nature*, Jan. 12, 2017; Clara Rodríguez Fernández, "Interview with Francis Mojica, the Spanish Scientist Who Discovered CRISPR," *Labiotech*, Apr. 8, 2019; Veronique Greenwood, "The Unbearable Weirdness of CRISPR," *Nautilus*, Mar. 2017; Francisco Mojica and Lluis Montoliu, "On the Origin of CRISPR-Cas Technology," *Trends in Microbiology*, July 8, 2016; Kevin Davies, *Editing Humanity* (Simon & Schuster, 2020).

2. Author's interviews with Francisco Mojica.

3. Sanne Klompe and Samuel Sternberg, "Harnessing a Billion Years of Experimentation,'" *CRISPR Journal*, Apr. 1, 2018; Eric Keen, "A Century of Phage Research," *Bioessays*, Jan. 2015; Graham Hatfull and Roger Hendrix, "Bacteriophages and Their Genomes," *Current Opinions in Virology*, Oct. 1, 2011.

4. Rodríguez Fernández, "Interview with Francis Mojica"; Greenwood, "The Unbearable Weirdness of CRISPR."

5. Kira Makarova . . . Eugene Koonin, et al., "A Putative RNA-Interference-Based Immune System in Prokaryotes," *Biology Direct*, Mar. 16, 2006

6. Author's interviews with Jillian Banfield and Jennifer Doudna;

Doudna and Sternberg, *A Crack in Creation*, 39; "Deep Surface Biospheres," Banfield Lab page, Berkeley University website.

7. Author's interview with Martin Jinek.

8. Blake Wiedenheft et al., "Structural Basis for DNase Activity of a Conserved Protein Implicated in CRISPR-Mediated Genome Defense," *Structure*, June 10, 2009.

Chapter Eight: The Yogurt Makers

1. Author's interviews with Rodolphe Barrangou.

2. Rodolphe Barrangou and Philippe Horvath, "A Decade of Discovery: CRISPR Functions and Applications," *Nature Microbiology*, June 5, 2017; Prashant Nair, "Interview with Rodolphe Barrangou," *Proceedings of the National Academy of Sciences*, July 11, 2017; author's interviews with Rodolphe Barrangou.

3. Rodolphe Barrangou . . . Sylvain Moineau . . . Philippe Horvath, et al., "CRISPR Provides Acquired Resistance against Viruses in Prokaryotes," *Science*, Mar. 23, 2007 (submitted Nov. 29, 2006; accepted Feb. 16, 2007).

4. Author's interviews with Sylvain Moineau, Jillian Banfield, and Rodolphe Barrangou. Conference agendas 2008–2012 provided by Banfield.

5. Author's interview with Luciano Marraffini.

Chapter Nine: Restless

1. Eugene Russo, "The Birth of Biotechnology," *Nature*, Jan. 23, 2003; Mukherjee, *The Gene*, 230.

2. Mukherjee, *The Gene*, 238.

3. Author's interview with Jennifer Doudna

Chapter Ten: Building a Lab of People

1. Author's interviews with Sam Sternberg, Jennifer Doudna.

2. Samuel Sternberg and Jennifer Doudna, "DNA Interrogation by the CRISPR RNA-Guided Endonuclease Cas9," *Nature*, Jan. 29, 2014; Sy Redding, Samuel Sternberg . . . Blake Wiedenheft, Jennifer Doudna, Eric Greene, et al., "Surveillance and Processing of Foreign DNA by the *Escherichia coli* CRISPR-Cas System," *Cell*, Nov. 5, 2015.

3. Blake Wiedenheft, Samuel H. Sternberg, and Jennifer A. Doudna, "RNA-Guided Genetic Silencing Systems in Bacteria and Archaea," *Nature*, Feb. 14, 2012.

4. "How Scientists Present the Importance of Their Research," *BMJ*, Dec. 19, 2019; Olga Khazan, "Carry Yourself with the Confidence of a Male Scientist," *Atlantic*, Dec. 17, 2019.

5. Author's interviews with Blake Wiedenheft, Jennifer Doudna; Blake Wiedenheft, Gabriel C. Lander, Kaihong Zhou, Matthijs M. Jore, Stan J. J. Brouns, John van der Oost, Jennifer A. Doudna, and Eva Nogales, "Structures of the RNA-Guided Surveillance Complex from a Bacterial Immune System," *Nature*, Sept. 21, 2011 (received May 7, 2011; accepted July 27, 2011).

Chapter Eleven: Starting a Company

1. Author's interviews with Rachel Haurwitz, Jennifer Doudna.

2. "Kit for Global RNP Profiling," NIH award 1R43GM105087-01, for Rachel Haurwitz and Caribou Biosciences, Apr. 15, 2013.

3. Author's interviews with Jennifer Doudna, Rachel Haurwitz; Robert Sanders, "Gates Foundation Awards $100,000 Grants for Novel Global Health Research," *Berkeley News*, May 10, 2010.

Chapter Twelve: Making Connections around the World

1. Author's interviews with Emmanuelle Charpentier. This chapter also draws from Uta Deffke, "An Artist in Gene Editing," *Max Planck Research Magazine*, Jan. 2016; "Interview with Emmanuelle Charpentier," *FEMS Microbiology Letters*, Feb. 1, 2018; Alison

Abbott, "A CRISPR Vision," *Nature*, Apr. 28, 2016; Kevin Davies, "Finding Her Niche: An Interview with Emmanuelle Charpentier," *CRISPR Journal*, Feb. 21, 2019; Margaret Knox, "The Gene Genie," *Scientific American*, Dec. 2014; Jennifer Doudna, "Why Genome Editing Will Change Our Lives," *Financial Times*, Mar. 24, 2018; Martin Jinek, Krzysztof Chylinski, Ines Fonfara, Michael Hauer, Jennifer Doudna, and Emmanuelle Charpentier, "A Programmable Dual-RNA–Guided DNA Endonuclease in Adaptive Bacterial Immunity," *Science*, Aug. 17, 2012.

2. Author's interview with Emmanuelle Charpentier.

3. Author's interview with Emmanuelle Charpentier.

4. Elitza Deltcheva, Krzysztof Chylinski…Emmanuelle Charpentier, et al., "CRISPR RNA Maturation by Trans-encoded Small RNA and Host Factor RNase III," *Nature*, Mar. 31, 2011.

5. Author's interviews with Emmanuelle Charpentier, Jennifer Doudna, Erik Sontheimer; Doudna and Sternberg, *A Crack in Creation*, 71–73.

6. Author's interviews with Martin Jinek, Jennifer Doudna. See also Kevin Davies, interview with Martin Jinek, *CRISPR Journal*, Apr. 2020.

Chapter Thirteen: Success through Teamwork

1. Richard Asher, "An Interview with Krzysztof Chylinski," *Pioneers Zero21*, Oct. 2018.

2. Author's interviews with Jennifer Doudna, Emmanuelle Charpentier, Martin Jinek, Ross Wilson.

3. Author's interviews with Jennifer Doudna, Martin Jinek.

Chapter Fourteen: Dueling Papers and Presentations

1. Author's interviews with Jennifer Doudna, Emmanuelle Charpentier, and Martin Jinek.

2. Jinek et al., "A Programmable Dual-RNA–Guided DNA Endonuclease in Adaptive Bacterial Immunity."

3. Giedrius Gasiunas, Rodolphe Barrangou, Philippe Horvath, and Virginijus Šikšnys, "Cas9–crRNA Ribonucleoprotein Complex Mediates Specific DNA Cleavage for Adaptive Immunity in Bacteria," *PNAS*, Sept. 25, 2012 (received May 21, 2012; approved Aug. 1; published online Sept. 4).

4. Virginijus Šikšnys et al., "RNA-Directed Cleavage by the Cas9-crRNA Complex," international patent application WO 2013/142578 Al, priority date Mar. 20, 2012, official filing Mar. 20, 2013, publication Sept. 26, 2013.

Chapter Fifteen: How Gene Editing Works

1. Author's interviews with Jennifer Doudna; Doudna and Sternberg, *A Crack in Creation*, 242.

2. Sheryl Gay Stolberg, "The Biotech Death of Jesse Gelsinger," *New York Times*, Nov. 28, 1999.

3. Srinivasan Chandrasegaran and Dana Carroll, "Origins of Programmable Nucleases for Genome Engineering," *Journal of Molecular Biology*, Feb. 27, 2016.

Chapter Sixteen: The Gene-Editing Race

1. Author's interviews with Martin Jinek and Jennifer Doudna.

2. Author's interviews with Jennifer Doudna and Martin Jinek.

Chapter Seventeen: Doudna's First Competitor

1. Author's interviews with Feng Zhang. This section also draws from Eric Topol, podcast interview with Feng Zhang, Medscape, Mar. 31, 2017; Michael Specter, "The Gene Hackers," *New Yorker*, Nov. 8, 2015; Sharon Begley, "Meet One of the World's Most Groundbreaking Scientists," *Stat*, Nov. 6, 2015.

2. Galen Johnson, "Gifted and Talented Education Grades K–12 Program Evaluation," Des Moines Public Schools, September 1996.

3. Edward Boyden, Feng Zhang, Ernst Bamberg, Georg Nagel, and Karl Deisseroth, "Millisecond-Timescale, Genetically Targeted Optical Control of Neural Activity," *Nature Neuroscience*, Aug. 14, 2005; Alexander Aravanis, Li-Ping Wang, Feng Zhang . . . and Karl Deisseroth, "An Optical Neural Interface: In vivo Control of Rodent Motor Cortex with Integrated Fiberoptic and Optogenetic Technology," *Journal of Neural Engineering*, Sept. 2007.

Chapter Eighteen: Doudna's Second Competitor

1. This section is based on author's interviews and visits with George Church and also Ben Mezrich, *Woolly* (Atria, 2017); Anna Azvolinsky, "Curious George," *The Scientist*, Oct. 1, 2016; Sharon Begley, "George Church Has a Wild Idea to Upend Evolution," *Stat*, May 16, 2016; Prashant Nair, "George Church," *PNAS*, July 24, 2012; Jeneen Interlandi, "The Church of George Church," *Popular Science*, May 27, 2015.

2. George Church Oral History, National Human Genome Research Institute, July 26, 2017.

3. Nicholas Wade, "Regenerating a Mammoth for $10 Million," *New York Times*, Nov. 19, 2008; Nicholas Wade, "The Wooly Mammoth's Last Stand," *New York Times*, Mar. 2, 2017; Mezrich, *Woolly*.

4. Author's interviews with George Church and Jennifer Doudna.

Chapter Nineteen: The Race Heats Up

1. Josiane Garneau . . . Rodolphe Barrangou . . . Philippe Horvath, Alfonso H. Magadán, and Sylvain Moineau, "The CRISPR/Cas

Bacterial Immune System Cleaves Bacteriophage and Plasmid DNA," *Nature*, Nov. 3, 2010.

2. Davies, *Editing Humanity*, 80; author's interview with Le Cong.

3. Author's interviews with Eric Lander, Feng Zhang; Begley, "George Church Has a Wild Idea . . ."; Michael Specter, "The Gene Hackers," *New Yorker*, Nov. 8, 2015; Davies, *Editing Humanity*, 82.

4. David Altshuler, Chad Cowan, Feng Zhang, et al., Grant application 1R01DK097758-01, "Isogenic Human Pluripotent Stem Cell-Based Models of Human Disease Mutations," National Institutes of Health, Jan. 12, 2012.

5. Author's interviews with Dana Carroll; Dana Carroll, "Declaration in Support of Suggestion of Interference," University of California Exhibit 1476, Interference No. 106,048, Apr. 10, 2015.

Chapter Twenty: Photo Finish

1. Author's interviews with Feng Zhang; Fei Ann Ran, "CRISPR-Cas9," *NABC Report* 26, ed. Alan Eaglesham and Ralph Hardy, Oct. 8, 2014.

2. Le Cong, Fei Ann Ran, David Cox, Shuailiang Lin . . . Luciano Marraffini, and Feng Zhang, "Multiplex Genome Engineering Using CRISPR/Cas Systems," *Science*, Feb. 15, 2013 (received Oct. 5, 2012; accepted Dec. 12, 2012; published online Jan. 3, 2013).

3. Author's interview with George Church.

4. Prashant Mali . . . George Church, et al., "RNA-Guided Human Genome Engineering via Cas9," *Science*, Feb. 15, 2013 (received Oct. 26, 2012; accepted Dec. 12, 2012; published online Jan. 3, 2013).

5. Pandika, "Jennifer Doudna, CRISPR Code Killer."

6. Michael M. Cox, Jennifer Doudna, and Michael O'Donnell, *Molecular Biology: Principles and Practice* (W. H. Freeman, 2011). The first edition cost $195.

7. Detlef Weigel decision letter and Jennifer Doudna author response, *eLife*, Jan. 29, 2013.

Chapter Twenty-One: Commercializing CRISPR

1. Author's interviews with Andy May, Jennifer Doudna, and Rachel Haurwitz.
2. George Church interview, "Can Neanderthals Be Brought Back from the Dead?," *Spiegel*, Jan. 18, 2013; David Wagner, "How the Viral Neanderthal-Baby Story Turned Real Science into Junk Journalism," *The Atlantic*, Jan. 22, 2013.
3. Author's interviews with Jennifer Doudna, George Church, and Emmanuelle Charpentier.
4. Author's interviews with Jennifer Doudna.
5. Editas Medicine, SEC 10-K filing 2016 and 2019; John Carroll, "Biotech Pioneer in 'Gene Editing' Launches with $43M in VC Cash," *FierceBiotech*, Nov. 25, 2013.
6. Author's interviews with Jennifer Doudna, Rachel Haurwitz, Erik Sontheimer, and Luciano Marraffini.

Chapter Twenty-Two: Patents

1. *Diamond v. Chakrabarty*, 447 U.S. 303, U.S. Supreme Court, 1980; Douglas Robinson and Nina Medlock, "*Diamond v. Chakrabarty*: A Retrospective on 25 Years of Biotech Patents," *Intellectual Property & Technology Law Journal*, Oct. 2005.
2. Author's interviews with Andy May and Jennifer Doudna.
3. Provisional patent application U.S. 2012/61652086P and published patent application U.S. 2014/0068797A1 of Doudna et al.; Provisional patent application U.S. 2012/61736527P (Dec. 12, 2012) and granted patent US 8,697,359 B1 (Apr. 15, 2014) of Zhang et al.
4. Alessandra Potenza, "Who Owns CRISPR?," *The Verge*, Dec. 6,

2016; Jacob Sherkow, "Biotech Trial of the Century Could Determine Who Owns CRISPR," *MIT Technology Review*, Dec. 7, 2016; Sharon Begley, "CRISPR Court Hearing Puts University of California on the Defensive," *Stat*, Dec. 6, 2016.

5. Patent Trial Board Judgment and Decision on Motions, Patent Interference Case 106,048, Feb. 15, 2017.

6. Judge Kimberly Moore, decision, Patent Interference Case 106,048, United States Court of Appeals for the Federal Circuit, Sept. 10, 2018.

Chapter Twenty-Three: When Friends Drift Apart

1. Author's interviews with Jennifer Doudna and Emmanuelle Charpentier.

Chapter Twenty-Four: Creating Happy, Healthy Babies

1. Doudna and Sternberg, *A Crack in Creation*, 198; Michael Specter, "Humans 2.0," *New Yorker*, Nov. 16, 2015; author's interview with Jennifer Doudna.

2. Author's interviews with Sam Sternberg and Lauren Buchman.

3. Author's interviews with George Church and Lauren Buchman.

Chapter Twenty-Five: The Ethics of Genetic Engineering

1. Paul Berg et al., "Potential Biohazards of Recombinant DNA Molecules," *Science*, July 26, 1974.

2. Alan Handyside et al., "Birth of a Normal Girl after in vitro Fertilization and Preimplantation Diagnostic Testing for Cystic Fibrosis," *New England Journal of Medicine*, Sept. 1992.

3. Gregory Stock and John Campbell, *Engineering the Human Germline* (Oxford, 2000), 73–95; author's interviews with James Watson; Gina Kolata, "Scientists Brace for Changes in Path of Human Evolution," *New York Times*, Mar. 21, 1998.

4. Council of Europe, "Oviedo Convention and Its Protocols," April 4, 1997.

Chapter Twenty-Six: Guidelines, Regulations, and the Government

1. Author's interviews with David Baltimore, Jennifer Doudna, Sam Sternberg, and Dana Carroll.

2. David Baltimore et al., "A Prudent Path Forward for Genomic Engineering and Germline Gene Modification," *Science*, Apr. 3, 2015 (published online Mar. 19).

3. Nicholas Wade, "Scientists Seek Ban on Method of Editing the Human Genome," *New York Times*, Mar. 19, 2015.

4. Puping Liang . . . Junjiu Huang, et al., "CRISPR/Cas9-Mediated Gene Editing in Human Tripronuclear Zygotes," *Protein & Cell*, May 2015 (published online Apr. 18).

5. Author's interviews with Ting Wu, George Church, Jennifer Doudna; Johnny Kung, "Increasing Policymakers' Interest in Genetics," pgEd briefing paper, Dec. 1, 2015.

6. George Church, "Encourage the Innovators," *Nature*, Dec. 3, 2015.

7. Author's interviews with Jennifer Doudna, David Baltimore, and George Church; *International Summit on Human Gene Editing*, Dec. 1–3, 2015 (National Academies Press, 2015); Jef Akst, "Let's Talk Human Engineering," *The Scientist*, Dec. 3, 2015.

8. R. Alto Charo, Richard Hynes, et al., "Human Genome Editing: Scientific, Medical, and Ethical Considerations," report of the National Academies of Sciences, Engineering, Medicine, 2017.

9. Françoise Baylis, *Altered Inheritance: CRISPR and the Ethics of Human Genome Editing* (Harvard, 2019); Jocelyn Kaiser, "U.S. Panel Gives Yellow Light to Human Embryo Editing," *Science*, Feb. 14, 2017; Kelsey Montgomery, "Behind the Scenes of the National Academy of Sciences' Report on Human Genome Editing," *Medical Press*, Feb. 27, 2017.

10. Consolidated Appropriations Act of 2016, Public Law 114-113, Section 749, Dec. 18, 2015; Francis Collins, "Statement on NIH Funding of Research Using Gene-Editing Technologies in Human Embryos," Apr. 28, 2015; John Holdren, "A Note on Genome Editing," May 26, 2015.

11. Heidi Ledford, "CRISPR, the Disruptor," *Nature*, June 3, 2015. Danilo Maddalo . . . and Andrea Ventura, "In vivo Engineering of Oncogenic Chromosomal Rearrangements with the CRISPR/Cas9 System," *Nature*, Oct. 22, 2014; Sidi Chen, Neville E. Sanjana . . . Feng Zhang, and Phillip A. Sharp, "Genome-wide CRISPR Screen in a Mouse Model of Tumor Growth and Metastasis," *Cell*, Mar. 12, 2015.

12. James Clapper, "Threat Assessment of the U.S. Intelligence Community," Feb. 9, 2016; Antonio Regalado, "The Search for the Kryptonite That Can Stop CRISPR," *MIT Technology Review*, May 2, 2019; Robert Sanders, "Defense Department Pours $65 Million into Making CRISPR Safer," *Berkeley News*, July 19, 2017.

Chapter Twenty-Seven: He Jiankui

1. This section is based on Xi Xin and Xu Yue, "The Life Track of He Jiankui," *Jiemian News*, Nov. 27, 2018; Jon Cohen, "The Untold Story of the 'Circle of Trust' behind the World's First Gene-Edited Babies," *Science*, Aug. 1, 2019; Sharon Begley and Andrew Joseph, "The CRISPR Shocker," *Stat*, Dec. 17, 2018; Zach Coleman, "The Businesses behind the Doctor Who Manipulated Baby DNA," *Nikkei Asian Review*, Nov. 27, 2018; Zoe Low, "China's Gene Editing Frankenstein," *South China Morning Post*, Nov. 27, 2018; Yangyang Cheng, "Brave New World with Chinese Characteristics," *Bulletin of the Atomic Scientists*, Jan. 13, 2019; He Jiankui, "Draft Ethical Principles," YouTube, Nov. 25, 2018, youtube.com/watch?v=MyNHpMoPkIg; Antonio Regalado, "Chinese

Scientists Are Creating CRISPR Babies," *MIT Technology Review*, Nov. 25, 2018; Marilynn Marchione, "Chinese Researcher Claims First Gene-Edited Babies," AP, Nov. 26, 2018; Christina Larson, "Gene-Editing Chinese Scientist Kept Much of His Work Secret," AP, Nov. 27, 2018; Davies, *Editing Humanity*.

2. Jiankui He and Michael W. Deem, "Heterogeneous Diversity of Spacers within CRISPR," *Physical Review Letters*, Sept. 14, 2010.

3. Mike Williams, "He's on a Hot Streak," *Rice News*, Nov. 17, 2010.

4. Teng Jing Xuan, "CCTV's Glowing 2017 Coverage of Gene-Editing Pariah He Jiankui," *Caixan Global*, Nov. 30, 2018; Rob Schmitz, "Gene-Editing Scientist's Actions Are a Product of Modern China," *All Things Considered*, NPR, Feb. 5, 2019.

5. "Welcome to the Jiankui He Lab," http://sustc-genome.org.cn/people.html (site no longer active); Regalado, "Chinese Scientists Are Creating CRISPR Babies."

6. Cohen, "The Untold Story"; Begley and Joseph, "The CRISPR Shocker"; author's interviews with Jennifer Doudna; Jennifer Doudna and William Hurlbut, "The Challenge and Opportunity of Gene Editing," Templeton Foundation grant 217,398.

7. Davies, *Editing Humanity*, 221; George Church, "Future, Human, Nature: Reading, Writing, Revolution," Innovative Genomics Institute, January 26, 2017, innovativegenomics.org/multimedia-library/george-church-lecture/.

8. Author's interview with Jennifer Doudna.

9. Medical Ethics Approval Application Form, HarMoniCare Shenzhen Women's and Children's Hospital, March 7, 2017, theregreview.org/wp-content/uploads/2019/05/He-Jiankui-Documents-3.pdf; Cohen, "The Untold Story"; Kathy Young, Marilynn Marchione, Emily Wang, et al., "First Gene-Edited Babies Reported in China," YouTube, Nov. 25, 2018, https://www.youtube.com/watch?v=C9V3mqswbv0; Gerry Shih and Carolyn

Johnson, "Chinese Genomics Scientist Defends His Gene-Editing Research," *Washington Post*, Nov. 28, 2018.

10. Jiankui He, "Informed Consent, Version: Female 3.0," Mar. 2017, theregreview.org/wp-content/uploads/2019/05/He-Jiankui -Documents-3.pdf; Cohen, "The Untold Story"; Marilynn Marchione, "Chinese Researcher Claims First Gene-Edited Babies," AP, Nov. 26, 2018; Larson, "Gene-Editing Chinese Scientist Kept Much of His Work Secret."

11. Cohen, "The Untold Story."

12. He Jiankui, "Draft Ethical Principles of Therapeutic Assisted Reproductive Technologies."

13. He Jiankui, "Designer Baby Is an Epithet" and "Why We Chose HIV and CCR5 First," The He Lab, YouTube, Nov. 25, 2018.

14. He Jiankui, "HIV Immune Gene CCR5 Gene Editing in Human Embryos," Chinese Clinical Trial Registry, ChiCTR1800019378, Nov. 8, 2018.

15. He Jiankui, "About Lulu and Nana," YouTube, Nov. 25, 2018.

Chapter Twenty-Eight: The Hong Kong Summit

1. Author's interview with Jennifer Doudna.

2. Cohen, "The Untold Story."

3. Author's interviews with Victor Dzau, David Baltimore, Jennifer Doudna.

4. Author's interviews with Jennifer Doudna; Robin Lovell-Badge, "CRISPR Babies," *Development*, Feb. 6, 2019.

5. Second International Summit on Human Genome Editing, University of Hong Kong, Nov. 27–29, 2018.

6. He Jiankui session, the Second International Summit on Human Genome Editing, Hong Kong, Nov. 28, 2018.

7. Author's interview with Matthew Porteus.

8. Author's interviews with Jennifer Doudna, David Baltimore.

9. Author's interviews with Matthew Porteus, David Baltimore.

10. David Baltimore et al., "Statement by the Organizing Committee of the Second International Summit on Human Genome Editing," Nov. 29, 2018.

Chapter Twenty-Nine: Acceptance

1. Author's interview with Jennifer Doudna and dinner with her and Andrew Doudna Cate.

2. Author's interview with Jennifer Doudna.

3. "Proposal for an IGI Sickle Cell Initiative," Innovative Genomics Institute, February 2020.

4. Eric S. Lander et.al., "Adopt a Moratorium on Heritable Genome Editing," *Nature*, Mar. 13, 2019.

5. Kay Davies, Richard Lifton, et al., "Heritable Human Genome Editing," International Commission on the Clinical Use of Human Germline Genome Editing, Sept. 3, 2020.

6. "He Jiankui Jailed for Illegal Human Embryo Gene-Editing," Xinhua news agency, Dec. 30, 2019.

7. Philip Wen and Amy Dockser Marcus, "Chinese Scientist Who Gene-Edited Babies Is Sent to Prison," *Wall Street Journal*, Dec. 30, 2019.

Chapter Thirty: Regulating Gene Editing

1. Matt Ridley, *Genome* (Harper Collins, 2000), chapter 4, powerfully describes Huntington's and the work of Nancy Wexler in researching it.

2. Liza Mundy, "A World of Their Own," *Washington Post*, Mar. 31, 2002; Michael J. Sandel, *The Case against Perfection* (Harvard University Press); Marion Andrea Schmidt, *Eradicating Deafness?* (Manchester University Press, 2020).

3. Francis Fukuyama, "Gene Regime," *Foreign Policy*, Mar. 2002.

Chapter Thirty-One: Doudna's Ethical Journey

1. David Cyranoski, "CRISPR Gene-Editing Tested in a Person for the First Time," *Nature*, Nov. 15, 2016.
2. "Single Ascending Dose Study in Participants with LCA10," ClinicalTrials.gov, Mar. 13, 2019, identifier: NCT03872479; Morgan Maeder . . . and Haiyan Jiang, "Development of a Gene-Editing Approach to Restore Vision Loss in Leber Congenital Amaurosis Type 10," *Nature*, Jan. 21, 2019.
3. Matthew Porteus, "A New Class of Medicines through DNA Editing," *New England Journal of Medicine*, Mar. 7, 2019; Sharon Begley, "CRISPR Trackr: Latest Advances," *Stat Plus*.
4. Author's interviews with Jennifer Doudna; Doudna and Sternberg, *A Crack in Creation*, 222–40; Hannah Devlin, "Jennifer Doudna: 'I Have to Be True to Who I Am as a Scientist,'" *The Observer*, July 2, 2017.

Chapter Thirty-Two: The Front Lines

1. Robert Sanders, "New DNA-Editing Technology Spawns Bold UC Initiative," *Berkeley News*, Mar. 18, 2014; "About Us," Innovative Genomics Institute website, https://innovativegenomics.org/about-us/. It was relaunched in January 2017 as the Innovative Genomics Institute.
2. Author's interviews with Dave Savage, Gavin Knott, and Jennifer Doudna.
3. Author's interview with Jennifer Doudna. The competition was run by First Robotics, a nationwide program created by the irrepressible Segway inventor Dean Kamen.
4. Interviews, audio and video recordings, notes, and slides provided by Jennifer Doudna, Megan Hochstrasser, and Fyodor Urnov; Walter Isaacson, "Ivory Power," *Air Mail*, Apr. 11, 2020.
5. Jonathan Corum and Carl Zimmer, "Bad News Wrapped in

Protein: Inside the Coronavirus Genome," *New York Times*, Apr. 3, 2020; GenBank, National Institutes of Health, SARS-CoV-2 Sequences, updated Apr. 14, 2020.

6. Alexander Walls . . . David Veesler, et al., "Structure, Function, and Antigenicity of the SARS-CoV-2 Spike Glycoprotein," *Cell*, Mar. 9, 2020; Qihui Wang . . . and Jianxun Qi, "Structural and Functional Basis of SARS-CoV-2 Entry by Using Human ACE2," *Cell*, May 14, 2020; Francis Collins, "Antibody Points to Possible Weak Spot on Novel Coronavirus," NIH, Apr. 14, 2020; Bonnie Berkowitz, Aaron Steckelberg, and John Muyskens, "What the Structure of the Coronavirus Can Tell Us," *Washington Post*, Mar. 23, 2020.

Chapter Thirty-Three: Testing

1. Shawn Boburg, Robert O'Harrow Jr., Neena Satija, and Amy Goldstein, "Inside the Coronavirus Testing Failure," *Washington Post*, Apr. 3, 2020; Robert Baird, "What Went Wrong with Coronavirus Testing in the U.S.," *New Yorker*, Mar. 16, 2020; Michael Shear, Abby Goodnough, Sheila Kaplan, Sheri Fink, Katie Thomas, and Noah Weiland, "The Lost Month: How a Failure to Test Blinded the U.S. to COVID-19," *New York Times*, Mar. 28, 2020.

2. Boburg et al., "Inside the Coronavirus Testing Failure"; David Willman, "Contamination at CDC Lab Delayed Rollout of Coronavirus Tests," *Washington Post*, Apr. 18, 2020.

3. JoNel Aleccia, "How Intrepid Lab Sleuths Ramped Up Tests as Coronavirus Closed In," *Kaiser Health News*, Mar. 16, 2020.

4. Julia Ioffe, "The Infuriating Story of How the Government Stalled Coronavirus Testing," *GQ*, Mar. 16, 2020; Boburg et al., "Inside the Coronavirus Testing Failure." Greninger's email to a friend is in the excellent *Washington Post* reconstruction.

5. Boburg et al., "Inside the Coronavirus Testing Failure"; Patrick Boyle, "Coronavirus Testing: How Academic Medical Labs Are Stepping Up to Fill a Void," *AAMC*, Mar. 12, 2020.

6. Author's interview with Eric Lander; Leah Eisenstadt, "How Broad Institute Converted a Clinical Processing Lab into a Large-Scale COVID-19 Testing Facility in a Matter of Days," *Broad Communications*, Mar. 27, 2020.

Chapter Thirty-Four: The Berkeley Lab

1. Author's interviews with Fyodor Urnov. Dmitry Urnov became a professor at Adelphi University in New York. He is an accomplished horseman who once accompanied three horses on a sea voyage when Nikita Khrushchev wanted to give them as a gift to the American industrialist Cyrus Eaton. He and his wife Julia Palievsky wrote *A Kindred Writer: Dickens in Russia*. They are also scholars of William Faulkner.

2. Author's interviews with Enrique Lin Shiao

3. Author's interviews with Fyodor Urnov, Jennifer Doudna, Jennifer Hamilton, Enrique Lin Shiao; Hope Henderson, "IGI Launches Major Automated COVID-19 Diagnostic Testing Initiative," *IGI News*, Mar. 30, 2020; Megan Molteni and Gregory Barber, "How a Crispr Lab Became a Pop-Up COVID Testing Center," *Wired*, Apr. 2, 2020.

Chapter Thirty-Five: Companies for the Common Good

1. Janice Chen . . . Lucas B. Harrington, Jennifer A. Doudna, et al., "CRISPR-Cas12a Target Binding Unleashes Indiscriminate Single-Stranded DNase Activity," *Science*, Apr. 27, 2018 (received Nov. 29, 2017; accepted Feb. 5, 2018; published online Feb. 15); John Carroll, "CRISPR Legend Jennifer Doudna Helps Some Recent College Grads Launch a Diagnostics Upstart," *Endpoints*, Apr. 26, 2018.

2. Sergey Shmakov, Omar Abudayyeh, Kira S. Makarova, Konstantin Severinov, Feng Zhang, and Eugene V. Koonin, "Discovery and Functional Characterization of Diverse Class 2 CRISPR-Cas Systems," *Molecular Cell*, Nov. 5, 2015 (published online Oct. 22, 2015); Omar Abudayyeh, Jonathan Gootenberg, Eric Lander, Eugene Koonin, and Feng Zhang, "C2c2 Is a Single-Component Programmable RNA-Guided RNA-Targeting CRISPR Effector," *Science*, Aug. 5, 2016 (published online June 2, 2016).

3. Author's interviews with Feng Zhang.

4. Alexandra East-Seletsky . . . Jamie Cate, Robert Tjian, and Jennifer Doudna, "Two Distinct RNase Activities of CRISPR-C2c2 Enable Guide-RNA Processing and RNA Detection," *Nature*, Oct. 13, 2016. CRISPR-C2c2 was renamed CRISPER-Cas13a.

5. Jonathan Gootenberg, Omar Abudayyeh . . . Cameron Myhrvold, Eugene Koonin, Feng Zhang, et al., "Nucleic Acid Detection with CRISPR-Cas13a/C2c2," *Science*, Apr. 28, 2017.

6. Emily Mullin, "CRISPR Could Be the Future of Disease Diagnosis," *OneZero*, July 25, 2019; Emily Mullin, "CRISPR Pioneer Jennifer Doudna on the Future of Disease Detection," *OneZero*, July 30, 2019; Daniel Chertow, "Next-Generation Diagnostics with CRISPR," *Science*, Apr. 27, 2018; Ann Gronowski, "Who or What Is SHERLOCK?," *EJIFCC*, Nov. 2018.

Chapter Thirty-Six: CRISPR-Based Coronavirus Tests

1. Author's interviews with Feng Zhang.

2. Feng Zhang, Omar Abudayyeh, and Jonathan Gootenberg, "A Protocol for Detection of COVID-19 Using CRISPR Diagnostics," Broad Institute website, posted Feb. 14, 2020; Carl Zimmer, "With Crispr, a Possible Quick Test for the Coronavirus," *New York Times*, May 5, 2020.

3. Goldberg, "CRISPR Comes to COVID"; "Sherlock Biosciences

and Binx Health Announce Global Partnership to Develop First CRISPR-Based Point-of-Care Test for COVID-19," *PR Newswire*, July 1, 2020.

4. Author's interviews with Janice Chen and Lucas Harrington; Jim Daley, "CRISPR Gene Editing May Help Scale Up Coronavirus Testing," *Scientific American*, Apr. 23, 2020; John Cumbers, "With Its Coronavirus Rapid Paper Test Strip, This CRISPR Startup Wants to Help Halt a Pandemic," *Forbes*, Mar. 14, 2020; Lauren Martz, "CRISPR-Based Diagnostics Are Poised to Make an Early Debut amid COVID-19 Outbreak," *Biocentury*, Feb. 28, 2020.

5. James Broughton . . . Charles Chiu, Janice Chen, et al., "A Protocol for Rapid Detection of the 2019 Novel Coronavirus SARS-CoV-2 Using CRISPR Diagnostics: SARS-CoV-2 DETECTR," Mammoth Biosciences website, posted Feb. 15, 2020. The full Mammoth paper with patient data and other details is James Broughton . . . Janice Chen, and Charles Chiu, "CRISPR–Cas12-Based Detection of SARS-CoV-2," *Nature Biotechnology*, Apr. 16, 2020 (received Mar. 5, 2020). See also Eelke Brandsma . . . and Emile van den Akker, "Rapid, Sensitive and Specific SARS Coronavirus-2 Detection: A Multi-center Comparison between Standard qRT-PCR and CRISPR Based DETECTR," *medRxiv*, July 27, 2020.

6. Julia Joung . . . Jonathan S. Gootenberg, Omar O. Abudayyeh, and Feng Zhang, "Point-of-Care Testing for COVID-19 Using SHERLOCK Diagnostics," *medRxiv*, May 5, 2020.

Chapter Thirty-Seven: Vaccines

1. "A Trial Investigating the Safety and Effects of Four BNT162 Vaccines against COVID-2019 in Healthy Adults," ClinicalTrials.gov, May 2020, identifier: NCT04380701; "BNT162 SARS-CoV-2 Vaccine," *Precision Vaccinations*, Aug. 14, 2020; Mark J.

Mulligan . . . Uğur Şahin, Kathrin Jansen, et al., "Phase ½ Study of COVID-19 RNA Vaccine BNT162b1 in Adults," *Nature*, Aug. 12, 2020.

2. Simantini Dey, "Meet Sarah Gilbert," *News18*, July 21, 2020; Stephanie Baker, "Covid Vaccine Front-Runner Is Months Ahead of Her Competition," *Bloomberg Businessweek*, July 14, 2020; Clive Cookson, "Sarah Gilbert, the Researcher Leading the Race to a Covid-19 Vaccine," *Financial Times*, July 24, 2020.

3. Author's interviews with Ross Wilson, Alex Marson; IGI white paper seeking funding for DNA vaccine delivery systems, Mar. 2020; Ross Wilson report at IGI COVID-response meeting, June 11, 2020.

Chapter Thirty-Eight: CRISPR Cures

1. David Dorward . . . and Christopher Lucas, "Tissue-Specific Tolerance in Fatal COVID-19," *medRxiv*, July 2, 2020; Bicheng Zhag and Jun Wan, "Clinical Characteristics of 82 Cases of Death from COVID-19," *Plos One*, July 9, 2020.

2. Ed Yong, "Immunology Is Where Intuition Goes to Die," *The Atlantic*, Aug. 5, 2020.

3. Author's interview with Cameron Myhrvold.

4. Author's interview with Cameron Myhrvold.

5. Cameron Myhrvold to Pardis Sabeti, Dec. 22, 2016.

6. Defense Advanced Research Projects Agency (DARPA) grant D18AC00006.

7. Susanna Hamilton, "CRISPR-Cas13 Developed as Combination Antiviral and Diagnostic System," *Broad Communications*, Oct. 11, 2019.

8. Catherine Freije, Cameron Myhrvold . . . Omar Abudayyeh, Jonathan Gootenberg . . . Feng Zhang, and Pardis Sabeti, "Programmable Inhibition and Detection of RNA Viruses Using Cas13," *Molecular Cell*, Dec. 5, 2019 (received Apr. 16, 2019;

revised July 18, 2019; accepted Sept. 6, 2019, published online Oct. 10, 2019); Tanya Lewis, "Scientists Program CRISPR to Fight Viruses in Human Cells," *Scientific American*, Oct. 23, 2019.

9. Cheri Ackerman, Cameron Myhrvold, and Pardis C. Sabeti, "Massively Multiplexed Nucleic Acid Detection with Cas13m," *Nature*, Apr. 29, 2020 (received Mar. 20, 2020, accepted Apr. 20, 2020).

10. Jon Arizti-Sanz, Catherine Freije, Pardis Sabeti, and Cameron Myhrvold, "Integrated Sample Inactivation, Amplification, and Cas13-Based Detection of SARS-CoV-2," *bioRxiv*, May 28, 2020.

11. Author's interviews with Stanley Qi.

12. Timothy Abbott and Lei [Stanley] Qi, "Development of CRISPR as a Prophylactic Strategy to Combat Novel Coronavirus and Influenza," *bioRxiv*, Mar. 14, 2020.

13. Theresa Duque, "Cellular Delivery System Could Be Missing Link in Battle against SARS-CoV-2," *Berkeley Lab News*, June 4, 2020.

Chapter Thirty-Nine: A Virtual Return to Cold Spring Harbor

1. Andrew Anzalone . . . David Liu, et al., "Search-and-Replace Genome Editing without Double-Strand Breaks or Donor DNA," *Nature*, Dec. 5, 2019 (received Aug. 26; accepted Oct. 10; published online Oct. 21).

2. Beverly Mok . . . David Liu, et al., "A Bacterial Cytidine Deaminase Toxin Enables CRISPR-Free Mitochondrial Base Editing," *Nature*, July 8, 2020.

3. Jonathan Hsu . . . David Liu, Keith Joung, Lucan Pinello, et al., "PrimeDesign Software for Rapid and Simplified Design of Prime Editing Guide RNAs," *bioRxiv*, May 4, 2020.

Chapter Forty: The Nobel Prize

1. Author's interviews with Heidi Ledford, Jennifer Doudna, Emmanuelle Charpentier.

Chapter Forty-One: The Next Scientific Horizon

1. Jennifer Doudna, "How COVID-19 Is Spurring Science to Accelerate," *The Economist*, June 5, 2020. See also Jane Metcalfe, "COVID-19 Is Accelerating Human Transformation—Let's Not Waste It," *Wired*, July 5, 2020.

2. Michael Eisen, "Patents Are Destroying the Soul of Academic Science," *It's Not Junk*, Feb. 20, 2017.

3. "SARS-CoV-2 Sequence Read Archive Submissions," National Center for Biotechnology Information, https://www.ncbi.nlm.nih.gov/sars-cov-2/, n.d.

4. Simine Vazire, "Peer-Reviewed Scientific Journals Don't Really Do Their Job," *Wired*, June 25, 2020

5. Author's interview with Emmanuelle Charpentier

★"A TRULY INSPIRING READ."

—*Booklist*, starred review

The remarkable group of female pilots who answered their country's call in its time of need during World War II—and why their story still matters today.

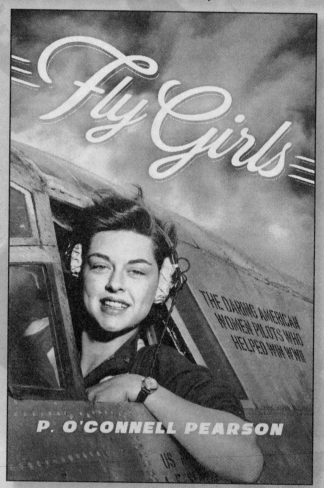